In *Modernism, Mass Culture, and Professionalism* Thomas Strychacz argues that modernist writers need to be understood both in their relationship to professional critics and in their relationship to an era and ethos of professionalism. In studying four modernist writers – Henry James, Theodore Dreiser, John Dos Passos, and Nathanael West – Strychacz finds that, far from being opposed to the ideas and expressive forms of mass culture, modernist writers in the period 1880–1940 are thoroughly caught up in them. Nevertheless, modernist writers seek to distinguish their ideas and styles from mass culture, particularly by making their works esoteric. In doing so, modernist writers are reproducing one of the main tenets of all professional groups, which is to gain social authority by forming a community around a difficult language inaccessible to the public at large. While their modernism arises out of the nature of their encounter with mass culture, that encounter frequently overturns commonly held notions of the nature of modernism. Finally, Strychacz explores his own world of academia and observes that the work of professional critics in the university reproduces the strategies of modernist writers.

CAMBRIDGE STUDIES IN AMERICAN LITERATURE AND CULTURE #65

Modernism, Mass Culture, and Professionalism

Books in the series

Continued on pages following the Index

Modernism, Mass Culture, and Professionalism

THOMAS STRYCHACZ

Mills College

CAMBRIDGE
UNIVERSITY PRESS

Published by the Press Syndicate of the University of Cambridge
The Pitt Building, Trumpington Street, Cambridge CB2 1RP
40 West 20th Street, New York, NY 10011-4211, USA
10 Stamford Road, Oakleigh, Melbourne 3166, Australia

First published 1993

Printed in the United States of America

Library of Congress Cataloging-in-Publication Data
Strychacz, Thomas F.
Modernism, mass culture, and professionalism / Thomas
Strychacz.
p.   cm. – (Cambridge studies in American literature and
culture ; 65)
Includes bibliographical references and index.
ISBN 0-521-44079-3
1. American fiction – 20th century – History and
criticism – Theory, etc.   2. Modernism (Literature) – United
States.   3. West, Nathanael, 1903–1940 – Criticism and
interpretation.   4. James, Henry, 1843–1916 – Criticism and
interpretation.   5. Dreiser, Theodore, 1871–1945. American
tragedy.   6. Dos Passos, John, 1896–1970. U.S.A.   7. United
States – Popular culture – History – 20th century.
8. Criticism – United States – History – 20th century.
9. Authority in literature.   I. Title.   II.   Series.
PS379.S76   1993
813'.509 – dc20   92-44711
                                                              CIP

A catalog record for this book is available from the British Library.

ISBN 0-521-44079-3   hardback

Contents

Acknowledgments

I owe much to the many people who have read, guided, critiqued, and helped shape this work. I would particularly like to thank Lee Mitchell and Alvin Kernan at Princeton University for the care and time they bestowed on an embryonic version of this book; their patient criticism and advice shines out, I think, in everything good about this book. Bob Weisbuch at the University of Michigan read the manuscript and offered invaluable advice; Helen Maxson likewise read, provoked, and believed. At Mills, I am grateful for two summer grants that enabled me to finish rewriting the manuscript and for the support of my colleagues. Marilyn Chandler, as ever, came through with comments and a powerful (and much-needed) sense of "you can do it." A special thanks to Laurie Duesing, who gave the manuscript the most thorough reading of its life, and who was right in every respect about changes major and minor.

I owe most to Kathryn Reiss, who read version after version of the manuscript and whose love and enthusiasm kept me going; to my father for teaching me about what it means to work; and to my mother for her love of language. She would have been proud. To these three people this book is dedicated.

Finally, a word for my sons Nicholas and Daniel, who have always made the writing and rewriting of this book seem worthwhile, and who anyway love to see their names in print.

1

Modernist Writers and the Ethos of Professionalism

In 1902, William Dean Howells addressed the sad lack of literary centers in the United States. Envisaging New York as the inheritor of Boston's literary pre-eminence, he wrote that in Boston "journalism desired to be literary, and here [New York] literature has to try hard not to be journalistic" ([1902] 1968, 179). For a would-be literary center, suggested Howells with his usual dry wit, one dilemma seemed insurmountable: Was it even possible to conceive of literature in the newspaper capital of America? Howells was entering a debate already raging about the status of literature in an era of best-sellers and burgeoning newspaper circulations. Often the debate was conducted in strictly adversarial terms. "Why is daily newspaper work so antagonistic to literary writing?" demanded the journalist and critic W. J. Henderson, who went on to describe a copyeditor wreaking violence on an aspiring young writer's "glittering web of language" (1890, 713). At the other extreme, Henry Walcutt Boynton argued that "between literature and 'the higher journalism' the partition is extremely thin" and located the work of his contemporary, E. L. Godkin, "upon the border regions between literature and journalism" (1904, 19, 21). And Richard G. Moulton, an Englishman who came to the United States in order to pursue an academic career, seemed to find this border region quite mystifying: "The grand literary phenomenon of modern times is journalism, the huge apparatus of floating literature of which one leading object is to review literature itself" ([1888] 1989, 64). Like Henry James, who decried in "Criticism" (1893) the disproportion of reviewing to writing worthy of being reviewed, Moulton claimed that it is "natural enough" that "the review should tend to usurp the position of the literature for which reviewing exists" (64) – despite the fact that the category "literature," for Moulton, seems occupied already by that "grand literary phenomenon" of journalism.

Seventy years later, beset by the twentieth-century revolution in electronic forms of mass communication, Allen Ginsberg lamented that

> literature . . . has been mocked, misinterpreted and suppressed by a horde
> of middlemen whose fearful allegiance to the organization of mass stereo-

type communication prevents them from sympathy . . . with any manifes-
tation of unconditioned individuality. I mean journalists, commercial
publishers, book-review fellows, multitudes of professors of literature, etc.,
etc. ([1959] 1970, 26)

Ginsberg's vision of mass conspiracy suggests the evolving complexity of an
antagonism earlier writers had begun to perceive. Publishers, book reviewers,
professors – that despairing "etc., etc." reminds us that instances could multiply
indefinitely – occupy and extend Boynton's border regions. As an adjunct to an
oppressive system, the "higher journalism" now institutionalized in publishing
houses and universities constitutes a threat to free literary expression that
Ginsberg, during the censoring of *Howl,* had already experienced firsthand. In
essence, Ginsberg's comments are Howells's and Henderson's writ large. Ginsberg also insists on an adversarial relationship, in this case between the "unconditioned individuality" of literary principles and the "middlemen" of mass
culture. Most importantly, he also takes on the role of cultural arbiter, assuming
the power to set limits to spheres of influence even as "mass stereotype communication" seems to have grown out of all control.

For Howells, Henderson, Boynton, Moulton, and Ginsberg, the status of
literature assumes a paradoxical quality. They recognize a threat to literary
writing, yet the convergence of mass culture and literature actually functions to
restore the difference between them. And this is true even though few of these
writers would reach a consensual definition of literature. Certainly Henderson
would have found great difficulty in canonizing Ginsberg's manic *Howl* alongside those whose "glittering web of language" constitute, for him, literary
expression. But literature, these writers imply, can and must be more closely
defined because of countervailing cultural forces. The very concept of the
"literary," at first glance colonized by alien antiliterary meanings, is actually
consolidated by its structural propinquity to positions we can only define as
marginal and other. Even Boynton, who professes at times scarcely to know
literature from journalism, enjoins, in the rest of his essay, stricter definitions, as
he says, "Wherever in a journal personality emerges and fully expresses itself,
literature emerges. Wherever in literary forms the occasional, the conventional,
the partisan, the indecisive personality, are felt, journalism is present" (16).
Similarly, Moulton's confusion rapidly dissipates, and what appears at first to be a
signal failure to categorize the literary is redeemed by a rhetoric of appropriation
that separates and stabilizes the significances of literature and nonliterature:
"Now in journalism testing and valuation of literary work have a real and
important place. It has thus come about that in the great preponderance of
ephemeral over permanent literature the machinery adapted to the former has
become applied to the latter" (64). In the twentieth century, writers have
asserted similar discriminations so frequently that literature and mass culture
have come to seem mutually dependent categories: One emerges from and helps

determine the shape of the other. Tacitly or, as in the case of the above examples, quite consciously, some variation on the theme of mass culture (the higher journalism, mass stereotype communication) has been used to fashion cogent but flexible definitions of literature whose specific characteristics are organized around *what they oppose.*

This is true even though the proposition that literature exists as an absolute category has come under increasing attack by many critics and critical movements, which have assaulted, refashioned, and augmented traditional canons, aesthetics, and definitions to the extent that Leslie Fiedler's provocative question "What was literature?" (in a book by that title) seems quite accurate. Feminist critics, for instance, have introduced popular romances of the nineteenth and twentieth centuries for academic consideration; structuralist analyses have commonly drawn on popular forms like the detective or Gothic novel; and the postmodern novel, critics write, makes its engagement with mass culture a constitutive element of the text. We need only cite the New Journalism or the generic difficulties of classifying works like Margaret Mitchell's *Gone With the Wind* or Harriet Beecher Stowe's *Uncle Tom's Cabin* to see how conceiving of a popular work as "literature" is enough to disrupt the very notion of literariness. We need only remark on the historical fluctuations in the evaluation of such writers to sense how fully concepts of the literary are constrained by historical and cultural conditions. As Barbara Herrnstein Smith has observed, "Although it is clear that the *term* 'literature' retains idiomatic viability in a number of contexts, it is also becoming clear that those contexts are irreducibly various, that there is no essential trait or quality – formal or functional – that marks the 'literariness' of a text, and that there is therefore no particular, self-evident set of texts that can be, or ever could be, assembled under that label" (1989, 2).

Smith's argument against a single, unified, essentialist concept of literariness is a complex and theoretically powerful one; certainly we cannot say that literature exists, like Borges's Library of Babel, *ab aeterno,* or that any one definition can serve to crystallize its boundaries. Yet if the term and concept "literature" is historically determined, so are the contemporary efforts to contest or overthrow it. To dwell on present controversies about lines of literary demarcation may blind us to the ways in which the concept remains more than idiomatically viable – indeed, indispensable – in today's academia. As Alvin B. Kernan has noted, today's library catalogues, publishing houses, bookstores, journals, and university departments do distinguish literature from popular fiction and journalism, even though individual works may prove unclassifiable, giving literature "objective status, making it solidly, really there" (1982, 12). Perpetuating literature in this way probably no longer entails the cultural baggage of humanism and conserving universal values it once did. Decisions to publish a Penguin Classic or a Norton Critical Edition may be primarily economic and pragmatic. But somehow literature has been stabilized as an objective fact of our culture; college departments afford it respectability; students study it for their major; institutions fund it; critics contend its boundaries; many of the "middlemen" whom Allen Ginsberg decries are precisely those who do most to produce and perpetuate a concept of literature and to prevent that concept from slipping toward popular writing or journalism. Literary studies exist as a profession even as professional literary critics have argued increasingly about what their object of study really is — arguments that paradoxically consolidate their object of study, given that they are contesting a terrain that most other people in the United States cannot or will not even recognize as meaningful. The arguments, that is, produce within their institutional frameworks (disciplines, departments, professional journals, conferences) the very domain they seek to question. The category of literature thus functions within real institutions to produce real effects. For instance, it enables — perhaps forces into being — American studies departments and the Popular Culture Association, institutions whose power and survival depend on a distinction that can with little effort be theorized out of existence. If our recent discussions about literature have raised profound epistemological and ontological problems, in a quieter way they also concern the way that critics and other readers work to make literature (whatever it is) a meaningful and powerful organizing category within our professional institutions, penetrating every aspect of the ways in which we teach, write, form associations, and articulate our most pressing intellectual and professional problems.

The concept of literature, then, exists not in any single group of texts or definitions but in a set of structural relationships now situated within and alongside the academy, which may be activated on demand to demarcate a boundary line — friable, flexible, yet still relevant — between worthwhile texts and those considered worthless, or less useful, or deserving of different forms of treatment. This latter category of nonliterary texts is usually associated with mass culture. That similar structural relationships apply even when that association is explicitly not made, however, can be seen in the case of a critic like Leslie Fiedler, whose typical shock tactics often consist of alternately invoking and obscuring the relevance of such categories. The catholicity of Fiedlerian categories like "Literature, both high and low" (1982, 129), as he puts it in *What Was Literature?,* soon dissolves under closer inspection. In fact, "authentic literature" (70) for Fiedler takes shape from the mythic meeting of white and black. Within the framework of this monomyth, modernist art (or "High Art") is consigned to the marginal position of an "antibourgeois and disreputable experimentalism" and the "wan and genteel" avant-gardism of T. S. Eliot (71). Fiedler's narrative of American literature appears to transgress conventional academic distinctions between "High" and "Low" while actually keeping intact an entire critical apparatus created to legitimate new differences between authentic art (variously characterized as majority, Low, pop) and inauthentic art (under the rubric High, minority, elite, modernist, and so on). The term "literature" thus performs a double role for Fiedler, evoking on the one hand a minority art for an academically powerful readership and on the other signifying a transcendently real category defined largely by its popular appeal and by the efforts of academic critics to resist it. Far from subverting literature, Fiedler readmits it in the guise of "High Literature" and then projects it as a principle of opposition to a more authentic literature associated with mass or majority culture. Yet it is Fiedler, not any mass audience, legitimating this new literary standard. How else to explain the arbitrary exclusion of the demonstrably popular Rod McKuen from the ranks of the great cultural myth makers (83, 94)? Once a work's authenticity is seen to depend on a critic's expert opinion rather than on its mass appeal, the hegemony of the mass audience is irredeemably broken. By appearing to capitulate to popular taste, Fiedler does not subvert standards (though he claims in a chapter title to be doing so) so much as rewrite them, and in such a way that his canon seems just as narrow and idiosyncratic as the ones he attacks: Twain and Stowe are in, Eliot and James are out.

Such questions about literature, canon, and critical authority impinge directly on the larger issues of this work, which have to do with the contemporaneous development of mass culture, the writing strategies that legitimate American modernist texts, as well as the critical acts that legitimate those writing strategies. For, like modernist writers, today's critics are forced to situate the literary work in some meaningful relationship to mass culture or to ignore it entirely – which is to mystify the relationship rather than circumvent it. The modernist writers were the first to articulate the complex formation of forces that have characterized literary institutions in the twentieth century. As Howells, Henderson, Boynton, Moulton, and many others had seen by the end of the nineteenth century, the literary text would emerge in an age of mass culture as contextual; it would constantly negotiate with other media and other texts; it would have to be situated in some relationship, however adversarial, to the massive production of words, sounds, and images by – in T. E. Adorno's phrase – "the culture industry." As very few recognized, on the other hand, literary production in the twentieth century was to be shaped and legitimated by professional associations of writers, literary magazines, and by the rise of the university. Modernist writing, in particular, responded to a new discourse of professionalism, characterized by obscurity and esoteric knowledge, which throughout the emerging socioeconomic institutions of America was granting professionals "a privileged or exclusive right to speak in and about their domain," as Magali Sarfatti Larson writes (1984, 35). I argue that the kind of text we usually call modernist was shaped profoundly by a convergence of professional discourse and the rise of mass culture. In this respect, modernist texts are historically related to the processes governing the establishment of authoritative discourses in American mass society.

I argue further that our professional *critical* enterprises exhibit very similar discursive roles within an age of mass culture and that in order to gain a fuller understanding of modernism we need to recognize the fact that modernist writing in general demonstrates a hidden relationship to the recently formed and still organizing profession of literary studies. This relationship can be, and usually is, overlooked − not because it is buried too deep but because it pervades too thoroughly the everyday literary significances we read out of texts and inscribe into our critical discourse. The critic's work is crucial to my argument, in part because modernist writing could not otherwise have amassed the cultural authority it undoubtedly possesses, in part because that work is so rarely acknowledged. A series of profound complicities draws together the critic and modernist writer by virtue of their common historical relationship to the vast web of cultural and economic formations of the twentieth century. They share, in particular, a predilection toward esoteric writing as a way of marking out a distinct space apart from what is perceived to be the clear, simpleminded productions of mass culture. We might say that creative writers criticize mass culture, whereas critics create (or activate) those meanings and legitimate them as culturally authoritative (the play on words suggesting that the authority of modernist writing did not spring to life full-blown but developed out of particular historical engagements with specialized academic audiences). Throughout this work I describe not only how authors write in mass culture in an effort to write it off, but how the critical act of writing replicates that process.

The texts I consider, on a purely formal level, suggest that the rise of mass culture and its new expressive forms decisively affected the ways in which modernist writers went about composing works appropriate to the twentieth century. John Dos Passos's *U.S.A.,* Henry James's *The Reverberator,* and Theodore Dreiser's *An American Tragedy* incorporate and manipulate newspaper texts. Nathanael West's *The Day of the Locust* takes on the perceived fragmentation and incompletion of Hollywood film culture; and West claimed that *Miss Lonelyhearts* took its form from the art that has always been associated with the newspaper: the comic strip. Under the acid test of mass culture, many unsuspected resemblances emerge from this group of writers: Dreiser, conventionally labeled a naturalist, does not employ the same narrative devices as Henry James, but *An American Tragedy* transforms mass-cultural expression in the same way, and to the same ends, as *The Sacred Fount.* For the same reasons, Dos Passos's *U.S.A.* can be viewed as occupying the same cultural field as *The Sacred Fount,* despite Dos Passos's socialist affiliations in the early 1930s and despite the fact that Dos Passos harshly criticized the kind of cultural heritage James admired and epitomized. This move toward seeing the modernist text as irrevocably linked to and penetrated by the dense, complex social formations of a burgeoning mass culture is a crucial one, for it denies the common view of modernism as being merely antagonistic to the cultural formations it defines itself against. Renato Poggioli, to take one typical example, asserts "as an absolute principle that the genuine art of a bourgeois society can only be antibourgeois" (1968, 120). Fredric Jameson, too, argues that the nature of modernist writing depends on a "distinction between high and so-called mass culture," its function "consisting at least in part in the securing of a realm of authentic experience over against the surrounding environment of philistinism, of schlock and kitsch, of commodification and of Reader's Digest culture" (1984, 64). For Jameson and many other critics, it is postmodern writing that consistently transgresses the putative boundaries between high art and mass culture.

Though modernist writing in the period 1880–1940 is characteristically distinct from the forms of expression emerging from mass culture, I argue that writers in search of a realm of authentic experience had to write within that context and that the marks of that cultural refashioning are inscribed within their texts. The formal strategies of modernism were conceived dialogically; modernism and mass culture, the authentic and the inauthentic, must be theorized together and situated within the authoritative discursive structures of American society. Modernist writers articulate an opposition between them and mass culture only to disguise larger relations of power within which the products and forms of mass culture are vital to the shaping of modernist discourse. The strategic borrowings practiced by American modernists mean that their work is more than just the inscription of difference into the cultural terrain; it constitutes a set of accommodations so thoroughgoing that the paradigmatic literary–nonliterary and authentic–nonauthentic structures with which most critics work are set in question. Hence, although I am concerned with the issue of how modernists create and critics recognize cultural differences, I also work to revive mass culture as a constant and vital presence in these novels. Mass culture and inauthenticity are so easily made to cohabit that the correspondence rarely needs to be invoked; it exists among the interstices of cultural significations and practices, everywhere shaping and determining that which is known and written about as authentic art. It is precisely this precondition for recognizing authenticity that modernist writing addresses – and often seriously disrupts.

This discussion raises the question of how the structures, forms, and linguistic strategies of modernist texts are shaped by their encounters with that "other" cultural terrain of consumer capitalism. Jean Piaget provides a useful preliminary model in *Structuralism,* in which he distinguishes between "assimilation" as a process in which a system "comes to incorporate new objects into itself," and "accommodation" as a "process whereby the schemes of assimilation themselves become modified in being applied to a diversity of objects" (1971, 63). A text organized around a principle of assimilation would incorporate, say, the technique of D. W. Griffith's film-montage, as though by a process of osmosis, leading to a smooth, invisible capture of structural features originating in an altogether different medium. Most critics view modernist works this way. Faulkner's work, for instance, might be seen as cinematic, but what is really important is not the fact of Hollywood filmmaking or the undigested remains of particular films. All of that is divested during Faulkner's act of transformation, which composes scenes around film technique so seamlessly that one might never recognize the influence. It is as if the specific nature of the act of borrowing excises the fact of borrowing. When an influence is recognized, critics invariably propose a formal appropriation that in no way implies an ideological sellout. Quite the opposite: critical reading after reading suggests that an author's appropriation of formal elements signals the disruption of his or her ideological contexts. While Faulkner's work might seem cinematic in some abstract sense, then, it will not be held to owe its existence to Hollywood. A structural principle of accommodation, on the other hand, signifies works that are rough-edged and discontinuous, and whose assimilative processes bear witness to the work of transformation. Their schemes of assimilation bespeak their changed or changing functions. In these works, material and techniques borrowed from mass culture obtrude in the act of "writing in"; the narratives, to use Mikhail Bakhtin's terminology, voice their "heteroglossia," their status as relational, dialogic texts. These texts, in my reading, thus share common ground with those that Jameson designates as postmodern.

These neat categories break down, however, on the grounds that we can see assimilation as a disguised form of accommodation. The expressive forms of mass culture leave their traces in all modernist texts, if only in the work their authors must perform to exclude them. In what I have called assimilation, mass culture is written off, as it were, before it is written in; but the echoes of excluded language, forms, and images nonetheless invest the text, occupying the interstices of the work if not the textual surface. Signs of this appear most obviously in works where the voices of mass culture barely interrupt. James's image of the journalist in *The Sacred Fount,* for instance, invites us to observe a whole network of secret liaisons between mass cultural and modernist writing practices. Likewise, in T. S. Eliot's *The Waste Land* (1922), a fragment like "O O O O that Shakespeherian Rag" summons a context of all that the poem purports not to be. We do not need Eliot's own mordant recorded reading of this line to reveal that four "O"s add up to vacuity in popular music and that ragtime has ripped up more than Shakespeare's name. The text makes room for a voice from another realm, an act that constellates anew every allusion and disjunction we have witnessed so far. Indeed, the act seems to parody Eliot's famous account of the symbiotic relationship between tradition and the individual talent. As we apprehend the culture that must have gone into the making of the "Shakespeherian Rag," we begin to realize the pressure it must have exerted on the poem from the start. It illuminates every fragment borrowed or created afresh, every poetic structure that would accrue greater authority than a sum of zeroes. We might also note the silent pressure the line exerts on us as critics. Since Eliot tells us nothing about the song beyond its mere appearance in the text, other strategies – a common sense of a particularly esoteric kind – must have already come into play to allow us to read "O" as zero.[1]

Two major theses arise from this model of assimilation and accommodation, only one of which I shall argue in this book. One might, first of all, write an account of modernist writing in which various writing strategies articulate a history of exclusions and acts of silencing; an account of works in which an historical engagement with a consumer-driven mass culture has disappeared underground. This might include works that seem to hold no obvious relation to the expressions of mass culture as well as those in which cinematic technique or radio or jazz forms function as barely more than a useful metaphor. The works that interest me most, however, are those in which the act of accommodation is most pronounced and whose authors' literary designs are most bound up with, compromised and inspired by the mass culture from which they desired to secede. These texts confront the widest cultural divide of the twentieth century as both a structuring principle and a problematic, and bring into the open the crucial critical acts of reading and the legitimating practices whereby literary significances are fashioned, refashioned, disputed, and affirmed. And they allow this opening-up because they invite us to see, by way of a series of narrative gaps, hesitations, and incompletions, the acts of transformation that authors and critics alike undertake in order to establish points of difference between the originality of a (modernist) text and the origin of its formal techniques in mass culture. In the works I study, I narrow the spectrum of possible points of difference by arguing that they are articulated in direct relation to the specific modes of mass culture these texts accommodate. For example, I view Dos Passos's modernism in relation to the mass cultural forms and ideological attributes we find, or think we find, in the Newsreels; and I view West's modernism in *Miss Lonelyhearts* in relation to the comic-strip form that he claimed structured the novel.

We might say that the process of assimilation disguises the shaping of one cultural terrain into another, whereas the act of accommodation highlights the transformative act while problematizing it. By taking seriously the irruption into these texts of mass cultural material – not as a de facto sign of authorial intervention, but as a sign of a network of formal and ideological complicities between author and consumer culture – I question the epistemological grounds that enable us to insert a critical wedge between cultural realms. But calling into doubt the epistemological foundation of our interpretive acts does not negate the actual, real-life, day-to-day business of legitimating critical practices and writings. As often as I question our strategies of knowing about literature, I insist on their real, objective basis within the profession of literary studies. As an ever-changing structural principle, accommodation guarantees the recognition and preservation of difference and thus constitutes a strategy for the fashioning of a separate (though constantly shifting) literary realm. This model thus sketches out a tripartite relationship: a complex accommodation within the modernist text of culturally powerful expressive forms; a reciprocal relationship between modernist writers and the institution of literary studies; and a crucial though covert liaison of both critics and modernist writers to the social and discursive formations of consumer capitalism. We will not understand the nature of modernist texts without examining the ways in which they have been and are read and legitimated. Nor will we understand twentieth-century modes of legitimation without examining the ways in which esoteric writing, in particular, comes to be valued in an age of mass culture.

This account of modernism exists in a strong – though skeptical – relationship to academic attempts to reassess the function and power of mass culture, which, until the past couple of decades, could be said to guarantee the idea of "culture" for both the political left and right. Cultural conservatives (Matthew Arnold through T. S. Eliot, F. R. Leavis, E. D. Hirsch, and beyond) discover in a trivial and trivializing mass culture an argument for reading and teaching the best that has been thought and said in the world. Similar critiques can be found in dozens of academic publications as well as in the media. They come to the fore in every battle for freedom of the press, in every account of televised electoral debates, as well as in every attack on the psychologically debilitating effects of TV violence, commercials, videos and video games, Hollywood's catering to the lowest common denominator, and so on. On the left, T. E. Adorno and the Frankfurt School level an equally virulent attack on mass culture, now shaped by the capitalist economy that conservatives would prefer to ignore, so that, ironically, as Andreas Huyssen writes, "20th-century capitalism has 'reunified' economy and culture by subsuming the cultural under the economic, by reorganizing the body of cultural meanings and symbolic significations to fit the logic of the commodity" (1986, 21). Art, for Adorno, comprises an autonomous realm that dialectically reflects – and negates – the affirmative power of the culture industry. That critique remains alive on the left in the works of thinkers like Fredric Jameson and Jean Baudrillard, theorizing the cultural, psychological, and economic phenomena of a postmodern age in terms of simulacra, hyperspace, and schizophrenia – and yet with still greater angst.[2] So completely does mass culture exercise hegemony over American life, in Antonio Gramsci's sense of moral, intellectual, and artistic leadership of society, that critics on the left have seemed increasingly pessimistic about the value of any kind of social critique. Within a radically fragmented, schizophrenic, and disorienting culture, the manipulation of desires, aspirations, values, and perceptions continues unexamined – or if examined, only from within the academy, whence the most virulent attacks on mass culture are routinely ignored, repressed, and occasionally packaged for mass consumption by those controlling mass publication and programming.

But powerful new bodies of work within the academy have sought to redefine the purpose, value, and relevance of mass culture in more affirmative ways. These theories explain the hegemony of popular forms of expression by accepting that popular culture (rather than the pejorative-sounding "mass culture") provides authentic experiences, gratifies desires, and provides a real, lived, and shared sense of being-in-the-world.[3] New theories about the postmodern condition, beginning in the realm of aesthetics but quickly becoming applicable to other political, psychic, and financial economies, have portrayed a radically decentered, heterogeneous cultural landscape characterized by the demise, in Jean-François Lyotard's already famous term, "*les grands récits*" of Western culture.

A work like Jim Collins's recent *Uncommon Cultures,* for instance, celebrates the final demise of a "Grand Hotel" of culture whereby a single, approved group of texts could pass for High Culture, while the kind of works enjoyed by the majority of people were dismissed as worthless. As Collins puts it, the "co-presence of such contradictory hierarchies . . . makes 'the official hierarchy' difficult to identify" (1989, 25), and undermines our ability to construct a cultural center from which to observe, categorize, and hierarchize all cultural production. In such an atmosphere, it has become increasingly possible to read literature as a formation of mass culture, rather than as a set-apart and culturally privileged body of texts – often with major consequences for our understanding of literary work in other periods. I shall consider in the next section some of the more important attempts to construct a new narrative of American literature at the turn of the century based on the hegemony of the mass market.

New assessments of mass culture have not only heightened the debate over literariness, and thus over the modernist writing that has provided us with our most authoritative and long-lasting definitions of literary expression in the twentieth century, but have raised the question of how aesthetic, cultural, and literary criteria promulgated within the enclave of the academy can be said to be culturally authoritative at all. By the end of the nineteenth century intellectuals were already articulating feelings of inadequacy as they observed the burgeoning, high-energy world of mass journalism, and those feelings have only intensified as the contempt many academics harbor toward the banality and formulaic repetitiveness of mass culture gives way to a sense of being a second-class citizen, divorced from the arenas of real life and real power experienced by journalists, scriptwriters, freelance writers, and those in charge of TV programming. Such a fear underwrites Andrew Ross's recent attempt to transcend what he calls a dialectic of disrespect, whereby a popular anti-intellectualism confronts an educated contempt for mass culture.[4] Ross calls for "specific" or "organic" intellectuals (in Michel Foucault's and Gramsci's terms respectively) – or simply "new intellectuals," in his own terms – who will be able to eschew outmoded cultural oppositions and transcend the limitations of their own intensely specialized languages in order to "shift from context to context, whether it involves the use of specialized knowledge in an occupational field or the use of generalized persuasion in speaking through the popular media." They will be informed, moreover, by the "pragmatic, democratizing possibilities ushered in by new technologies and new popular cultures" (1988, 127).

The remainder of this chapter and the subsequent analyses of works by James, Dreiser, Dos Passos, and West draw on this contemporary skepticism about the privilege of literary texts and professional critics. Yet my examination of the historical and discursive features of professionalism suggests that the identities I trace between professional readers and modernist writers are neither arbitrary, nor circumstantial, nor likely to disappear in the near future. Indeed, it is worth noting that, though both Ross and Collins argue against the kind of cultural privilege hitherto associated with intellectuals and the kind of high cultural endowment typically celebrated by intellectuals, both postmodern agendas recuperate traditional prerogatives of academic professionals. Intellectual work, for instance, is still adjudged appropriate to certain local arenas; though assigned a relatively minor role in a radically decentered cultural space, it is to survive as one among many forms of cultural production. New intellectuals are to recognize and align themselves with the hegemony of mass culture – though only in certain specific situations – and thus to stand forth with more power than they previously possessed. Specialized and popular face off across as deep a divide as ever before; that divide is in fact confirmed in the ability of the new intellectuals to cross (but not destroy) boundaries. These writers, in short, envisage a strikingly decentered and heterogeneous landscape – a chessboard of postmodern culture – in which the notion of cultural authority is both suspect (because there can be no one authoritative perspective) and preserved in decentered form (for there is no single perspective to overturn the legitimating strategies practiced by each individual area of culture). The following pages elaborate the significance of this second possibility: that the specialized work and arcane languages that circumscribe the voice and appeal of intellectuals nevertheless constitute the foundation of their powerful right to speak about cultural matters.

I

Frank Norris, speaking of the American public and its reading habits, wrote in 1903 that "the great presses of the country are for the most part merely sublimated sausage machines that go dashing along in a mess of paper and printer's ink turning out the meat for the monster" ([1903] 104–5). So much for one of America's greatest technological and cultural achievements, the giant, speedy printing presses and the monstrous public they were able to capture. But after the last decade of the nineteenth century, in which circulation battles between Joseph Pulitzer's *New York World* and William Randolph Hearst's *New York Journal* attained new levels of ferocity, Norris's hyperbole might be forgiven. Yellow journalism, sensational stunts and muckraking campaigns, crusades and pseudoevents were employed in a (successful) effort to sustain circulation drives. New techniques arose for presenting the news for consumption – dramatic headlines, subheadings for making reports easier to assimilate, front page photographs, comic strips, and huge Sunday supplements – all of which showed how information might be packaged as fully as any consumer product on the market. Journalism, advertising, popular writing, and later the movie industry all showed increasing ties to the corporate model of production and participated in the drive toward consumerism. Popular novels, for instance, were frequently produced efficiently in writing "factories," as though "Taylorized." Books were disseminated through new technologies of distribution: book clubs, ad campaigns, extensive reviews. Hollywood, too, employed an efficient conveyor belt model to assemble movie scripts and productions piecemeal, like a Model T Ford; communal scripts played down the significance of individual creativity to corporate effort, much to the dissatisfaction of writers with literary pretensions in Hollywood script factories.[5]

A link between a developing mass market and consumer-oriented cultural forms had certainly begun to emerge in America by the 1830s.[6] The American Romantics, as many critics have demonstrated, were aware of changing conditions of production, sensing the different requirements of a mass audience as well as the new status of the text as a commodity in the marketplace.[7] "By 1855," as John Tebbel remarks, "America had already far surpassed England in sales, so that while it was most unusual to sell more than 10,000 copies of even the best fiction in Great Britain and Ireland, it was not at all out of the ordinary to sell 50,000 copies of even a moderately good book in America" (1974, 215). But it was the period after the Civil War, with the launching of paperbacks, dime novels, cheap reprints, "libraries" of classics, and mass magazines – innovations that responded to and greatly encouraged the formation of a mass audience – that gave most dramatic impetus to the consolidation of mass culture. And the development of mass culture seemed to increase exponentially toward the end of the century. Richard Altick notes that by 1885 the four American magazines with circulations over 100,000 sold an aggregate of 600,000 copies a month; by 1905, the number of such magazines had increased fivefold, selling an aggregate of 5,500,500 per month (1989, 227).

The measure of this transformation in American culture is as familiar as the reasons put forward to explain it. On the one hand, the spread of education and literacy in this period effected enormous gains in the size of reading publics.[8] On the other, massive industrial growth, the expansion of cities, and improved communication and transportation networks led to the emergence of a national marketplace, a development that was sustained by the ability of companies to reach and influence mass audiences through the channels of the new mass media. Advances in mass communication had startlingly immediate (and highly visible) effects: the introduction of linotype machines in 1885 and of speedier presses capable of supplying an audience of millions allowed the rapid growth of journalism. The fact that the circulation of the New York World rose from about 15,000 in 1883 to 150,000 in 1885, the first two years of Joseph Pulitzer's ownership, and had reached over a million by the end of the century, testifies not only to his drive but to an intricate convergence of technology and literacy.[9] In the same decades, Thomas Edison and William K. Dickson made the first crude moving pictures, and inventions by Heinrich Hertz and Guglielmo Marconi led to the development of the radio. New technologies spurred new audiences; by 1908, there were already about 10,000 nickelodeons in America. By the end of the century, the technology, technological expertise, and marketing techniques necessary for the development of mass culture were substantially in place.

Still more interesting are the familiar and influential accounts by cultural historians of a thoroughgoing reorientation of American culture in the Progressive Era. A crisis of cultural authority emerged as people's traditional relations to work, leisure, the city, and cultural pursuits began to warp under the rapid development of consumer capitalism. As Richard Wightman Fox and T. J. Jackson Lears have pointed out, selfhood became "fragmented, diffuse, and somehow 'weightless' or 'unreal'" as new urban environments and technologies unsettled traditional patterns of life (Fox and Lears, 1983, xiii). The drive to shape a new sense of self and create new sources of authority in American life took various forms. For our purposes, the most important of these was the rise of professional elites to guide the new social and psychological patterns of consumer society. Fox and Lears note the "emergence of a new stratum of professionals and managers, rooted in a web of complex new organizations (corporations, government, universities, professional associations, media, foundations, and others)" (xi). As the rationalization of American economic and social life unfolded in the last thirty years of the nineteenth century, professional groups arose to manage new corporate and bureaucratic structures of power, and in the process attained a powerful economic and social status. The authority achieved by professionals, however, was limited by their complicity with the structures of corporate capitalism they sought to guide and control. As supposedly expert guides to new and disorienting social structures, professionals were themselves subject to widespread fears of a "weightless" existence. One consequence was the rise of what Jackson Lears calls the "therapeutic ethos": "a new gospel of therapeutic release preached by a host of writers, publishers, ministers, social scientists, doctors, and the advertisers themselves" (Fox and Lears, xi). Anxious to restore a powerful and coherent sense of self, professionals advocated therapy in many different ways: the creation of a "muscular" culture of strength and martial valor, a return to traditional ideals of craftsmanship, and a "recovery of the primal, irrational forces in the human psyche" (Lears 1981, 57).

This reading of the Progressive Era, whereby cultural expression is subsumed under a massive reorientation of society toward bureaucratic organization, professional endeavors, and demands for a "muscular" culture, has proved particularly fruitful for analysts of mass culture. As Christopher Wilson has argued powerfully in *The Labor of Words,* the image of the literary writer as a genteel amateur writing in seclusion – and for the love of writing – became increasingly difficult to support. Although Frank Norris staunchly declared that to "make money is not the province of a novelist" (1986, 1151), Norris and many others were well aware that their work had become commodified, ever more subject to the whims of the marketplace. (They were also well aware of the financial benefits accruing to the professionalized writer willing to be associated with the market.) Educated Americans also sensed a deep dissatisfaction with discourses that have traditionally confirmed the status of literature – a dissatisfaction that in many cases led them toward the discursive and ideological practices of journalism. Journalism, in fact, obsessed many educated Americans in their thinking about cultural roles. The journalist became something of a culture hero – tough, uncompromising, at once reporter, investigator, and man of action, and a surprisingly consistent refrain was that the journalist's role in society demonstrated, by contrast, all that was wrong with the traditional literary life. As Jay Martin has noted, the poet George Cabot Lodge specified the problem with almost comic fervor: "I don't do anything here, nothing tangible. I work five hours a day or six, and what on – a miserable little poetaster. I want to get home and get some place on a newspaper or anything of that kind, and really do something" (1967, 15).

Unease with the "effeminate" and nonprofessional aspects of literary endeavors is evident throughout the late nineteenth century, and certainly led to a transformation of sociological conditions of authorship and in literary discourse.[10] Christopher Wilson argues that literary writers "came to see their craft predominantly as a product of technical expertise rather than inspiration, viewed the market as the primary arbiter of literary value, and were guided principally by an internalized sense of responsibility to their public" (1985, 204). One result, Wilson argues, is that authors began to "aspire to the ideal of *reportage.*" The reporter became the "high priest of 'experience,' the expert on 'real life,'" and the literary writer wished to follow the reporter into the "muck of American life" (17). Writers also entered the muck of American business life. Throughout the field of writing, whether authors perceived themselves to be literary writers or bound over to the current Grub Street, a new tough-mindedness about the writer's professional affiliations was apparent. The formation of writers' societies, new copyright laws, the increasing importance of literary agents, and a growing attention on the part of writers to the minutiae of contracts and marketing were all indications of changing attitudes toward the marketplace.[11] Wilson grounds his study in well-documented historical and sociological transformations. Many writers at the turn of the century began their careers as apprentice reporters. Of the four writers I examine, only Nathanael West had no newspaper experience, and the list of other writers who did (Crane, Cather, Hemingway) could be extended almost indefinitely.[12] Wilson's account thus suggests that we "cannot overlook the strategic positioning of Progressive Era news reporting in not only providing a literary apprenticeship . . . but in charting out new terrain for literature as a whole" (38).

The term "apprenticeship," which appears in numerous considerations of the literary production of this era, strikes the keynote of this particular critical perspective. Connoting an intimate but youthful student–master relationship, "apprenticeship" allows for the possibility of more mature (literary) work while assuming that a later style emerged out of an early encounter with journalism. Journalism marks a point of origin for writers whose later work, however far it extends an early training in newspaper writing strategies, remains indebted to that training for its authority and distinctive American flavor. Many different elements of American journalism are figured into this equation: a vivid, colorful, "storytelling" style; a tendency toward hard, direct prose and factual accuracy; a professionalization of relationships in the writing business; and the cult of real experience embodied in the reporter's everyday work. It is important to note that in these critics' work the interdependency of reporter and author helps to explain not only the latter's writing strategies but their source of cultural authority. With the passing of the ethos of genteel, amateur writing, these critics assume, the sources of literary power must be discovered elsewhere; and the journalist, dealer in raw experience as well as advocate of a new style, seems a prominent guide to a crude but energetic national literature. These assumptions derive much of their explanatory power from a new faith in the hegemony of forms of writing created for the mass market – a faith that is justified if cultural authority depends on one's ability to sway a mass audience. From the critics' point of view, theories of a literary apprenticeship to journalism (like the current interest in extending the canon to more popular forms of writing) has the advantage of associating academic work with writing that seems tangibly linked to dominant American ideologies and structures of power.

Most of these critics, however, covertly sketch quite another narrative of literary production – a counternarrative that closely resembles the structure of accommodation I have described. As an example, let us take Alan Trachtenberg's essay "Experiments in Another Country: Stephen Crane's City Sketches" (1982), an interpretation of Crane's earlier reportage and fiction that should be telling because Crane, who not only wrote fiction and newspaper reports concurrently but sought self-consciously to perform a tough male role in his pursuit of "real life," appears in life and fiction to exemplify a professional writer's ties to journalism. Trachtenberg's careful, penetrating analysis of stories like "The Men of the Storm" and "An Experiment in Misery" suggests that these apprentice works drew on key features of 1890s journalism: colorful and vivid slice-of-life portrayals of personal experiences in the city, probing at urban mysteries that the newspaper sensationalized as much as explored. Insofar as these sketches were written for publication in the newspapers, Trachtenberg appears to be on solid enough ground for constructing a powerful argument about the symbiosis of literary work and journalistic experience. From the first, however, Trachtenberg seems concerned about claiming too much for Crane's sketches: "Considering their origins as newspaper sketches," he remarks, "these mainly short, deft impressions of New York street life seem more like apprentice work than finished inventions" (141). Although the newspaper must be taken into account as a "given of the experimental situation," at a deeper level the "form provided a challenge, a barrier to be overcome." And although journalism enabled him to develop new techniques, defining his "literary problem from within such conventions posed certain difficulties; literalism, sensationalism, sentimentality were the ogres of the newspaper story Crane had to slay in his own work" (143). Trachtenberg's evenhanded approach transforms Crane's apprenticeship into a complex set of good and bad influences, some of which would continue to exert a positive influence over his writing, others of which would strengthen his writing only in their excision.

Relying again on criteria of experience and intimacy with the mass market-place, Trachtenberg argues that, at best, "within the logic of the newspaper lies a possible condition for the salvation of the word – in the new relationships it fosters between writer and world, between writer and reader." In the next sentence, though, Trachtenberg changes tactics: "Crane accepted the conditions of newspaper production and produced within it work that, with the complicity of his careful reader, converts the data of street life into memorable experience. He thus transvalues, or as Benjamin would put it, 'alienates' the apparatus of production and forces his reader to become an accomplice" (149). But who is Crane's reader? An anonymous and neutral reader forced to become Crane's accomplice? Or the newspaper reader whom Trachtenberg has already situated within the "'public' that is the collective identity each isolated urban conscious-ness is invited to join" (141)? Or the careful reader, whose special attributes and sociological conditions of reading Trachtenberg nowhere specifies? A careful reader surely cannot be conflated with those isolated urban consciousnesses who may not even recognize (as we certainly do) that the public they are invited to join is only a public in quotation marks – a travesty of a public. But if Crane's careful reader is not identical with his original newspaper readers, to what extent does the logic of the newspaper and the relationships it fosters contribute to the salvation of the word?

Even if Trachtenberg had not specified a careful reader, we (as critics) would naturally know the name of that anonymous reader as "Trachtenberg," perhaps Walter Benjamin as a kind of ghostlike presence often invoked in this essay, and most likely the critical consciousness reading the essay. The new relationships Trachtenberg is really invoking have to do with careful readers, subtle reading strategies, and an understanding of alienating writing strategies that transcends that of any bourgeois newspaper reader in the 1890s. It is only because of this set of relationships that Trachtenberg can propose the formative power of journalism. His readings of newspaper culture, in fact, always imply this com-petent but silent audience. Although he explains in great detail the connection between the newspaper and the mysteries of late-nineteenth-century urban life, he never states the grounds upon which the problems of the newspaper can be perceived as literalism, sensationalism, and sentimentality (the ogres that Crane needs to slay). Nor, for that matter, does he explain how to recognize a "finished invention" from the newspaper sketches Crane wrote in the early nineties – a necessary knowledge, since without it we could not possibly recognize the compromised, incomplete status of the sketches. In fact we do know: not because Trachtenberg tells us, but because our common sense as careful readers ensures that no critical reading has to argue for the sensationalism and sentimentality of the newspaper. It is a given before we even read this essay, a given that Trachtenberg does not even consider needs explanation (and he is right). Like

Crane, according to Trachtenberg, we have "no illusions about the newspaper and the degradation of literature it represents" (149). Thus even if we cannot guess what Trachtenberg means by "finished invention" and "literature," we do know (our common sense tells us) that a story like "An Experiment in Misery" will be different from any newspaper production – including itself! Given our preconstituted knowledge about reportage, we automatically discount the story's origins as a newspaper sketch in our final evaluation. Rather than reading the sketch as no more than a mere newspaper sketch, we discover its originality in its transformation (by careful readers like us) out of the newspaper medium. We are not surprised, consequently, to see that Trachtenberg labels the sketches "proto-literary" rather than the most polished and highly elaborated examples of newspaper art.

Other stories of Stephen Crane's point up even more dramatically how limited the interpretive power of these critical strategies might be. "The Open Boat" (1897), for instance, which draws attention in its brief introduction to the tale's being the "Experience of Four Men," is based on Crane's experience of surviving the sinking of the *Commodore* and his subsequent thirty-hour voyage in a dinghy to safety. Crane first published his recollections in the New York *Press* on January 7, 1897, under the title "Stephen Crane's Own Story," later rewriting and publishing it in June 1897 as "The Open Boat." At first sight the story meets journalistic criteria for action, realism, and accuracy of detail; it seems, above all, "masculine" writing. Yet "action" is misapplied to a story that deals insistently with the constraints placed on action. "By the very last star of truth," remarks the narrator, "it is easier to steal eggs from under a hen than it was to change seats in the dinghy" (1968, 281). Male action and valor, in fact, are reduced to near-paralysis and grim repetition ("They rowed and they rowed"), while natural phenomena refuse to respond to human desires and perceptions: "Slowly and beautifully the land loomed out of the sea" (276), observes the narrator, as though the emergence of land had nothing to do with the relative position of the human observers.

The introduction also implies the indeterminacy that invests the whole story. It is a tale told "after the Fact," where "after" could signify either a causal relationship ("based on, closely following") or a chronological one ("later than") or both together. Moreover, it is "A Tale *Intended* to be after the Fact" (my italics), an odd figure of speech that seems to rule out reading "after" as referring to chronology: Why, otherwise, would Crane only intend a relationship to fact that already existed concretely in time? But then why trouble to connote chronology in the first place? What Crane intends by a tale based on fact also becomes increasingly mysterious as the tale unfolds. He is not asserting an ideal of journalistic objectivity, nor even following the tendency of journalism in the 1880s and 1890s toward relating a "good story." Rather, "The Open Boat" actively engages the question of the status of facts and fictionality, as demonstrated most obviously by the struggles of the men in the boat to interpret signs of rescue on shore. "What's that idiot with the coat mean? What's he signalling, anyhow?" asks one of the men; "Well, I wish I could make something out of those signals. What do you suppose he means?" asks another. We never find out: Facts signify as facts only within the appropriate context, as when the narrator turns to his audience to note, "It is fair to say here that there was not a life-saving station within twenty miles in either direction; but the men did not know this fact." Not knowing, the men therefore do not register this fact as a fact; their fact is their limited perception: "There was the shore of the populous land, and it was bitter and bitter to them that from it came no sign" (278). We do not need to read Crane's original report of the wrecking of the *Commodore* to recognize that this story does not "reproduce" the newspaper sketch of the time; by questioning the very categories by which the story assigns meaning, Crane proclaims its distance from both the original facts of the wrecking and from the sensational newspaper story of the period. Its status as a story about fact, fiction, and the limitations of action alone preserves its difference from reportage.

What I have done here is read back into "The Open Boat" the careful reader whom Trachtenberg everywhere implies but nowhere specifies in his reading of Crane's sketches. I have emphasized aspects of "The Open Boat" according to a critical discourse that values complexity, subversion, and indeterminacy and that transforms this tale told "after the Fact" into a metafiction; if the survivors of the shipwreck feel at the end of the story that "they could then be interpreters," we feel (with more angst) that we should be interpreters of a story that demonstrates just how problematic our task really is. In the process, the relationship of Crane to the more colorful, "masculine," and naturalistic literary approach critics have adduced for this period becomes increasingly questionable. Reportage still functions in this intrepretation of the story, but as a level of discourse having to do with fact, objectivity, "masculine" writing, which is accommodated and subjugated within (this is one way of putting it) a narrative about narrative modes, in which reportage has lost its privileged claims to truth and cultural primacy. Certainly "The Open Boat" casts great doubt on critical models that seek to hold journalism (and other forms of writing appealing to the mass market) responsible for literary production around the turn of the century. However much Crane demonstrated in his life the new career opportunities available to a writer, and however much Crane's story pays tribute to the outdoor life, current explanations of how a story like "The Open Boat" might relate to a new professional ethos remain unsatisfactory.

One way of putting this is that "The Open Boat" is closer to a modernist paradigm than to the realist or naturalist paradigm invoked by most critics. More precisely, I chose to locate the story within a modernist frame of reference to draw attention to those elements that subtly incorporated and transformed newspaper rhetoric and logic. But that choice was not an arbitrary one. Sedimented into the literary canon by years of accumulated critical statements, the story can scarcely be viewed any longer as merely the best that the late-nineteenth-century newspaper has to offer. It is by the same token misleading to locate the story's cultural authority *now* in a "masculine," professionalized culture of journalism. Its readership, and the readership of those who write most powerfully about it, is quite different. The critical acts of reading and writing by critics who set out to ground writers thoroughly in sociological conditions of authorship have already, as we read, embedded a putative set of original relationships between author and audience into a discourse composed of different practices and legitimative principles. I do not mean to suggest either that our critical horizon has merely displaced that of Crane and his contemporary readers. In fact the opposite is true: Our critical horizon emerges out of the relationship of historical forces already at work in Crane's time to produce small, competent professional groups within a social framework characterized by corporate forms of power and a burgeoning mass culture. The relations of power that really work to make "The Open Boat" and "An Experiment in Misery" culturally authoritative are not those endowed by a newspaper context (as real and tangible as these appear), but the conjunction of accommodatory writing strategies and a critical establishment capable of reading those strategies powerfully. If, as I argue, that conjunction best defines modernist writing, "An Experiment in Misery," as odd as it sounds, is not only protoliterary but protomodernist in the way it functions (or we make it function) to become more – and more powerful – than the newspaper story it in fact was.

Models of literary production that describe the hegemony of the mass market thus seem inadequate on at least four counts. First, they oversimplify writers' attitudes toward mass culture, the mass market, and the desirability of reaching a huge audience. Second, as a corollary, they fail to account for the impulse toward esoteric writing strategies in many writers (including those commonly labeled naturalist) who underwent an "apprenticeship" to journalism. Third, they ignore the particular way these strategies incorporate and subvert the languages, forms, and ideologies specific to mass culture. Fourth, and perhaps most important, they fail to recognize ways in which writers might maintain cultural hegemony in spite of widespread perceptions about the dominance of mass culture. By focusing on the mass market, in other words, these studies ignore the fact that the newly forming structures of the marketplace allowed for a special kind of esoteric writing and, what is more important, made it possible for this kind of writing to assume cultural authority. It is because critics do not recognize that the history of literary meanings and practices has followed a quite different path than the one their sociological studies define that they persist in attributing the authority of turn-of-the-century writing to professionalized forms of writing for the mass market.

Henry James, in fact, proves to be a more reliable guide to the implications of the reorganized mass marketplace in his provocative essay "The Question of the Opportunities" ([1898] 1984). The essay begins by stating point-blank the premise that professionals, writing within a mass culture, must compromise the quality of their work. Thus, drawing attention to the existence of the largest reading public in history within the "great common-schooled and newspapered democracy" of America, he first laments that "literature for the billion will not be literature as we have hitherto known it at its best." Immediately, however, he envisages this public "breaking up into pieces." He continues, "The public we somewhat loosely talk of as for literature or for anything else is really as subdivided as a chess-board, with each little square confessing only to its own *kind* of accessibility." That situation, James observes, might lead to "individual publics positively more sifted and evolved than anywhere else, shoals of fish rising to more delicate bait." Among those individual publics, then, exists one we can firmly talk of as "for literature" (now in its restricted, exclusive sense of literature *not* for the billion) that can rise to the esoteric work of James's late years and to the work of the modernist movements he helped to fashion.

A mass audience of readers, James perceives, exists more as theory than as fact, and the exigencies of twentieth-century publishing have indeed shown that financial success depends on reaching a specific, well-defined group of readers – one of many mass audiences – rather than aiming at some amorphous mass readership.[13] James also grasps one of the key issues behind the creation of modernist writing strategies: the power of esoteric writing to deny even the theoretical legitimacy of a mass audience and to replace it with a readership fashioned by its cultural, linguistic, and literary competence. For reading material on the mass market, exclusion is a matter of taste – the publisher of *Playboy* magazine targets a specific male audience that will presumably not be interested in *Ladies' Home Journal,* even though the latter magazine is perfectly comprehensible to a male reader. James's notion of "accessibility" suggests something very different: the possibility that certain linguistic and formal strategies will be accessible to one audience based on its competence and thus guarantee their unavailability to another. This has the effect, incidentally, of orienting esoteric writing in a new relationship to the mass market of fiction, rather than removing it. Writing specifically for one subdivision of the chessboard mass audience, the literary writer may restrict but simultaneously guarantee the salability of any piece of writing. Although James remains vague about the specific constitution of these audiences, it is a matter of historical fact that a readership teaching within or educated by the university has carried the banner "for literature" in the cultural chess game that James's metaphor presages.

Unlike many postmodern theorists, James does not read heterogeneity as decenteredness; he views the fragmented mass audience as at once heterogeneous and centered. The fact that most audiences are off reading literatures for the billion actually helps to constitute one audience and one form of literature whose characteristics are more than usually delicate and evolved. James envisages a situation, in other words, in which the differentiations made by a multitude of audiences (each preoccupied with its own form of preferred literature) give way before the differentiations made by people who matter in terms of their capacity to speak for cultural matters. James's formulation is indubitably elitist, but I want to argue that it is also more accurate than postmodern visions of radical heterogeneity. In fact, to anticipate a point it will take the next sections to explore fully, esoteric forms of discourse possess a power that is hegemonic rather than marginal or, in Raymond Williams's term, "residual," allowing small groups of people to exercise a power out of all proportion to their actual size.

The question of how a certain discourse gains hegemony within particular structures of power, becomes institutionalized, and thus grants power to particular groups, is crucial to a comprehension of cultural authority. How does a work like James's *The Sacred Fount* accrue authority and how does it differ from a work by Lincoln Steffens? How do modernist writers create and critics observe distinctive forms of writing and how is it that such writing becomes authoritative? How, in other words, do writers and critics make difference *make a difference?* My answer is to reintroduce the socioeconomic transformations of Progressive Era America while emphasizing an alternative model of professional power that rests on the discursive practices of professionals, rather than upon their economic relationships to the mass market or on their yearnings for "real life." Any account of the historical processes governing the establishment of authoritative discourses in American consumer society must include a description of how universities at the end of the nineteenth century institutionalized specialized discourses and communities of competence as part of an attempt by the middle class to maintain social power, particularly by way of powerful professional groups that enjoy a reciprocal relationship with the university. This relationship between professional power and the university as legitimating agent is crucial to an understanding of how literary writers and critics, by privileging certain forms of writing, have preserved a form of cultural authority within the complex of forms, ideologies, and media we call mass or popular culture.

II

We have seen that a culture of professionalism arose out of the massive reorientation of American society toward corporate capitalism and as a response, at least in part, to a crisis of identity and authority among the middle classes. Professional institutions, as Thomas L. Haskell remarks, were "a way to *insure* that each audience would find its proper guide" (1977, 36). Professionals were able to establish new sources and kinds of authority, not least of which was their avowed autonomy within new corporate and bureaucratic structures. Certainly, the common perception that professionals constitute uniquely neutral, impartial groups existing outside conventional class divisions, standing apart from corporate modes of production, has accorded them great prestige. Their ability to organize themselves into tightly knit groups, each secure in its difference from other groups and from the public at large, certainly strengthens that impression, as does the nature of their product. As Stuart Culver has noted, professionals constantly articulate a need for "distinguishing service from commodity" (1984, 120). They claim, in other words, that the business of professionals is not to manufacture commodities but to produce a uniquely intangible service based on their possession of unquantifiable knowledge. In an economy where any object can, potentially, be mass produced, and where human beings themselves tend to become reified along with objects in the marketplace, professionals look to provide a distinctive and noncommodified service – though there is a great deal of argument about the extent to which professionals really do constitute a unique and privileged class.[14]

Historians have reached a loose consensus about the genesis of a culture of professionalism and about the special attributes of professional authority. The rise of the university, which began to take on its modern form in the 1870s, was indispensable to professional power. Post–Civil War crises of individual, civic, and economic authority led to social unrest on many levels. As Thomas Bender has pointed out, one specific result was an "erosion of public culture" (1984) in urban environments as mass immigration and a developing mass culture disrupted intellectual communities traditionally based within the city. Confronted by suddenly inexplicable economic and social transformations, communities of thinkers reformed within university departments to manage and guide in expert fashion the social, cultural, and economic systems of America. The university, which, as Barton Bledstein writes, "came into existence to serve and promote professional authority in society" (1976, x), became the most important institution of this movement. If traditional forms of discourse about the city were no longer applicable to a mass urban experience, the university promised to restore to intellectuals an authority based on new methods of analysis, powerful scientific models, and complex, specialized languages.[15] The university formalized bodies of esoteric knowledge, bestowed credentials on those who mastered that knowledge, and spread its ideologies by training an energetic corps of people who would take up socially prominent positions. The institutionalization of this knowledge guaranteed, moreover, that the failure or malfeasance of individual practitioners could be discounted: The university protected the legitimacy and continuity of professional discourse itself.

The key to this institutionalization of professional power is the ability to employ expert knowledge. Professionalization involves defining a body of what Eliot Freidson calls "formal knowledge," legitimating it by virtue of its association with institutions of higher education, and accrediting those who studied and used this knowledge. All discourses formalized within the university institute an organized, coherent body of knowledge, sets of laws, special techniques of analysis, and (as Foucault reminds us) an organizing sense of what kinds of knowledge, information, and questions must be excluded from consideration. The special nature of this higher knowledge – opaque discourse, jargon, a great amount of information to be remembered and processed, an arcana of traditions, values, and responsibilities, many of which are not specified in writing – limits the number of individuals able to possess it and therefore make the process of accreditation significant to the individual and to the community at large.[16] The "possession of scarce knowledge and skills," according to Larson, is the "principal basis on which modern professions claim social recognition and economic rewards" (1977, 136). Thus lawyers are not lawyers merely by virtue of their affiliations to professional associations or by virtue of their credentials, but because they have studied a special, esoteric body of knowledge that necessarily sets them apart from those who have not. Likewise, a special competence in reading literature and mastering a certain canon of texts, once approved and credentialed by adjudicating bodies within the university, allows a graduate student to become a professional scholar or critic. Moreover, literary critics may lay claim to being professionals despite their difficulty in claiming an absolute truth-value to their statements about a particular work; they may in fact have disclaimed any such allegiance to stable, determinate truths. But no critic working with a credo of indeterminacy could attain professional status without elaborating this credo in appropriately complex fashion.

Two other points necessarily follow. First, a key characteristic of professional discourse is its inaccessibility to a mass public. Second, esoteric knowledge presupposes the formation of a "community of competence" – a group of experts distinguished by their shared competence in a particular body of knowledge. The university establishes the means by which an individual might gain power from a group that is organized, has well-established goals and protocols, and is thus in every way distinguished from the undifferentiated power of the mass.[17] And it is characteristic of such groups that they become self-perpetuating. As Donald Scott puts it, a professional group secures "an effective monopoly over a particular body of knowledge, [and] arrogates to itself the authority to determine what constitutes knowledge in the field" (1983, 13). Professionals demonstrate their competence to fulfill an institutionalized course of study and assume the authority it confers and, in the process, validate the continuing pertinence and power of the guiding body of knowledge. Demonstrable competence is a double-edged strategy that separates members of a profession from mass society and, as a consequence, empowers the discourse that constitutes their original authority by associating it with the professional's new social status. The acquisition of competence within a community of inquirers, then, at once delimits the boundaries of expert power and bestows almost unlimited power on an expert within a particular field. As Larson argues: "Characteristic of the occupations that apply esoteric knowledge (of myth and theory, or technique and ritual) is, by definition, their struggle for a privileged or exclusive right to speak in and about their domain. The 'intellectuals' in any field of activity . . . are those who act with the conviction – or, at least, as if they were convinced – that the right to speak is a form of power" (1984, 35).

Among the many consequences of a culture of professionalism is the creation of "market shelters" to protect the specific economic interests of professionals.

De facto monopolies on the exercise of certain forms of speech, and expert techniques, justified by accreditation and the existence of professional associations, give professionals the opportunity to practise without having to compete in the mass market (as, say, a maker of breakfast cereal must). Professionals may perform their tasks without capital and without producing a readily definable commodity. In this sense, professionalization holds out the opportunity of practising outside the exigency of market forces. Professional authority is created by possessing, in Larson's evocative phrase, "symbolic capital" (1984, 61), which allows its possessors to float their expert insight, information, and special languages as pseudocommodities, and which derives value from the prestige investing the specialized and esoteric knowledge that experts possess rather than from market operations.[18] A work of literary criticism, for instance, offers its writer and publisher little in the way of financial reward – by the strict laws of the capitalist economy, few (generally subsidized) university presses could succeed. But there is no doubt that a large amount of "symbolic capital" thus accrues to writer, publisher, and university department which simply cannot be explained by the money involved or by the business relationships between writer and publisher.

In what ways does this particular model of professionalism open up discussion about modernism? First and foremost, this concept of professionalism offers an alternative way of describing a writer's newly emerging set of relationships to a mass market. It displaces the concept of a professional as a "non-amateur, involved with financial considerations" (loosely Wilson's definition) to a narrower definition of "having status based on the possession of symbolic capital."[19] But there is an important caveat: Clearly, literary writers cannot be easily categorized as professionals in the senses that I have outlined above. In 1884 the popular writer Walter Besant wondered "How can that [fiction] be an Art which has no lecturers or teachers, no school or college or Academy, no recognised rules, no text-books, and is not taught in any University?" (7). While the teaching of literature has somewhat dramatically answered Besant's question, it is still true that in the twentieth century creative writers require no higher education, are subject to no system of credentialing, and do not possess the automatic prestige accorded to the traditional professions (law, medicine) or to those working in scientific fields of knowledge. And despite the proliferation of authors' associations in this century, only in the loosest sense can writers be considered experts in a "field." Stuart Culver, in an essay on Henry James, the Society of Authors, and late-nineteenth-century concepts of literary professionalism, argues against the relationship I am beginning to define. He finds that there are "obvious affinities between the legal notion of copyright and the profession's definition of intellectual property," but that the author's property right "differentiates writing from true professional service by leaving the writer in an entrepreneurial role, concerned with the market value of a particular commodity" (1984, 122). Henry James (in the prefaces), according to Culver, "insists on the author's amateurism not to set fiction apart from commerce, but, conversely, to demonstrate more clearly how his authority is conditioned by the commodity status of his texts" (125–6). To Culver, then, the fact that professionalism signifies the possession and use of intellectual property precludes considering literary writers as professionals who must eventually be concerned with presenting their work as commodities on the market.

Modernist writers could not be considered professionals in the sense that Culver and I employ. Nonetheless, I break sharply from Culver in arguing that there is a profound identity between the structure of professional discourses and of modernist writing strategies emerging out of a shared matrix of historical imperatives, and that the economic and social rewards accruing to professionals are comparable to the cultural rewards (the symbolic capital) accruing to modernist writers. Writers and professionals alike have attempted to demarcate a space that exists culturally, economically, and linguistically apart from mass culture and the imperatives of the mass market. And they have done so in fundamentally similar ways: First, because all function within and by virtue of a special, esoteric discourse; and second, because all exist symbiotically with the university as the primary legitimator of professional activities in the twentieth century. This symbiosis is far from self-evident. Though we can hardly conceive of a medical doctor without several years of rigorous training at medical school, even the recent rise of creative writing workshops is not convincing evidence that writers need the university for training. But, as I shall explain more fully in the next section, the university has dramatically altered the constitutive processes by which critics, writers, and an educated audience apprehend literature. We (as critics) can hardly conceive of the significance of the terms "literature" and "modernism" outside today's communities of professionally trained critics. This statement is doubtless a loaded one in the sense that this book is being produced within and for that very same community. By the same token, the question of what literature would mean without the signifying structures institutionalized in university departments can only be posed rhetorically. This does not mean that modernist writers should be conflated with professional critics, though it does at least suggest that, whatever concepts of literature exist outside the academy, within it discussions of literariness must always be constituted by what is possible and impossible to say within the limits of our professional discourse. To speak of a culturally authoritative text in the twentieth century is to speak of the discursive practices, embedded within specific institutions, by which it is produced and recognized as valuable.

The nature of this discursive identity between professionalism and literature clearly demands more elaboration. It would be a mistake to consider modernist writers as professionals in the same sense as literary critics and thus to simply conflate one kind of writing with another. The modernist writers belonged to no particular all-embracing group bound by common laws and language, nor were they housed or trained in specific institutions. But I am arguing for a historically concrete relationship rather than a mere analogy (that complex modernist writing, in other words, in some ways happens to resemble a true professional discourse). Both emerge at approximately the same time in response to a common historical necessity. If a body of formal knowledge underpins a professional's power within a mass society, then the idiom of modernist writing – arcane allusion, juxtaposition, opaque writing, indeterminacy, and so on – performs precisely the same function within mass culture. If the nature of that knowledge grants professionals the right to speak about their subject, then the particular strategies of modernist texts give their writers a cultural prerogative to be heard – to speak, as it were, for literature, and to be understood as so speaking by a receptive audience. And if modernist writers did not go about their task with quite the same organizational zeal as professionalizing occupations at the end of the nineteenth century, then the advent of societies of authors, little magazines and, by the 1920s, a direct relationship to university-based literary studies, would provide writers with an increasingly elaborate infrastructure and sense of community.

The point that demands the most thorough examination in light of this professional model is the issue of linguistic difference. Fredric Jameson has argued that

> it is enough to evoke the fad for rapid reading and the habitual conscious or unconscious skimming of newspaper and advertising slogans, for us to understand the deeper social reasons for the stubborn insistence of modern poetry on the materiality and density of language. . . . So also in the realm of philosophy the bristling jargon of seemingly private languages is to be evaluated against the advertising copybook recommendations of "clarity" as the essence of "good writing." (1971, 24)

We might add modernist fiction to Jameson's list of seemingly private languages. The modernist emphasis on the "materiality and density" of language and complex narrative strategies requires from its readers skill, patience, and competence. Modernism organizes a special kind of relationship between text and reader that depends upon an ability to marshal specific competences (such as the ability to spot and decipher an allusion). Less obviously, modernism evinces a recognition that this kind of writing is demanding. After this recognition a number of responses are possible: One may choose not to read this kind of writing, or deride its implicit elitism, or set out to enjoy the intellectual challenges it poses. These responses, however, are only available after one has registered the difference of this kind of writing from others that are always available in newspapers, magazines, and popular fictions. In the same way, one can scarcely refuse to acknowledge the ways in which a doctor's interpretation and labeling of symptoms differs from a layperson's, even if one then chooses not to trust the doctor's diagnosis. That acknowledgment by educated and un-educated alike that a particular discourse demands special skills, and can therefore be performed or understood only by those who are specialized, lies at the foundation of professional power and cultural power in the twentieth century.

The value of esoteric language to literary writing emerges more clearly when we examine the profession with which literary writing was obsessively compared at the end of the nineteenth century: journalism. We have already noted that the occupation itself was becoming professionalized, requiring some degree of training for new recruits and often emphasizing its fact-based, scientific outlook.[20] But the characteristic accessibility of journalistic discourse suggests, somewhat paradoxically, the limitations of its power. (I am speaking of journalese rather than of a discourse about journalism, which might be extremely complex, but for that very reason would not be accessible to a mass audience.) The typical newspaper article – or, indeed, movie or popular novel – aimed at a mass audience is constructed, on the whole, so that the medium of language should pose no obstacle to the audience. The medium should not disrupt the delivery of its message, and so it facilitates the consumption of content as anonymously and transparently as possible. Once we begin to note the language of a newspaper report (or the structure, setting, of a movie) above and beyond its consumable content, the easy transmission of information is broken, and the apparently seamless narrative of facts disrupted. And once we begin to observe or supervise our own reading or watching habits, we find we are performing a rather different task: reading, perhaps, a work of New Journalism (or discovering an *auteur* director's idiosyncratic idiom), where we are forced to pay attention to the author's metacritical activities. The transparency or clarity of journalism not only aids consumption; it becomes, as it were, itself supremely consumable – and as such it facilitates reaching a mass audience.

The last point may seem obvious, but its implications are not. The demand for direct, intelligible language separates journalism from one of the key sources of what I have described as professional power: mastery of a discourse that is not readily accessible to a wide number of people. In this sense, journalism occupies a marginal position as a profession. As Michael Schudson correctly observes, "Nothing in the training of journalists gives them license to shape others' views of the world. Nor do journalists have esoteric techniques or language. . . . To criticize a lawyer, we say, 'I'm not a lawyer, but – ' and to question a doctor, we say, 'I'm no expert on medicine, but – .' We feel no such compunction to qualify criticism of the morning paper or the television news" (1978, 9). This is not by any means to suggest that anyone can write to the precise requirements of the newspaper, but that, compared to a doctor's or lawyer's jargon, journalese is not immediately, recognizably different from everyday speech. As Schudson's example aptly indicates, the authority of doctors and lawyers is such that a layperson can scarcely speak about their field or in their language. Indeed, posing a legal challenge to such professionals almost invariably means consulting other professionals who possess competence in that area: another lawyer, other doctors in a malpractice suit. The reason we are able to criticize the morning paper so freely is not merely because we do not trust journalists as guides, but that journalistic language guarantees our access and comprehension. As the materiality of language is constantly being put at the service of something else – encouraging comprehension, gaining a wide readership, and thus selling news – journalists necessarily abdicate their right to speak authoritatively about their own medium. If journalists' pretensions to objectivity won them social status at the end of the nineteenth century, then the very nature of their language militated against the establishment of this particular professional function. The organization of journalism excluded a discursive terrain that would be richly worked by those interested in creating a new hegemony over the use of language.

This ideal of clarity seems applicable to most expressive forms of mass culture. It is worth noting, however, that the fashioning of these forms does not preclude borrowing techniques we would normally associate with modernism in literature and art. Popular novels might occasionally use a Faulknerian stream of consciousness; modern advertising frequently employs montage, split-screen fragmentation, or fantasy images in surreal combinations. These borrowings comprise what Thomas Crow calls, in reference to the visual arts, a "process of mass-cultural recuperation": Avant-garde modernism creates new techniques and opens up areas of authentic experience which are then mined by the culture industry and "re-packaged in turn for consumption as chic and kitsch commodities" (1983, 254, 253). Nevertheless, even in these cases technique is used primarily to open a channel to the commodity in question. A TV commercial that focused on or laid bare its processes of construction to the exclusion of the commodity sold would necessarily be self-defeating, as would a popular fiction that subsumed its plot in a stream of consciousness of Faulknerian complexity. In the sense that these techniques are meant to further the consumption of commodities (a salable object, an entertaining narrative), it might be argued that opacity itself is placed within a framework that must redeem and clarify it. Even when an ad successfully plays upon unconscious fantasies, the purpose and goal of such play can never be in doubt. A soft drink commercial that flashes images (a body, a bottle, water) so quickly as to render them almost incomprehensible to the conscious mind, for instance, will possess a subtext too obvious to need displaying (Buy this drink so that you may enter this world of enticing images). This subtext ensures that appropriated modernist techniques function according to a formula that never varies from ad to ad and that they are therefore as consumable as "transparent" journalese.

So far, I have argued for a particular and historically significant relationship between literary modernism and the kind of discourses legitimated by professional power – a relationship arising from the perceived value of esoteric writing strategies and the communities of competence they create. Intuitively, however, complex creative writing seems different in kind, and created for significantly different ends, than the bodies of formal knowledge that grant authority to professional groups. That intuitive sense of difference needs now to be accounted for. Allon White has claimed that modernist "obscurity," for the first time in literary history, becomes *"constitutive of the very being"* of literature: "Modernist obscurity is not due simply to the unfamiliarity of the protocols upon which it is based. It is rather that a key protocol upon which it is based is obscurity" (1981, 16, 17). White's distinction is a key one, for it suggests that no amount of familiarity with modernist strategies will ever allow us to "crack the code" and arrive at determinate meaning – unless we accept, along with White, that a law of radical uncertainty is the only meaningful determination we can make of the text. The text, as it were, evades our attempts to control and limit meaning. White also suggests, perhaps taking his cue from various statements by writers such as Flaubert and Joyce on the aloofness or even absence of the artist, that modernist obscurity dismantles, on the grounds of intentionality, another form of authority: "It was precisely the intention of the author, and the concomitant authority which this gave him over his own work, which modernist obscurity brought into doubt" (22). Both lines of argument converge in a model of textual indeterminacy whereby author and reader lack authority to single out and substantiate discrete meanings; in its infinite interpretability, the text forces us to displace meaning into a rhetoric of slippage, *différance,* and the *jouissance* of textual play.

These observations make literary modernism sound quite different from professional discourse, in which obscurity seems to pose practical rather than epistemological problems. To follow White's rhetorical usage, one might hypothesize that professional discourse poses problems of *difficulty* (where the problems are ultimately solvable) rather than of *obscurity* (where the problems have no single and discrete answers) (White, 17). A statute, for instance, might be couched in difficult language (for nonlawyers) and legal theorists might even disagree about its ultimate significance and use, but one might argue that the intention behind the statute was not to create obscurity; at worst, it might have been constructed to offer a certain latitude in interpretation. Similarly, medical jargon would nullify its practical applications if its difficulty stood in the way of labeling, interpreting, and treating symptoms. The complexity of the languages of law and medicine might instead be justified by the need to render complex or unusual situations clearly. In both examples, the authority of legal and medical practitioners depends on a perception by all concerned that the supporting body of formal knowledge, however dense and inaccessible to a layperson, provides a functional, objective, and meaningful basis to expert power. To expose the basis of that power as an arbitrary managing of indeterminacies – to see it as a mere will to power – could constitute something of a professional crisis. Such is potentially the case in the legal profession, in fact, where recent attempts to subject legal documents (particularly the Constitution) to literary theories of textual indeterminacy have occasioned much impassioned debate.[21]

But the distinction between difficulty and obscurity is neither absolute nor clear-cut across the whole terrain of professional activities. On the one hand, different disciplines within the academic profession demand different standards of truth and determinacy. One can doubt the availability and legitimacy of historical, literary, or cultural truths more easily than scientific truth without disrupting the disciplinary codes that constitute their field of knowledge; one available paradigm in the former disciplines is precisely the indeterminacy of humanly constructed knowledge or narrative. On the other hand, there is a functional difference between professional practice and the predominantly theoretical study of formal knowledge encouraged within the university. University practices of open debate, teaching multiple perspectives, and the confinement of research to specialized (and often rarefied) areas of inquiry have fostered the sense that academic studies, in the humanities at least, have only an oblique, almost parasitical relationship to professional practice. And members of disciplines tied directly to professional occupations, such as law, probably have more freedom to consider their field of knowledge as suspect, partial, unscientific, or indeterminate than do those engaged in professional practice. Legal theoreticians might, for instance, debate the interpretability of the Constitution without having any effect on the way in which judges hand down decisions or on the prestige and financial reward attaching to the practice of law. While theoretical studies undoubtedly do gradually transform the way professionals perceive and practice their vocations, the greatest value of such studies might be said to lie in the fact that their defining order of knowledge warrants such analysis, argument, and elaboration. What academic professionals must maintain is not so much a claim to objective truth, however important this may be to individual disciplines, but the codes, perspectives, and discourse that make permissible an expert's claims to truth or denial of truth. To disclaim one's ability, *as an academic,* to know the meaning of the Constitution is thus not to destroy one's claim to expert knowledge but to deploy one's resources anew within a controlling frame of reference. In particular, one has spoken for the authority of that frame of reference to elicit such studies – even those that appear hostile to prevailing protocols – and thus to demarcate a boundary between expert agreement or disagreement and inexpert opinion. For the purposes of controlling (and patrolling) a field of knowledge within the academy, one's ability to resolve problems and ratify solutions is, or can be made to be, inconsequential if irresolution and skepticism can be parlayed into expert inquiry. One may speak at will in favor of obscurity within the confines of an academic discipline as long as the key consequence of that speaking is to establish the difficulty of a particular set of disciplinary codes and to exclude a majority of others from speaking knowledgeably about them.

There are thus profound affinities between the exercise of professional power within the academy and the strategies of the modernist text insofar as each depends on an esoteric discourse distinguishable from mass-produced writings in order to construct and maintain intellectual authority on the one hand, and cultural authority on the other. The cultural authority of the modernist text, however, itself depends largely on the complicitous but frequently covert relationship between literary writing and the university. Departments of literature, by virtue of their relationship with the university as the primary legitimating agent of intellectual endeavors in America, are perfectly positioned to preserve functional concepts of literature by means of selection, exclusion, and legitimation – in particular, by providing criteria that exclude serious consideration of mass culture. In some ways, literary studies have functioned like the system of royal patronage in the Renaissance, whereby writers' work gained significance and prestige from its association with an aristocracy. It would not be too much to say that the university has established in our century the legitimacy and continuity of a cultural realm that we can readily identify as meaningful, valuable, and worthy of careful analysis, and has done so in large measure by canonizing modernist writers and their aesthetic principles. This does not argue for an intentional complicity on the part of writers and university professors to carve out and preserve a privileged cultural space between them. Nor, on the other hand, does it suggest that literature in the twentieth century exists to fill a need for the university system, however hard it may be to conceive of "literature" without it. If that were the case, one would expect literature and the literary establishment to be much more homogeneous than they are. While the development of the modern university and literary modernism were contemporary phenomena, my point is not that university studies simply influenced modernist writing. Rather, both responded to the new sources, relations, and formations of power that were beginning to transform American society around the turn of the century – a new insistence on the power of experts and their possession of symbolic capital.[22]

Literature and the study of literature in the university are linked most clearly by the fact that writers gain ideological legitimacy from a group of professional critics devoted to interpreting a special order of discourse which, by definition, warrants interpretation. Departments of literature bestow patronage on texts demanding enough to validate the pursuits of their members. Such an identification of literature with the university does not necessarily mean that the reader invoked by modernist texts is the literary critic, though there is a sense in which some modernist writing entertains that possibility – sometimes in tongue-in-cheek ways, like the footnotes T. S. Eliot appended to *The Waste Land* or like James Joyce's (self-?) deprecatory study of the pedagogue in Stephen Dedalus. But the creation of departments of literary studies has had far-reaching effects on the nature and reception of the literary text. By their very nature, the products of mass culture are endorsed by the sheer numbers of readers and viewers: by becoming a best-seller or by Nielsen ratings or by box office returns. By contrast, the writing and study of "literature" depends on the confident assertions of professional writers, who assume, as Peter Nagourney writes, "a hierarchy of 'texts' based upon the imposition of distinction, conferring admission to the pantheon of classics, by a relatively small group of critics and teachers" (1982, 99). University departments of literature have replaced mass audiences with a coterie of sympathetic readers and established the teaching of privileged texts as a bastion against a mass audience's endorsement of best-sellers. Most important, critics have replaced or, perhaps more precisely, supplemented the notion of taste with a battery of formal, aesthetic, and ideological strategies designed to prove the value of those texts we choose to call "literary." It is telling that critics rarely talk of taste as a criterion of judgment, preferring to rely on a text's canonicity or to invoke textual properties that somehow speak for the value of the text: ambiguity, profundity, subversiveness, complexity, and so on. Such terms give critics an advantage over the uncritical likes and dislikes of a mass audience, which lacks the sophisticated vocabulary and bodies of arcane knowledge that bestow authority on literary professionals.

The nature of this relationship does not rule out the presence of many voices dissenting from the protocols of professional endeavors. Avant-garde literature, as well as avant-garde theory, has frequently created consternation in university circles. In his discussion of the profession of literary studies, Gerald Graff points out a continuing fear of overspecialization and obscurity among university professors that has frequently led to a symptomatic desire for a homogeneous and accessible conversation about cultural matters (1987, 88–93). Many aspects of our contemporary professional scene testify to a continuing pursuit after consensual decisions about the meaning, value, and canonical status of the literary work: Great Books courses that give the impression of a stable canon, the search for (or struggle to restore) a Great Tradition, finding recent expression in books like Allan Bloom's *The Closing of the American Mind* (1987) and E. D. Hirsh's *Cultural Literacy* (1987) and still more recently in Page Smith's *Killing the Spirit* (1990) and Roger Kimball's *Tenured Radicals* (1990). Gerald Graff and Reginald Gibbons, in a fairly typical statement, recently wrote that "contemporary academic criticism as a whole is lacking not only in its usefulness to the reader of an imaginative work, but also in its applicability both to the literary culture generally and to the largest pedagogical responsibilities of the university" (1985, 10). Graff and Gibbons go on to inveigh against the "superprofessionals" who celebrate the increasingly recondite reaches of literary studies; and later in the same volume Wendell Berry adds to the chorus by condemning contemporary criticism as "too specialized" (207). From the other end of the political spectrum, recent publications like Andrew Ross's *No Respect* (1989) and *Universal Abandon?* (1988) and Bruce Robbins's *Intellectuals: Aesthetics, Politics, Academics* (1990) testify again to fears of overspecialization in the ivory tower. Such writers correctly gauge the fragmentation of cultural studies and raise significant questions about the ethics of professional behavior. What they fail to address sufficiently is the fact that the structure of professional discourse works toward specialization, subdivision, and abstruse expression. Exponential increases in jargon-ridden terminology, proponents of indeterminacy, struggles to speak for particular points of view, departments divided – all of these have actually tended to consolidate rather than to disrupt the authority of intellectuals. The profession is shaping up like the chessboard that Henry James imagined as the twentieth-century writer's public. We find it harder to speak to each other across disciplinary divides but, by the same token, each discipline and subdiscipline enjoys an increased ability to set its own agenda and legitimate its specialized work. This does not answer important questions about professional ethics, but it does suggest (a somewhat unpopular view at the moment) that the contemporary spirit of crisis is misleading. Institutionally and professionally, twentieth-century literary studies have been and still are extremely powerful.

To examine the entire history of the relationship between literary modernism and literary studies lies well beyond the scope of this work, and is in some of its aspects too well known to require much rehearsing. The ensuing narrative, therefore, should be seen as a sketch, revisionary only in its emphasis, rather than a thorough discussion of the role of the academy. Formalism, by the 1940s and 1950s, dominated university departments of literature; the New Critics, indeed, were supremely aware of the legitimating function of the university and were able to use it to empower their own methodologies, canonical figures and texts (Gerald Graff 1987, 152–3; and Grant Webster 1979, 95). Not incidentally, that canon focused heavily on modernist writers. The New Critics derived intellectual momentum from the critical writings of the Anglo-American modernists, notably from T. S. Eliot's poetics of impersonality. A crucial essay like Eliot's "Tradition and the Individual Talent," together with Henry James's Prefaces and "The Art of Fiction," allowed formalist scholars to elaborate a criticism grounded in the autonomy of the text. That formalist move toward excluding historical and biographical considerations was, according to Grant Webster, an important step in the consolidation of a particularly stable canon: "The advantage of accepting the Formalists' strategy of exclusion is that one is free to detach the work of literature from its origins in the author and the historical context, and to use each individual poem and novel as a building block to construct an autonomous realm of literature, or a 'tradition'" (80).

If the doctrine of textual autonomy offered formalists a way of distinguishing literary values from a bleak, technological environment, then it is also true that this strategy encouraged canon formation and the elaboration of a body of complex protocols. And if the doctrine of impersonality was necessary to enshrine the text, then it also offered a way of establishing experts in interpreting and knowing about texts. Esoteric writing strategies functioned as a means of institutionalizing an elite readership capable of using new interpretive modes and promoting a situation in which reader, author, and text maintain hegemony over a wide range of cultural matters. Canon formation, theory building, and cultural definition proceeded hand in hand. Though many formalists held science and traditional scholarly practices (philology, bibliographical studies, literary history) in contempt, the progressive articulation of complex theories seemed to take critical statements out of the realm of subjective evaluation, bestowing on them immense practical significance for the teaching of literature. Formalist theories of the text were nowhere more powerful than in the class-room, where readings of texts presented in the guise of practical criticism gave them an aura of objectivity, usefulness, and future applicability. As Vincent B. Leitch has pointed out, formalist principles did, at least, promise entry on the part of students and professional critics to a body of complex work of which modernist writing was the most vital component (Leitch 1988, 24–7). Though schools of critical thought (many of them politically opposed to the New Critical agenda) have proliferated since the 1940s, none has seriously challenged that conjunction of literary study and specialization. Indeed, as close reading has given way to the current obsession with theory, theorizing an end to specialization seems the self-consuming approach most writers take toward their goal.

If the New Critics awakened most fully to the potential of esoteric readings, that interpenetration of literary writing and critical study was already becoming clear by the 1920s. Little magazines of the teens and twenties published avant-garde fiction and poetry alongside critical manifestoes. Ezra Pound established a significant part of his reputation on his abilities as a critic. T. S. Eliot's many-faceted role as poet, critic, and editor of the influential magazine *The Criterion* (1922–39), which was crucial in guiding the taste of a minority, educated public, helped to lay out the principles the New Criticism would later formalize. The New Criticism also looked back to writer-critics like Robert Penn Warren, Allen Tate, John Crowe Ransom, who formed the nucleus of the Southern Agrarians and, in the 1930s and 1940s, also propounded their views in important journals such as the *Southern Review, Kenyon Review,* and *Sewanee Review.* The political dimensions of these critical practices have been fully established in analyses of the attraction of right-wing politics to many modernist writers and of the Southern Agrarians' revolt against technology, urban environments, and the "cheapness and triviality of public taste" (Donald Davidson, as quoted in Hoffman, Allen, and Ulrich 1947, 121). The conservative and authoritarian aspects of these critical systems have been frequently condemned in the past two decades – and rightly so. But here I want to concentrate on the professional dimensions of their work. We might argue, in fact, that the authoritarianism of their work took its voice from the principle that I believe lies at the root of professional power in the twentieth century: the possession of "symbolic capital" in the form of recondite language, theories, and works. As antagonistic as many formalist critics were to an urban, managerial society, their work ultimately forged a covert relationship with that society's structures of authority.

But we can push this narrative back even further. By the end of the nineteenth century, the trend of literary studies already pointed toward the progressive validation of esoteric language and toward, not incidentally, the institutionalization of an authoritative opposition to mass culture.[23] By the beginning of the twentieth century, as Graff writes, MLA Convention addresses "start to bewail the disappearance of the sense of solidarity and shared goals that had supposedly marked the first generation of modern language scholars of the eighties and nineties." Alexander R. Hohlfield, chairman of the MLA Central Division, lamented in 1902 that the "increasing specialization" of critical discourse was "decreasing the number of occasions when a considerable proportion of those present are capable of joining in a discussion" (Graff 1987, 110–11). Hohlfield was identifying those elements of professional discourse that had arisen out of philological studies in the university and that were predominantly text-based and research-oriented.[24] As Graff describes in some detail, the power of "generalists" within the university was bound to wane before professional scholars: the former's commitment to a "common literary culture" which had already broken down meant that "merely to invoke the catchphrases of that culture – literature's mysterious essence and so forth – was an ineffective tactic" (89). Professional scholars responded to the overall trend of the modern university toward professionalized activities and fields; they were able to embrace specialization with their methodologies and critical apparatuses. By also controlling graduate studies they were able to institutionalize a mechanism whereby forthcoming teachers would perpetuate – indeed require for their legitimacy – a similar professionalized outlook. This did not necessarily imply, as Geoffrey H. Hartman puts it nicely, a "managerial society full of technicians, operators, language therapists, a department of discourse control and emendation" (1980, 3), but certainly does imply the esoteric languages and abstruse knowledge that together buttress an ethos of specialization. The genealogy of contemporary theoretical practices must be traced not just to French theory or the New Criticism but to the socioeconomic transformations already under way by the end of the nineteenth century.

Several implications of this narrative, brief as it is, must now be addressed. First, to perceive the academic establishment as if it once constituted a unified and coherent field of cultural beliefs and discursive practices that is only now fragmenting misjudges the extent to which specialization (and thus fragmentation) is built into the professional model from the start. The humanist notion of a Great Tradition and a unified culture cannot easily be reconciled with professional practice. But neither can professional practice be easily separated from esoteric writings. If on the one hand the notion of a Great Tradition (shaky to begin with) must founder on the increasing diversity of critical approaches, it seems likely on the other that some principle of canon formation based on esotericism and complexity will remain intact. Second, as a corollary, the authority of modernist literary practices lies not in the fact of a Grand Hotel of culture or in their self-professed claims to it, but in the properties of recondite (professional) discursive practices that predate and underwrite the modernist movement itself. It is thus no historical accident that James's narrative and linguistic strategies were accepted so readily by later critics – and not just because of his undoubted, often-acknowledged influence on them. Rather, James's work became central because it adheres to a discourse of obscurity and complexity that happens also to constitute the primary discourse of professional academic studies. Both preserve an identity of purpose and strategy for speaking authoritatively. This would suggest that James is fated to remain as a cornerstone of the literary academic establishment, whatever shape it is to take, much longer than the staunchest supporters and opponents of canon subversion may suppose. If so, cultural conservatives worried about the overthrow of existing canons have less to fear than they thought. Alternative, subjugated canons will not gain widespread recognition until their works can be convincingly represented as rich, many-sided, and, in Henry James's term in "The Art of Fiction," as *discutable* as anything in the Master's oeuvre. But the continued hegemony of a Henry James in the canon will not rest on the preservation (or re-emergence) of a unified Great Tradition but on the continued legitimacy of the formal and rhetorical protocols most conducive to professional work.

This is at once to concur with and to revise Barbara Herrnstein Smith's remarks about the collapse of stable criteria for judging literariness. First, struggles within the academy between generalists and critics, critics and theorists, left and right, suggest that literary criteria have always been a matter for debate. Second, meanings historically assigned to literature cannot be overturned as easily as they are challenged. Nowhere am I arguing for the apotheosis of modernist writers; but neither can we ignore the intricate, dense, pervading web of significations that underwrite the convergence of complex (modernist) writing and definitions of literature. This statement has many implications for professional ethics, for political actions undertaken within the academy, and for pedagogy. The one question I will explore more fully, since it bears directly on issues of cultural authority, is that of the canon. The model of professionalism I have outlined strongly suggests that the body of works accounted worthwhile will not only conform to various criteria of complexity but will be limited in size. If any text could be admitted to the canon, there would be no *specific* body of works or set of legitimizing criteria with which professional critics could work.[25] This would subvert the very basis of professional power, which depends for its legitimacy on its reciprocal relationship with a body of legitimate texts. Theoretically, one could imagine a situation in which any text could be deemed worthwhile and professional legitimacy thus preserved by an extreme extension of, rather than a removal of, criteria already in existence. Practically speaking, the elimination of the concept of "nonworthwhile" could not occur without abandoning the underpinnings of professional power or without first securing the complicity of all professional endeavors. In the first case we are contemplating thousands of people giving up their primary access to power; in the second, we are imagining a nationwide economic collapse severe enough to restructure the entire socioeconomic fabric of the United States. Thus, while there are very good professional reasons for extending and diversifying the canon on the grounds of further possibilities for specialization, there is an even stronger counterbalancing force that seeks to limit the canon to special kinds of text that enhance professional inquiries.

Lillian S. Robinson anticipates many of these points in her article "Treason Our Text: Feminist Challenges to the Literary Canon" (1983), in which she cites Nina Baym's attempts to open up the canon by reading and discussing hundreds of nineteenth-century popular fictions by women. She notes Baym's discomfort with the results in her introduction to *Women's Fiction: A Guide to Novels By and About Women in America, 1820–70:* "Reexamination of this fiction may well show it to lack the esthetic, intellectual and moral complexity and artistry that we demand of great literature" despite the fact that Baym "cannot avoid the belief that 'purely' literary criteria, as they have been employed to identify the best American works, have inevitably had a bias in favor of things male" (113). Baym collides both with the traditional canon and with her own predisposition to judge according to standards that have in our century successfully isolated popular fictions from "literature." In Baym's case, this predisposition clearly arises not from political conservatism but from a sense of the conservatism of canon formation, which imposes certain limits on what can be deemed good or culturally valuable in ways that are no less real for seeming arbitrary. Baym's value judgments are far from arbitrary in the sense that they are constituted and endowed with life and objective reality within a specific cultural and historical milieu. Her own training may militate against such a radical substitution of, say, E.D.E.N. Southworth for Henry James. Moreover, it is Baym's previous well-known work with canonical authors that has enabled her to bring these popular fictions before a larger audience. Which is to say that defenses of popular fiction can be made but are difficult if not impossible to maintain if they must be undertaken within an academic discourse that has in the first place legitimated the nonpopular as culturally worthwhile and authoritative. Robinson, well aware of this problem, recognizes that the new feminist canons (letters, diaries, journals, as well as popular fictions) have "not challenged our received sense of appropriate style" and that until "the aesthetic arguments can be fully worked out in the feminist context, it will be impossible to argue, in the general marketplace of literary ideas, that the novels of Henry James ought to give place – a *little* place, even – to the diaries of his sister Alice" (118). Quite so. But the current marketplace of literary ideas is constituted according to criteria – particularly, as Robinson says, "'complexity' criteria" (118) – that preempt wholesale revisions and strictly govern possible extensions of the canon. These new aesthetic ideas would have to be maintained, not against Henry James, but against the controlling discourse that voiced, gave shape to, and legitimated the ideas in the first place. E.D.E.N. Southworth and Alice James might one day be assimilated to the literary canon, but it would not, I argue, be possible under criteria such as popularity or (in Robinson's enigmatic phrase) "honest writing."

Even more interesting for this question of canon formation is the case of Houston A. Baker's *Modernism and the Harlem Renaissance* (1987), which sets out to revise the prevailing opinion that the Harlem Renaissance should be faulted for its "'failure' to produce *vital, original, effective,* or 'modern' art," presumably, Baker adds, "in the manner . . . of British, Anglo-American, and Irish creative endeavors" (xiii). Baker's point reminds us of Baym's: "the very *histories* that are assumed in the chronologies of British, Anglo-American, and Irish modernisms are radically opposed to any adequate and accurate account of the history of Afro-American modernism, especially the *discursive* history of such modernism" (Baker, xvi). If so, then the very criteria we use to elevate James Joyce as a distinctive modernist – his labyrinthine word games and collage structure, for example – must confine (to use Baker's and Foucault's term) the works of Jean Toomer, Nella Larsen, or Claude McKay to the realm of nonmodernism. They are modern but not modernists, and are thus tacitly or otherwise marked out as failures, not because they try to be modernists and fail, but because modernist writers of the Anglo-American and Irish variety (and the critics who have come after them) have created our most persuasive definitions of what it means to be a successful literary writer. In a cultural field in which modernist principles of art dominate the assignation of meaning to literature, writers like Toomer and Larsen are at a double disadvantage. I am not so much concerned with Baker's assessment of the problem, however, as with the rhetorical steps he takes to present the Harlem Renaissance as a successful modernism, for although Baker seeks to subvert "Literature with a capital and capitalist L" (8), his own discursive practices are far from subversive in today's academia.

African-American modernism, Baker claims, originates with Booker T. Washington's ten-minute address to the Negro exhibit of the Atlanta Cotton States and International Exposition on September 18, 1895. The address demonstrates the strategies that Baker designates as characteristic of this modernism: the mastery of form and the deformation of mastery (15). Baker's complex argument focuses on Washington's appropriation of the minstrel mask, which in the first place comprised a misappropriation of African-American vernacular for the purposes of denying and repressing the true humanity of black people before a white audience. Booker T. Washington, as Baker puts it, "changed the minstrel joke by stepping inside the white world's nonsense syllables with oratorical mastery" (25): His speech mastered the mask's form in such a way as to deform the voice of power and exploitation speaking through the mask. Washington deconstructs the mask, as it were, in the process of oratorically assuming it. Attributing to Washington a "revolutionary *renaming*" (25) and suggesting his relevance to strategies like "mastery of form, deformation of mastery" intimates Baker's own discursive strategies, which are to elevate Washington's stock by employing principles not dissimilar from those used to justify the canonical status of a Joyce or Woolf. Mastery of form, wordplay, complexity: These criteria take us back via the back door to the Anglo-American and Irish modernism we thought had been subverted along with "Literature with a capital and capitalist L." Baker, as canny a rhetorician as Washington is orator, pulls off something of a rhetorical coup. He convinces us that the Harlem Renaissance demands a separate discursive history, then begins to supply one by tactics that are most convincing when closest to those avowedly left behind. Baker's own mastery of academic form and rhetoric persuades us not only that he is conversant with the legitimating criteria of literary discourse but that he has selected a thinker whose aspirations are valuable and profound enough to be worth legitimating.

To summarize: One can argue, from a remove, that definitions of the literary are contradictory, theoretically unsupportable, and hopelessly riddled with narrow and frequently prejudiced judgments palmed off as eternal and transcendent, and that as a consequence Henry James is no more literary or worthwhile than E.D.E.N Southworth. Second, one can argue that within the institutions of academia James has always been accepted as more valuable than Southworth and that, whether we like it or not, James will continue to be a more powerful figure as long as powerful interpretive communities support him and use him to support them in their effort to perpetuate their legacy of what is true, significant, and beautiful. This argument runs close to Stanley Fish's in *Is There a Text in This Class?* (1980), in which interpretive communities, rather monolithic entities that "grow larger and decline [while] individuals move from one to another," are brought forward to explain how certain views are shaped and authorized (171–2). And one can argue, as I have, that despite the fact that different interpretive communities validate different models of literary analysis and different canonical texts, those models and canons will only become authoritative and meaningful because they function within, and function to preserve, a set of professional practices and discourses that systematically underpins all enterprises within the academy.

The discursive bond between esoteric creative and recondite critical texts grants modernist writing a kind of self-confirming authority even after that authority is exposed as historically and culturally constructed. Such is the case in the work of an influential canon-shaping critic like Hugh Kenner. His *The Poetry of Ezra Pound* (1951), as Kenner says himself, made Pound "a stock on the academic exchange: a safe 'subject'," showing how the poet "with his large and complex oeuvre might plausibly be written about" (1983, 372). *The Pound Era* (1971) completed this first step toward hagiography (for Kenner and Pound) by exploring in appropriately complex fashion Pound's cultural and literary ties – and, not insignificantly, by giving the era a title and focal point. Kenner's essay "The Making of the Modernist Canon," which purports to answer questions like "how did [the canon of literary modernism] get made? Is it made yet?" (365), is a fascinating reminiscence of his part in shaping the canon, but is most revealing in what his account leaves out. In fact, the essay does not really ask how a body of ideas, texts, strategies that we have come to call modernist was shaped;

that question Kenner has already answered prior to writing the essay. Kenner asserts, for instance, that F. R. Leavis's attempt to define a literary canon in his *New Bearings in English Poetry* (1931) was hamstrung by his failure to recognize "the unprecedented interdependence of prose modernism and verse modernism." "That was a central modernist discovery," Kenner claims, "that distinctions between 'prose' and 'verse' vanish before distinctions between firm writing and loose" (Kenner 1971, 365). But this is to put the cart before the horse – to announce a modernist discovery before revealing how modernism was constructed as a movement and set of texts, first by its participants and then, somewhat differently, by historians and literary critics. To select a group of writers on (in part) the basis of their stated preference for firm writing and label them modernist is one thing; but to suggest that the functional opposition between firm and loose writing exists as a transcendental category that merely needs discovering obscures the critical work necessary to validate such definitions. This "modernist discovery" represents Kenner's own invention, disseminated through the very real authority he holds within the institution of literary studies. To see that the modernist canon and principles of modernism can be construed in very different ways, we need only look to a critic like Fredric Jameson, whose determining paradigm is the relationship between modernism and the formations of a capitalist state. At other points in the essay, to give Kenner his due, he acknowledges the idiosyncrasy of his modernist canon. He admits, for instance, that Wallace Stevens makes an uneasy fit solely because of geographic location, which prevents him from supporting "the only story that I find has adequate explanatory power: a story of capitals, from which he was absent" (373). If every canon is a narrative with limited power to select, organize, and explain how one might "plausibly write about" certain features of an era, however, we could not expect F. R. Leavis to recognize a modernism not yet invented.

Kenner's work is such that we must recognize its power and influence within modernist studies, whatever we think about his critical sleights of hand. He has become what Grant Webster calls the Man of Letters: a critic "who is widely enough known for the writing of essays and books about literature that his opinion has personal authority and carries weight because it is *by him*" (1979, 32). Because Kenner has gained an authoritative voice, and because others may now invoke his name and work (often by dissenting with it) to extend or buttress their own, it might be said that the limitations of his narrative are practically of little consequence. His affiliations to academic structures of power are such that his work matters despite any criticisms brought against it, and his words matter however much they are exposed as rhetorical performances. Even if no other critic subscribes to the exact contours of Kenner's canon, that canon still possesses an objective validity; it becomes, to take Kenner's own words, hard currency on the academic exchange, potent in creating literature "with a capitalist L." His work, like the canon he has created (and like any canon, statement, value, or meaning embedded within our institutionalized critical practices), bears the paradoxical quality of being open to attack on many fronts yet demonstrably powerful, producing real consequences for people performing real tasks in real institutions.

Yet, as idiosyncratic as his canon sounds, Kenner's emphasis on an aesthetics of complexity is not fortuitous. Kenner writes that he was intent on discovering how Pound "with his large and complex oeuvre might plausibly be written about" (1983, 372); but it is also because Pound's oeuvre is large and complex that writing about it becomes plausible. It is for that reason that Wilson's *The Labor of Words,* which focuses on "literary" writers like Lincoln Steffens and Richard Harding Davis, or Marcus Klein's *Foreigners* (1981), which sets out to rewrite canonical history by promoting writers like Michael Gold, Dashiell Hammett, and Nelson Algren over the modernists, effectively create subcanons that do not significantly disturb inherited notions of literariness. The process of making a canon or perceptual model hegemonic, in other words, is not "up for grabs"; no one has carte blanche to form a community that will validate just any idea or to elevate by dint of persuasion just any figure to canonical status. It is possible that critics will transform Gertrude Stein rather than Ezra Pound into the eponymous figure of the early twentieth century and thus demonstrate anew the fact that canon formation is flexible and historically variable. Certain groups – feminists, for instance – might invest a great deal in revising the modernist canon in this fashion. But a similar reevaluation of, say, Dashiell Hammett, seems to me doubtful even at this present time of canonical and disciplinary transformation. If canonical changes come about within specific discursive formations that shape what is possible to be conceived of as appropriate and worthwhile, and if academic studies of literature have from their inception valued the difficult, esoteric, and complex over the popular, then Hammett will not easily find favor within the academy. And if critics were convinced of hitherto undiscovered complexities in Hammett, this would not disrupt the protocols that cause complex writing to be highly valued, culturally constructed though they undoubtedly are.

These questions of canonicity are worth pursuing at length because they bear directly on the problems faced by a contemporary critic in defining the literary text in an age of mass culture and indirectly on the problems faced by the writers themselves. To argue that the literariness of Dreiser's *An American Tragedy* rests on the specific forms of mass culture written into its text depends, in turn, on recognizing the formal and ideological elements of mass culture. But to "recognize" mass culture in this way is to bring to bear criteria that exist prior to and thus structure the reading of the text, allowing us to mark out as marginal, "other," what we already know to be nonliterary. This smacks of tautology. We find in the texts those literary qualities we already expect to see, and partly because our perceptual apparatus – woven into the fabric of what is possible and appropriate within our dominant institutions – has already attached authority to certain modes of writing. It would be difficult, for instance, to perceive the Newsreel sections of Dos Passos's *U.S.A.* as in any way compiled of valuable scraps of newsprint, as though the purpose of the exercise were to alert us to the formidable power and beauty of the newspapers. (In my chapter on Dos Passos, however, I test out exactly that possibility.) What makes the Newsreel sections worth reading and remembering – at least, so most of the critics writing about *U.S.A.* agree – is Dos Passos's disruption of newspaper-speak and newspaper ideologies, all by way of modernist strategies of fragmentation and juxtaposition.

The fact that the precise nature of this disruption is constituted during the process of reading does not make it any less true that we come to *U.S.A.* expecting to be able to perform certain kinds of interpretive acts. Applying to the text our knowledge of modernist writing strategies – intransigent language, innovatory narrative schemes, singularly complex structures and narrative voices, fragmentation, irony, self-referentiality, lack of closure, and so on – we "discover" the literary quality of the text. In Newsreel VII, for instance, early in *The 42nd Parallel,* one newspaper fragment reads "Find bad fault in Dreadnaught," which presumably concerns the material upkeep of the battleship. This supposition is actually far from self-evident; but it comes to seem self-evident as soon as we set out to reconstellate the fragment in the context of a dozen other ironic references (or what we assume are ironic references) to America's war industry as well as in the context of a dozen characters to be maimed, physically or mentally, in the First World War. The "bad fault" extends from the material to the ethical, from the political to the economic, and it is, we assume, the bad fault of the media to focus on one part of the whole and thus to mystify the true relationships between a damaged battleship and a corrupt body politic. Dos Passos's larger structure of complex interrelationships reveals the limited and incomplete nature of the original newspaper statement. This revelation hinges, nonetheless, on the particular interpretive models of modernism we bring to the text, which ensure that the answers we receive about the nonliterary are the right ones. If Dos Passos is correct in suggesting that the media mystify their true relationship to structures of power, the corollary is that he – and we as educated readers – mystify the oppositional dynamic whereby the literary is constituted as literary, the modernist as modernist. Thus we tend to accept as obvious Dos Passos's insight into and superiority to the bad-faith world of mass culture. This is not the wrong conclusion to draw, merely a predictable one, given the historical and cultural circumstances in which literary writing and literary studies have constituted their subject. It is in this sense that choosing four modernist writers and demonstrating that their modernism arises from the particularity of their encounter with mass culture begins to seem like a purely tautological and redundant critical act.

Luckily, the tautology becomes a productive one once we see it as historically appropriate rather than merely limiting. One paradoxical consequence of recent inquiries into canon formation has been to show how concrete are academic

institutions, how persuasive are the critical paradigms, definitions, and evaluations that most critics recognize to be historically and culturally specific. In fact,
so concrete and persuasive are these institutions and evaluations that no one
really needs to make a case for Dos Passos's artistic and cultural importance
before writing an essay about him. Nor, and for the same reasons, does one
generally need to argue for the importance of modernist writing to the construction of literary values in the twentieth century. Both of my statements could
of course be challenged. But how will they be challenged except within an
academic discourse that derives its key values (sometimes covertly) from complexity and esoteric knowledge – values, in other words, that pertain most visibly
to modernist writing? It is for that reason that challenges to the hegemony of
Joyce, Woolf, or Dos Passos from outside the academy – say within a newspaper,
political tract, or some underground publication – will automatically be excluded from serious consideration by virtue of the highly articulated, expert
languages of literary critics. Conversely, those recondite languages privilege an
expert (and thus elite) perspective even in the act of denying the primacy of elite
culture. In Hayden White's words, mass culture has been "confiscated, repressed
or otherwise sublimated by those who claim the role of being the creators of the
high cultural endowment" (1974, 772). Departments of literature have either
systematically excluded the voices of mass culture, rewritten them as hitherto
unrecognized forms of literature, or spoken of them as a necessary but necessarily impoverished part of the cultural landscape. But the point is that White
himself acknowledges that relationship of power in the act of critiquing it. The
authority of university analysts of mass culture – including those who seem most
sympathetic to it – hinges on their ability to speak from a position institutionally
and linguistically distinct from mass culture. In that sense, all writers within the
university, even those who seem to attack its purpose and rationale, perpetuate a
"cultural endowment" that confers authority on those able to speak knowledgeably about it. White's language alone, with its tip of the hat to deconstructive
criticism, proclaims its difference from the discourses of mass culture. If White is
not claiming the role of creating the "high cultural endowment," his language
speaks to (and can *only* speak to) co-members of a "community of competence" – and therein lies his authority. The critical gesture of surrendering the
concept of literary modernism suggests, at the moment of speaking or writing,
that one has not.

2

Fiction from a Newspaperized World

Henry James's The Reverberator

======

"He was connected (as she supposed) with literature. . . ."
Delia Dosson in *The Reverberator*

The Reverberator opens in a reading room boasting two newspapers in a "desert of green velvet" ([1888] 1979a, 4–5). To the eyes of Mr. Dosson, the novel's docile but wealthy father, the room was composed of "a fireplace with a great deal of fringe and no fire, of a window with a great deal of curtain and no light, and of the *Figaro,* which he couldn't read, and the New York *Herald,* which he had already read." Heavy with fringe and curtain, the darkened room would loom like a Gothic mansion out of Edgar Allan Poe were it not for the two newspapers that intimate, rather pathetically, the room's function. Indeed, their iconic value as conspicuous reading material is their only function. Delia, who already occupies the room, "seemed to be doing nothing as hard as she could," while Mr. Dosson inspects them by raising a "hopeless, uninterested glass to his eye." The journalist George Flack, also looking at the newspapers, merely evinces a professional interest in the date of the *Herald.* Images of lack pervade this reading room, without light, fire, books, or even the desire to read, and dramatically express the "newspaperized world" James mused about in his notebook entry of November 17, 1887, which lay the foundation for *The Reverberator.* In that original entry, James recalled the incident of a young American girl, Miss McClellan, whose "inconceivable letter [written to the New York *World*] about the Venetian society whose hospitality she had just been enjoying," led him to pronounce on the "strange *typicality*" of this particular *donnée* – an appropriate oxymoron for an inverted world.

> One sketches one's age but imperfectly if one doesn't touch on that particular matter: the invasion, the impudence and shamelessness, of the newspaper and the interviewer, the devouring *publicity* of life, the extinction of all sense between public and private. It is the highest expression of

the note of "familiarity," the sinking of *manners,* in so many ways, which
the democratization of the world brings with it. (1947, 82)

In the first scenes of the novel, that recognition of the incident as the "highest
expression" of the lowest democratization finds issue in yet more paradoxes. The
two newspapers simultaneously comprise all the room's reading and no reading
at all, for the room showcases the unreadable and the already read. Oddly, then,
the newspapers fulfil the room's function as they empty that function of all
significance. A given thing "has but to be newspaperised *enough,*" wrote James in
the Preface to the New York Edition of *The Reverberator,* "to return, as a quick
consequence, to the common, the abysmal air and become without form and
void" (1908, xiv–xv); and he referred to book reviewing in magazines as a
"deluge of doctrine suspended in the void" ([1893] 1986a, 232). Mr. Dosson,
Delia, Flack, and Francie, denizens of the newspaper culture they produce and
consume, fail to see the dynamic of mass culture that James recognizes throughout his career as being one of emptiness in the midst of plenty.

Despite the lugubrious nature of the first encounters in this (non)reading
room, the scene marks – commemorates perhaps – a crucial transition in literary
history. For nothing literary happens in this room, an omission that seems all the
more startling given the potential literary significance embodied in such spaces.
Alvin B. Kernan describes one such moment – the famous encounter between
King George III and Samuel Johnson in the library of the queen's house in
1767, related in James Boswell's *Life of Johnson* – as a symbolic adumbration of
the developing institution of literature in the eighteenth century. Questioning
Dr. Johnson about literary matters in the library, the king relinquished the
authority he exercised in other social spaces, so that Dr. Johnson "talked to his
majesty with profound respect, but still in his firm manly manner, with a
sonorous voice, and never in that subdued tone which is commonly used at the
levee and in the drawing room." In this new domain of writers and their
fabrications, it is the king who intrudes and Dr. Johnson who is free to command
with his voice. To Kernan, the whole scene evokes the late-eighteenth-century
development of freedom from a traditional system of patronage – a freedom that
would lead to new crises for writers subjected to the open market, but that was
also instrumental in creating new audiences and narrative possibilities, and
occasioning a new sense of authorial power (1982, 4–5).

In *The Reverberator,* a century later, two newspapers appear to supplant the
commanding voice of a Dr. Johnson just as surely as Johnson supplanted the
king's in the library he nominally owned. That usurpation seems more frighten-
ing because of the reverence middle-class Victorians accorded the private reading
space.[1] Private reading rooms invested the activity of reading with dignity and
value by providing it with an architectural space and with a function as real as
that of kitchen or dining room. Even though the texts thus read did not
automatically constitute an order known as the literary, these texts were at least

associated with a reading event experienced as possessing a special cultural significance. James's most striking image of mass-produced writing, the "regular train which starts at an advertised hour" and which must be filled by "dummies for the seasons when there are not passengers enough" ([1893] 1986a, 232), accurately describes a new orientation of writing and reading space. New reading habits suited to a daily commute to the workplace and to a leisure class accustomed to travel began to emerge in the form of newspapers and cheap paperbacks designed for portability and easy consumption. The rapid rationalization of American life in the home and workplace at the end of the nineteenth century had profound implications for the acts of reading and writing, all leading, in Christopher Wilson's term, to the "demise of the gentle reader" (1983). In *The Reverberator,* the relationship between the Dossons, James's American family abroad, and the Proberts, James's Europeanized Americans, seems to represent the spectrum of possibilities for reading in a world of mass-market productions.

The reading room of *The Reverberator* documents and dramatizes these transformations. Its foreign newspaper (hence unreadable) and its out-of-date newspaper (hence useless) portend the arrival of Mr. Dosson and Flack and await their disappearance, for both characters are constantly in motion: Flack rushing off "to give a turn to one of his screws" (29), the Dosson family's wanderings marked by a "trail of forgotten Tauchnitzes" (13). It is one of James's finest touches that Flack's "two horrible columns" (135) of scandalous revelations about the Proberts are read only by the Proberts. The Dossons, nonreaders in a culture saturated with print, must be introduced to an article they consider already passé. As Delia exclaims, "Lord, what a fuss about an old newspaper! . . . It must be about two weeks old" (153).[2] What distinguishes *The Reverberator* is its effort to reinvest the printed word with significance within a print culture increasingly hostile to the stability and authority of its own productions – a culture that empties its meanings of meaning in the process of making them. Although the novel begins within an emptied reading room, James's strategy is to reinscribe within the space of the text the protocols necessary to achieve a certain level of reading competence, so that the text itself becomes a kind of private reading room carrying with it its own rules of exclusion. This is not to side with the common view that James teaches literary excellence nor to accuse him of elitism, but to suggest that James affirms a certain kind of reading experience that has (by and large) come to be accepted as literary. *The Reverberator* does construct a literary order by accommodating the mass media it both invokes and derides; but we need to ask not only how this process of accommodation functions in James's text, but why it functions so well to construct a discourse we can now call literary.

Poor readers and nonreaders, discarded or unreadable newspapers, "horrible columns" of print and unspeakable intrusions into privacy – through these the novel illustrates the potential demise of traditional reading habits and of a world of readable print. But more threatening still is the fact that Flack and the Dossons claim the right to speak as though they were connected with letters and as though their writing products were literature; the notion of the literary is introduced brazenly by those who appear not to read at all. Early in the novel, for instance, we find Delia Dosson pondering her conception of literature:

> He [George Flack] was connected (as she supposed) with literature, and was not literature one of the many engaging attributes of her cherished little sister? If Mr Flack was a writer Francie was a reader: had not a trail of forgotten Tauchnitzes marked the former line of travel of the party of three? . . . She considered however that as a family they had a sort of superior affinity with the young journalist. (13)

As in the first scene, images of lack contradict a theoretical abundance. Francie's engaging "attributes" turn out to be predicated upon a trail of forgotten books, thus making nonsense of Delia's designation of her as a "reader." And the "if" clause, which Delia doubtless intends positively, casts associative doubt on Flack's ability as a writer and thereby on the nature of his connection with literature. Flack writes for money, and Delia's view of literature as one of the "engaging attributes" of her sister imputes to it a degrading exchange value. That "superior affinity" Delia proposes between her family and Flack arises from their tendency to misread the term "literature" as signifying all printed matter. Flack, not surprisingly, later writes off any distinction between novels and journalism with the sweeping "Well, it's all literature" (118), while Francie, who is "not skilled in composition," addresses her lover with a "painful sense of literary responsibility" (113).

George Flack, the new master of the emptied reading room, constantly promotes himself as the inheritor of traditional artistic and intellectual values now being transformed under his reign. According to James's notebook entry for *The Reverberator,* Flack "of course hasn't a grain of delicacy in his composition . . . he has no tradition of reserve or discretion – he simply obeys his gross newspaper instinct" (1947, 83). Yet Flack emerges in the novel as much more complex, for that gross newspaper instinct allows him to appropriate the rhetoric of a fine sensibility. To Francie, for instance, Flack styles himself as (to borrow a famous line from "The Art of Fiction") "one of the people upon whom nothing is lost." "I take in everything," he remarks at one point, "It all depends on my opportunity. I try and learn – I try and improve. Every one has something to tell, and I listen and watch and make my profit of it" (115). During the same conversation Flack states: "genuine, first-hand information, straight from the tap, is what I'm after. I don't want to hear what some one or other thinks that some one or other was told that some one or other repeated; and above all I don't want to print it" (117). Equally impressively, Flack claims for himself the democratic and enlightenment values traditionally associated with journalism. As an advocate of "enlightened enterprise," Flack claims that "you can't keep out the light of the

Press," adding, "Now what I am going to do is to set up the biggest lamp yet made and to make it shine all over the place" (61). In the "great shining presence" (22) of the Press, Flack's goal is self-confessedly that of knowledge, to which he aspires by artistic and even mystic means: Knowledge "came to him by a kind of intuition, by the voices of the air" (27). Flack's intuition is also the subject of his own boast: "I consider I have about as fine a sense as any one of what's going to be required in future over there" (61).[3]

It comes as no surprise that these assertions of professional and artistic integrity are consistently ironic. His remarks suggest the insidious financial "profit" to be made from the invasion of privacy implied by the penetrating glare of the Press's lamp – he prefaces that image by stating "That's about played out, any way, the idea of sticking up a sign of 'private' and thinking you can keep the place to yourself" (61), and we have already seen that he contributes to the darkness of the reading room. Moreover, Flack's "genuine, first-hand information" turns out to be (Francie's) second-hand news, further removed from its origin by the infusion of material from a co-writer, the shadowy Miss Topping. James's early description of Flack as "not a particular person, but a sample or memento" (14) has already prepared us to accept nothing he says or writes as original. Yet the scandal he causes among the Proberts suggests quite the opposite: Flack's "disgusting sheet" (137), distanced from the American Proberts by its linguistic vulgarity and from the French-speaking relatives by language, achieves its shattering effect by presenting to them the new, the outré, the other.[4] In the best tradition of the man of action, the journalist, Flack's energy and determination structure the narrative: His words provoke Francie's major confrontation with the Proberts, disrupt Francie's and Gaston's marriage plans, but also finally enable Gaston to break from constricting family ties. Although the novel concludes differently from the way James anticipated in his notebook (Flack was to have threatened to expose the Proberts' treatment of Francie in order to effect a reconciliation), James's assessment that the "newspaper dictates and triumphs" (1947, 84) is borne out by Flack's preeminence in James's narrative design. To view Flack as solely the object of James's satire, then, is to miss the extent to which Flack's presence constitutes the stuff out of which satire is made.

In his notebook, James wrote that his primary difficulty lay in imagining a group of people in a "newspaperized" Europe who would be "shocked enough for my dramatic opposition" (84). Dramatic opposition is what we appear to get in the figure of the Europeanized American, Mr. Probert, and his son Gaston, whose scandalized reaction to Flack's article opens the possibility that they focus on and promote principles of literariness. Like so many of James's fictions, *The Reverberator* associates reading with imagination, perceptiveness and ratiocination; and the refined Mr. Probert is above all a profound reader: "He read a great deal, and very serious books; works about the origin of things – of man, of institutions, of speech, of religion" (98). Arriving home after the dinner party for the two families, Gaston notes "the lamplight shining on [his father's] refined old head" (98) and proceeds to reflect on his family's "affinities with a society of conversation" where "there was a circle round the fire and winged words flew about and there was always some clever person before the chimney-piece, holding or challenging the rest" (98–9). The whole passage is replete with significant contrasts: the lamp-lit room against the Dossons' lamp-less "desert" of a reading room; the Proberts' affinities to conversation against the Dossons' "superior affinity" to the young journalist; "winged words" around the fire against the Dossons' forgotten books and fire-less reading room; Mr. Probert's books about the "origin of things" against Flack's mercenary desire to find and publish "genuine, first-hand information." A great reader, Mr. Probert seems about to step forth as the kingpin of a literary circle akin to that of Gustave Flaubert's, which Anne T. Margolis describes as fascinating James on his intro- duction to the circle in the early 1870s (1981, 27–8).

But Mr. Probert, according to his son, was also "the lightest and most amiable specimen of the type that liked to take possession of the hearthrug. People left it to him; he was so transparent, like a glass screen, and he never triumphed in argument. His word on most subjects was not felt to be the last (it was usually not more conclusive than a shrugging, inarticulate resignation)" (99). Oddly, George Flack comes to mind: James characterizes both Flack ("memento or sample") and Probert ("specimen of the type") as conventional, even caricatured, figures whose voices are diminished by the very nature of their authority. Mr. Probert's possession of the hearthrug, that is, depends on everyone's under- standing of his lack of command, while Flack's undoubted ability to subjugate the Dossons by his journalistic talent masks the fact that none of his words is either original or "the last." The contraction of Mr. Probert's social circle and his subsequent withdrawal from the world underline his failure to empower the "winged words." Our last glimpse of Mr. Probert finds him trying and failing (through illness) to translate the offending article into English for his son-in-law (137) and later making – a far cry from his erstwhile oratory – a "strange inarticulate sound" (144) in response to Francie's apology. The other Proberts share this problematic relationship to culture. Gaston, in particular, has as many pretensions to artistic status as Flack, and frequently seems just as ridiculous. The "sensitive plate" (45) in his head is no guarantee of fine perception. Lacking in artistic talent himself, his mode of consciousness is impressionistic in the most meager way: He confesses to Waterlow that the most important things that have happened to him were "simply half-a-dozen impressions – impressions of the eye." And he refuses to impart the content of this fine consciousness in ways that scarcely endear him to us: "If he knew [Francie's charm] was rare she herself did not. He liked to be conscious, but he liked others not to be."

The Reverberator, initially designed to pose refinement and privacy against "the invasion, the impudence and shamelessness, of the newspaper and the inter- viewer, the devouring *publicity* of life" (1947, 82), appears to satirize journalism and a lightweight aestheticism alike, and in such a way that Flack emerges as the more straightforward and sympathetic character. And although the two families attach different values to linguistic usage, James does not make it easy for us to privilege one mode of discourse over another, as the following little parable of reading suggests. The Dossons, Gaston claims,

> had not in the least seen what was manner, the minimum of decent profession, and what the subtle resignation of old races who have known a long historical discipline and have conventional forms for their feelings – forms resembling singularly little the feelings themselves. Francie took people at their word when they told her that the whole *manière d'être* of her family inspired them with an irresistible sympathy; that was a speech of which Mme de Cliché had been capable. . . . As to the high standard itself there was no manner of doubt; it was magnificent in its own way. (97)

In fact Gaston casts all manner of doubt on the high standard. As her name unambiguously implies, Mme. de Cliché's speech relies on conventions that constitute the total significance of the utterance. "Irresistible sympathy," her euphemism for contempt, does more than present sweetly to the plainspeaking Francie (who assumes she stands in the presence, as it were, of Mme. de Cliché's meaning) the bitter message of her family's unacceptability. The phrase also carries with it a host of meaningful attributes – gentility, largesse, good breeding and manners, condescension – that signify as part of a social grammar imperceptible to Francie. It is worth pointing out that because this grammar functions only for the Proberts, Mme. de Cliché's speech is largely self-referential: She speaks for the benefit of the Probert family's own self-worth and superiority. Her conventional forms justify the usage of conventional forms insofar as they signify, to the Proberts, not sympathy but a mode of using language that is socially coherent and satisfying. The literal content of her speech, in other words, is unimportant (we could imagine a dozen other phrases that would have served as well); its real value lies in preserving the principles, codes, and social legitimacy of the Proberts' discourse. In the sense that "irresistible sympathy" bespeaks nothing more than the decorum of speaking some such phrase, her speech becomes merely that which is always spoken: a cliché.

In a novel in which dramatic oppositions tend toward the complementary, Mme. de Cliché's clichés lead us back to Flack's. James characterizes Flack, like Mme. de Cliché, as nothing more than the discourse that has produced him; in the business of creating texts for mass consumption, the discourse of the mass is found inscribed in him. He bears, for instance, "a number, like that of the day's newspaper," and as "every copy of the newspaper wears the same label, so that of Miss Dosson's visitor would have been 'Young commercial American'" (14). Not surprisingly, Flack constructs his speech out of phrases so timeworn that they are barely noticeable as such: "straight from the tap" (117), "they're bound to have the plums!" (61), "what the American people want" (61), and so on. But if Mme. de Cliché's utterances self-consciously articulate a discourse of decorum and conventionality whose repetition preserves its currency, Flack's clichés go unrecognized by him and the Dossons. To the latter, the style of Flack's letter from Paris appears "lively, 'chatty,' even brilliant," though Mr. Dosson does wonder that the Proberts are not aware of "the charges brought every day against the most prominent men in Boston" (157). One of the covert meanings of newspaper discourse, Mr. Dosson implies, is that iteration reduces its power. The publication of Flack's letter shocks the Proberts because they cannot accept that its form, as a letter in a newspaper, brings into play certain conventional expectations, such as the ubiquity and transience of scandal, that defuse its catastrophic effect. The Proberts read the letter literally, which is to say, out of context; it is Francie and family, given to taking people "at their word," who recognize that even the most damning comment about the Proberts, when published in the context of the newspaper, rapidly vanishes into the void of pervasive iteration.

As a whole, the novel debates issues of reading and writing in a series of unstable oppositions. The darkened reading room in the first scene of *The Reverberator* prepared us for a world of bad (or non) readers implicitly counter-pointed by good – the readers or writers who would, figuratively speaking, stock the reading room with books and enable us to formulate a definition of literature to oppose Francie's. James constantly engages the question of literariness in the characters' reading habits, writing, perceptiveness, and rhetoric. The term "litera-ture," once placed in common currency by the likes of Flack and Delia, structures the way we read, say, the Dossons' slang ("ain't") and the way we expect we would read Flack's "two horrible columns." From the opening sentence of the novel, which leads us with Mr. Dosson to enter the "little *salon de lecture*," we are aware that an inquiry into forms of writing constitutes the novel's subject and special domain. Yet to conceive of the literary as being formed by a struggle between the Proberts and Dossons, reflective readers and bad readers, the private and the public, is to miss the complexity of *The Reverberator*. The Proberts misread Flack's letter (by missing its context) as much as Francie misreads the tenor of the Proberts' speeches and wishes. Similarly, Gaston's fine sensibility objectifies Francie, while Flack, crudely opportunistic as he is, seems genuinely shocked by Francie's imputation that he desires her father's money (63). The characters are unable to fill the vacancies articulated early in the novel. If Delia's evocation of the literary lacks substance, then no one else speaks for literature, despite the many who pretend to represent it. Nor is it enough to claim that Flack and Gaston, as types of the (failed) artist, embody aspects of the artistic temperament. Flack, for instance, all too clearly evinces an appropriation of the literary; it is represented as a characteristic of Flack's opportunism and egotism rather than as a vocation to which he is occasionally called.

The issue of privacy focuses the novel's debate over the nature of literariness. From the moment of the novel's inception, as described in James's notebook, Flack's letter was to be marginalized as "horribly vulgar" (1947, 82), not so much because of its association with the public as with publicity: a mode of writing that proclaims the condition of appearing before a public as the principle of its existence. In the notebook, James lamented the "mania for publicity" and the "devouring *publicity* of life, the extinction of all sense between public and private" (82), and associates privacy throughout with propriety, manners, and tradition. Although James opposes the "newspaperized American girl" to the "rigid, old-fashioned, conservative, still shockable and much shocked little society she recklessly plays the tricks upon" (82) – scarcely a society in which to repose all value – his own outrage about the exploits of Miss McClellan clearly identifies him with a culture of privacy. He makes the same point more explicitly still in a notebook entry about *The Bostonians* on April 8, 1883, in which a desire to write a "very *American* tale" led him to want to "*bafouer* the vulgarity and hideousness of this – the impudent invasion of privacy – the extinction of all conception of privacy" (47). This lament did not prevent James from later bemoaning in a famous letter to William Dean Howells (January 2, 1888) that *The Bostonians,* together with *The Princess Casamassima,* represented the nadir of public response to his work:

> I am still staggering a good deal under the mysterious and (to me) inexplicable injury wrought – apparently – upon my situation by my last two novels, the *Bostonians* and the *Princess,* from which I have expected so much and derived so little. They have reduced the desire, and the demand, for my productions to zero – as I judge from the fact that though I have for a good while past been writing a number of good short things, I remain irremediably unpublished. (1980, 209)

As Michael Anesko contends in *Friction with the Market* (1986), this letter, often interpreted as a renunciatory gesture of despair with his perceived audience, should be taken instead as evidence of James's constant and productive engagement with the literary marketplace. James continued to publish and to concern himself with the professional aspects of writing. Anne T. Margolis points out that James's professionalism soon reasserted itself: he accepted Edmund Gosse's advice to seek the aid of a literary agent, and went on to write *The Reverberator,* which might be seen as a deliberate return to the theme of the young American girl abroad that had already provided him, after the publication of "Daisy Miller" (1879), with a measure of celebrity. *The Reverberator* comprises a return to public demand in more ways than one, Margolis argues: James deliberately avoided the savage, confrontational tone of the notebook entries in order to cater to conventional expectations, while harking back to the strategies that already constituted public knowledge and estimation of his work (1981, 2–5). The failure of the Proberts to oppose significant modes of reading and writing to the crudeness of

Flack's column – to engage, that is, in a genuinely antagonistic and possibly controversial debate between literature and journalism after the fashion of his treatment of feminism in *The Bostonians* – could then be seen as a function of James's overriding concern with placating his audience (a strategy that Margolis implies leads to artistic failure).

But there is a more profound reason why the Proberts fail to associate their legitimate ideals of privacy with a notion of literariness. Both *The Reverberator* and James's notebooks explicitly identify publicity with the journalistic mode of expression; the "history of the age," according to Flack's hyperbole, is the "papers" (118). The structural relationship James sets up between publicity and privacy leads us to expect a dialectic or debate between opposed literary principles – a private discourse that would counteract Flack's capacity for public expression – which is never articulated among the characters. Privacy complements the idea of publicity, representing that which publicity preys on and destroys, yet lacks any direct relevance to operations of reading or writing. Publicity evokes a world of writing and reading, however poor; privacy, on the other hand, is the prerogative of a group of people, the Proberts, who affirm a social (and political) imperative that has only marginal significance for constructing viable principles of writing. The linguistic possibilities of the Proberts' conduct are, in fact, self-consuming. We have seen already that the speech appropriate to the "high standard" as expressed through the language of Mme. de Cliché and Mr. Probert is constantly put at the service of social equilibrium: Mr. Probert's easy mastery of the fireside circle and Mme. de Cliché's euphemisms express their sense that speech must be conformable to the maintenance of that circle and family ties. Their speech, which appears ideally suited to a plastic, malleable creative discourse because it "responded so little to fact" (97), instead subjugates its expressive possibilities to a limited number of social gestures. Their speech tends, in a maneuver of self-subversion, toward that which has already and always been said, and when the crisis of the *Reverberator*'s article forces them to confront an outrageous new world of publicity, Mr. Probert succumbs to inarticulacy and Mme. de Brecourt to stuttering repetition ("Let her go, let her go!" [142]). The Proberts are structurally positioned in such a way that they represent a negation of publicity rather than an affirmation of positive values and principles.

This position is rather different from the traditional sense of James as a cultural conservative in the spirit of Matthew Arnold.[5] In that spirit, the Proberts, rigid as they undoubtedly are, must stand for cultural values now endangered by a publicity-minded society. Such a statement adequately describes James's position in his notebook entries and in letters of the time. But the novel by no means affords an easy correlation between cultural probity and privacy however we define the meaning of that term for James. The manner in which the Proberts employ the ideals they self-consciously represent quite clearly compromises the integrity of those ideals; moreover, the ideals themselves seem to lack the authority they might be expected to possess in order to support a genuinely private discourse. In his notebook, James complained about the "extinction of all conception of privacy," but *The Reverberator* shows him working to define and critique a conception of privacy that still contributes to the Proberts' eminence in the French social hierarchy and still has the power to provoke Gaston's rebellion. At the same time, I want now to argue, James works to construct in the novel a position of what we might call affirmative publicity – a rhetorical position involving a constant negotiation between the terms "privacy" and "publicity," which allows James to introduce a third term into the duality of Dossons and Proberts. Since neither the Proberts nor the Dossons prepare us to formulate an adequate response to, say, Flack's "Well, it's all literature," and since more adequate responses certainly are possible, another discourse invisible to both families must somehow be operating. We recognize, as the Dossons do not, that Flack's sweeping statement fails to discriminate between literature and so-called literature in the newspapers; and we recognize too that the Proberts, who would scorn Flack's statement, would not be able to justify that scorn to our satisfaction by reference to any ideal they espouse within the novel. This third term requires us to look more closely at the issue of literary competence and the community that might be formed around it. We are in the position of formulating – of having to formulate – a definition of the literary that is nowhere absolutely stated within the conversations and debates of the novel, and which therefore must emerge from the productive engagement of reader and text. By evoking a concept of literature defined almost entirely by the nonliterary, the text encourages us to supply a significance at best intimated, at worst in the process of being lost, within the text itself.

Two interrelated questions are crucial here. We need to inquire into how we may construct a definition of the literary different from any posited by the characters or narrator of *The Reverberator,* while asking a more fundamental question about the historical preconditions for the kind of response to the literary I am claiming the novel elicits. In other words, how does the novel elaborate a concept that readers from James's time to ours have been able to recognize as the literary? This way of putting it seems to produce the worst kind of critical tautology, succinctly anatomized by Stanley Fish, among others, whereby a historically specific interpretation (in this case of literature itself) is read back into an alien text and then, by critical sleight of hand, given the appearance of universality. In fact the tautology here is a real one, for the strategies employed by James in *The Reverberator* foreshadow in important ways the kind of reading experience, usually attributed to canonical modernist texts, that has characterized critical discourse in an age of mass culture. The novel calls for a special kind of competence historically related to the emergence of covert, esoteric modes of writing and (through the critical activity) rewriting, which the late twentieth century has embedded within its evolving institutions. The novel's concept of the literary is susceptible to critical analysis in the sense that it is still available to us as, if not a universally acceptable, then at least a functional and comprehensible set of significations.

This is true, for instance, in James's trademark manipulations of narrative voice, which in this novel occur most frequently in the first two chapters. While the reading room darkens, the narrator plays variations on a theme of diverse perception:

> An observer of these two persons would have assured himself. . . .
> Delia made no movement whatever . . . so far as could be perceived. . . .
> A person with a delicate ear might have suspected. . . .
> If an auditor had happened to be present. . . .
> An observer would have gathered . . .
> The slightly surprised observer whom we have supposed to be present. . . .
> I forbear to say positively. . . .
> If it be objected to all this. . . .
> Her sister's attitude would have told you. . . . (3–15)

These startling transformations of the narrative voice demand a reader capable of asking the right kind of questions about this series of missing pronoun antecedents. How far is that democratic "we" synonymous with "you" (a close friend of the narrator's, introduced under the traditional protocol of the "dear Reader")? Is "I" the same observer as the "slightly surprised" one? And can the "person with a delicate ear" be identified with the "auditor" or that all-embracing "we"? Clearly, the reader is being called upon to play a variety of roles: now distanced from the narrative point of view, now introduced as a friend, now made gender-specific ("assured himself"), now made androgynous and a partner in the author's productions in that intimate "we." The first two chapters of the novel thus represent an adventurous foray into the rhetorical possibilities of pronoun usage and the flexibility of narrative voice. But they also call for a cooler, historical perspective on the exclusiveness of this kind of reading. "We" are being asked to join an elite audience – one that is, for instance, at cross purposes with James's pessimistic representation of a potential reading public in the Dossons, whose habits of nonreading absolutely disqualify them for negotiating his intricate rhetorical turns.

Such reading experiences suggest that our expertise as readers might "fill in" for the lack of explicit articulations in the text of literary values and definitions. Much more problematic is the question of how we can maintain a faith in the nonliterary (or what I called negative publicity) in the face of a radical doubt about how the characters and we, the readers, read the text of Flack's letter. The letter is crucial, for it promises to document, once and for all, the literary transgressions of the new journalism, as well as offering final evidence for an ironic reading of Flack's pretensions to literary stardom. But it is also, by the Proberts' imputation and by virtue of its disappearance from the novel, unreadable. James's novel, whose title fosters expectation that the novel will somehow feature the newspaper, in fact silences the voice of the piece of writing most germane to the development of its plot. More precisely, Flack's letter appears in paraphrase, courtesy of Mme. de Brecourt, who quotes only four words of his genuine and original voice (or of Flack and Miss Topping's composite voice): "rare old exclusives" and "store" (138). Published in the *Reverberator* to the Proberts' dismay, the letter is reduced to four words in the published text of James's *The Reverberator,* and now somewhat to our bewilderment. For these four words are insufficient to judge the contrasting critical judgments of the Dossons and Proberts. The same article that both disappoints the Dossons for its blandness and evokes admiration for being "brilliant" (157) appears to the Proberts as "two horrible columns of vulgar lies and scandal" (135), as a "most disgusting sheet" (137), as a "hideous sheet" (139). Given the absence of the original text and given the fact that James privileges neither the Dossons nor Proberts as expert readers, we have no textual grounds for interpreting Flack's writing as hideous or brilliant or anything else. At best, we can argue from pronouncements such as "Well, it's all literature" that a failure to discriminate what might be specifically literary about any text compromises the observations of Flack and the Dossons. This argument rests on the assumption that the ability to discriminate more and more finely is the product of a literary sensibility – an assumption that most critics would accept as defensible, or at least true for Henry James. But a principle of discrimination can be adduced in this novel only by a process of discrimination. We read from a preexisting "understanding" of Jamesian and literary discriminations to a discriminating view of Flack's hideous article and back out to a finer sense of what is nonliterary. But because there is so little (four words) to discriminate finely *about,* because the written text that documents the transgressions of journalism is (virtually) unobtainable, we must begin to see that what appears to be a transcendental principle of literariness derives at least in part from the critical protocols available to us. Indeed, can we even state that "Well, it's all literature" is not an adequate formulation, given that we cannot read the one piece of written evidence that would, once and for all, define the nonliterary? The sharp debate over literary values occasioned by this novel is such that our ability to make categorical statements like "discrimination is a literary value" is one of the points at issue.

In *The Reverberator,* such interpretive doubts about the nature of literary value multiply as fast as James appears to bracket them off and disappear as rapidly as James raises them. Let us return to Delia's – and the narrator's – thoughts on literature:

> He was connected (as she supposed) with literature, and was not literature one of the many engaging attributes of her cherished little sister? If Mr Flack was a writer Francie was a reader: had not a trail of forgotten Tauchnitzes marked the former line of travel of the party of three? (13)

In one sense Delia's first connection, interrupted by the narrator's parenthesis, never occurs. Reconstructed, "He was connected with literature" attributes to her a facility and confidence she never actually achieves during this little meditation on literature. The narrator's parenthetical "as she supposed" introduces a note of doubt later augmented by the conditional "if" and her two rhetorical questions (was not? had not? to which we answer no and then yes). The "if" clause in particular marks a hazardous exchange. If Francie is no reader, then Flack by the same token is no writer; or we might reread the thought as "If Mr Flack were a writer, Francie would be a reader"; or we might read Delia's facile equation of literary producers and consumers as betokening a monstrous ignorance of hierarchy – something also characteristic of Flack ("Well, it's all literature"). The narrator's "as she supposed," however, does not quite have the effect of "she was wrong." In a sense Flack must be connected with any notion of literature the novel constructs, given its dynamic of mutual definition whereby the literary appears by way of the nonliterary (in this case the journalistic). Likewise, since Flack to writing equals Francie to reading (so Delia supposes), there is a sense in which the trail of forgotten Tauchnitzes leads to the shrine of the literary: that which is not forgotten, that which is (at least) not a cheap, discardable reprint. The narrator's interjection needs to be fruitfully misread, as it were, in order to see that his ridiculing of Delia's assessment of Flack's literary connections might give way to a still finer discrimination of the ways in which she is unwittingly correct.

The point is that in the process of deriding Delia's pretensions to literary status, the passage raises precisely the issue of how readers read, identify, and objectify a concept of the literary. It indicates how a reader's connection to institutionalized literary meanings makes decidable the literary quality of a text. To scorn Flack's "Well, it's all literature" or to perceive the emptiness of the reading room brings into play a competence that must precede the reading of the text (otherwise our immediate apprehension of the problems of the reading room would be impossible). That competence need not be consciously exercised – indeed, the linguistic model of competence suggests that it rarely is. Comprehending the joke of "Well, it's all literature" does not depend on bringing to consciousness a precise set of inherited literary attributes but on registering a difference. Likewise, the interpolated "as she supposed," by casting doubt on Delia's perspicacity, introduces as a precondition of meaning the possibility of separating one value from another. The passage needs only to establish a relationship of difference between Delia's use of the term literature and any other to force an awareness of the inadequacy of using the term to refer to all writing. Nowhere does James define, or need to define, what literature is; it is enough that as the voices of the newspaperized world extend the sign "literature" to include all printed matter, the possibility of literature as recognizably other should emerge. If Delia's annihilation of a specifically literary realm seems a characteristic maneuver of a newspaperized society, in other words, so does James's accommodation of the newspaperized voice within a discourse that emphasizes its otherness become typical of the modern (and modernist) text. To note this process of accommodation as it unfolds is not (necessarily) to imply agreement with Jamesian literary principles culled from his works of fiction and criticism, his letters and notebooks, but to assert that the principle of difference integral to the process has been and will continue to be possible.[6]

This is true even though James's refusal to publish the text (Flack's letter) which he throughout seems to stigmatize as contemptible intimates a radical indeterminacy of meaning. Lacking Flack's letter, it appears that meaning can only be contextual; the letter is consequently wrenched from one interpretation to another: hideous, passé, brilliant. By the same token, no understanding of literature, including "Well, it's all literature," could be dismissed as incorrect or unsuitable. Literary significance would rest in the domain of taste, where any judgment might be justified as legitimate and where, potentially, any majority judgment might cause its interpretation to prevail. Yet the novel does not allow, I claim, any such sliding of the signifier "literature" as this contextualization of meaning might suggest, for an interpretive community exists that has been able, and continues able, to legitimate the kind of differential understanding of literature I am proposing here. Indeed, while the literary principles commonly adduced from James's work – the fine sensibility, the focus on meaningful (upper-class) experience, and so on – have always been at the center of critical dispute, the concept that literature exists in an oppositional relationship to mass culture (until very recently) has not. We do not need to subscribe to James's enunciated principles in order to assign value to the covert assumption of literature's superiority over mass culture on which the satire of *The Reverberator* depends. The shaping of this kind of interpretive community, indeed, develops in spite of professed doubts about literary meaning and about the kind of reading experience offered by James. What I called a theme of diverse perception does not imply a diverse audience and, noting that, it is quite likely that some readers would prefer to opt out. My point, however, is that one cannot opt out until one has been – and remains – coopted. One cannot close the book on James until one has unfolded his covert assessment of the reading room and his narrative countermeasures; and it is the fact of that unfolding, not one's like or dislike of the cultural principles involved, that keeps the book open.

Meaning is always contextual but not for that reason meaningless. We understand the irony of Delia's "[h]e was connected . . . with literature" because a set of structural oppositions have arisen in our age of mass culture that prevent us from finally equating Flack with literature, however much his statements occasionally chime with principles James elsewhere identifies as literary. And this helps to explain the disappearance of Flack's letter within James's text. An interpretive community that would provide the competence necessary to actualize the irony of "Well, it's all literature" is constituted in such way that the text of Flack's letter has been already read, its message already known. Flack's letter, its original text silenced, speaks after all in a reader's ability to mobilize a prior understanding of the literary crimes perpetrated by mass culture and to assume their repetition in any work Flack might produce. His writing must embody, we suppose, the stockpiled clichés that already invest his verbal pronouncements. Reading *The Reverberator* thus instigates a complex process of mutual actualization in which meanings are read out of the text by marshalling a preexisting competence, and which leads in turn to the perception of the text's literariness. The discovery that we can answer "of course not" to Flack's "Well, it's all literature" is a recognition involving both the perception of our ability to actualize that response as well as the momentary coming-to-consciousness of our cultural and ideological ties to Henry James.

Those ties are nowhere more evident than in the occluded but somehow already-read text of Flack's letter. The letter speaks most clearly to those who are able to read what is not present in the text. But even the attempt to read it against the grain – by speculating, for instance, that it opens up the possibility of a favorable reading of popular culture, represented by Flack – activates the kind of reading that is, so to speak, incommensurable with itself. One may rhetorically pose the possibility that *The Reverberator* deconstructs its own cultural pretensions; but as one does so, one is reconstructing the institutional and cultural differences that allow the novel to be still published and read. In part, no doubt, this is because of James's historic importance to the profession of literary studies. Recognized by contemporary avant-garde writers like Stephen Crane, Ezra Pound, and Joseph Conrad, lionized by the New Critics, and presently the focus of a whole industry of books, articles, and dissertations, James has inarguably achieved the pinnacle of literary standing. While it has always been possible to criticize James's work on a number of counts, it is extremely difficult to argue that James is nonliterary, precisely because the category of the nonliterary has largely been subsumed by the productions of mass culture. A critical work arguing that James's real strength lies in his assimilation of the popular (rather than his transformation of the popular) would be incorrect, not because the literary exists as a universally separable and identifiable idiom, but because there exists no firmly institutionalized structure of meanings and values to privilege this reversal of the literary and the popular. Again: The category of literature is really and objectively there, difficult as it is to define. I am merely arguing that our acceptance of principles and strategies generally regarded as literary – such as, in James's case, complexity, subtlety, and reversal of the conventional – emerges from a specific cultural and historical context in which a critical discourse also geared toward complexity, individual apprehension, and subtlety makes the cult of Henry James a virtual tautology.[7]

Oddly, *The Reverberator* comes as close to being written off as a popular potboiler, a vague reworking of the well-made play, an aberration – in other words, nonliterary – as any text in the Jamesian canon. To Margolis, for instance, as to almost all critics, the novel is "slight" and "strictly calculated to please the conventional expectations of all components of James's audience" (1981, 4–5). Moreover, the comedy of the son breaking away from the confines of his family in order to marry departs little from the well-made plot of nineteenth-century fiction and drama, though James occasionally dramatizes the limitations of that plot (the novel's conclusion portrays a very suspect relationship between Francie and the disoriented Gaston). But, crude as it is by comparison to *The Portrait of a Lady* and James's late works, *The Reverberator* confronts head on the issue of a literature colonized by (allegedly) oppositional cultural principles and poses the question of literature's survival through a relationship of accommodation. The complex dynamic whereby the demise of the literary ("Well, it's all literature") adumbrates its resurrection (of course, everything is *not* literature) is one we shall see repeated in the work of later writers, and it is in this sense that *The Reverberator* begins to fulfil the grandiose claims of "protomodernist" I have made for it. The novel concerns not so much the crisis of an emptied reading room as the writing of a new kind of (modernist) text. The novel sets in motion a sharp debate between literary and nonliterary principles that cannot help but foreshadow more obviously modernist strategies of accommodation. We see James beginning to figure out some key strategies – not for creating modernism but for *accommodating mass culture*. The fact that this is not a simple writing off – that Flack's letter could just possibly be read in a spirit far more sympathetic to the popular than has ever been possible before – testifies to the even more complex writing strategies and cultural crossings that are to come.

3

The Newspaperman Kicked Out

The Sacred Fount
and Literary Authority

"How on earth can I tell what you're talking about?" demands Ford Obert of *The Sacred Fount*'s ([1901] 1979b) supersubtle narrator. The question, repeated by a number of the narrator's mystified interlocutors in the novel, has been echoed more circumspectly by generations of critics since the turn of the century. For the efforts of the unnamed narrator to comprehend social relationships at the country house of Newmarch leads him and his audience into impossible tangles out of all proportion to the symmetry of his theory of energy-exchanges. The perceived youthfulness of Mrs. Brissenden, understood to have been leached from her younger and prematurely aging husband, leads him to approach the enigma of a suddenly more perceptive Gilbert Long by proposing the existence of a female victim at the sacred fount: Long's lover, whose presence at Newmarch must be signalled by her exhausted wit. Aided by Mrs. Brissenden and Ford Obert, the narrator undertakes a quest for the missing fourth person with an intensity that burdens every spoken word with the potential for volumes of exegesis. Readers of the novel have constantly inquired "how on earth can I tell what you're talking about?"; for, as the first conversational exchange in the novel suggests, "talking" constantly gives way to reading, and reading to "reading in":

> It came back to me as I sat there that when she mentioned Lady John as in charge of Brissenden the other member of our trio [Gilbert Long] had expressed interest and surprise – expressed it so as to have made her reply with a smile: "Didn't you really know?" . . .
> "Why in the world *should* I know?"
> To which, with good nature, she had simply returned: "Oh, it's only that I thought you always did!" And they both had looked at me a little oddly, as if appealing from each other. "What in the world does she

mean?" Long might have seemed to ask; while Mrs. Brissenden conveyed
with light profundity: "*You* know why he should as well as I, don't you?"
In point of fact I didn't in the least. (4)

Four questions confound the expected sequence of interrogation/reply. The first
question receives another question, the second (Long's) returns a statement that
only causes both Long and Mrs. Brissenden to appeal questioningly to the
narrator. At the same time, from the narrator's two imagined questions emerge,
first, no answer and, second, an answer that reveals the question's unanswerability.
Thus we have no way of knowing whether Long's silently posed question is
meant rhetorically. More to the point, we have no way of knowing whether the
narrator construes those appealing (but odd) glances accurately. His own questions must then be at once in question (because we may doubt his perceptions)
and unquestioned (because we have no alternative set of perceptions to draw
on). Determining the rhetorical status of Long's "What in the world does she
mean?" depends upon correctly interpreting his glance; but his glance is inter-
pretable only in terms of "What in the world does she mean?" We have reached,
in Paul de Man's term, an aporia: What in the world does he (Long? the
narrator?) mean with his "What in the world does she mean?"?

Just as the playfully redundant "might have seemed" (why not "seemed"?)
doubly distances Long's words, so do all of the characters in *The Sacred Fount*
recede before us. Dialogue, for instance, more often than not suspends communal discourse between characters; it comprises, as Sergio Perosa puts it,
"interviews suddenly interrupted, half-sentences and broken talks, inconclusive
verbal duels, hints quickly denied, flimsy suggestions, sudden suspensions, false
clues, tentative assumptions" (1978, 78). Unfortunately, we are often unsure
about what comprises dialogue. "How could a woman who had been plain so
long become pretty so late?" (5) wonders (or remarks?) James's narrator. This, he
alleges, is "just what he [Long] had been wondering." Long's actual quoted
remark, "I didn't place her *myself*" (my italics), situates his perception in a
dialogic relationship that we hear only textually but which, we suppose, sounded
out to Long. In other words, does the narrator confidently appropriate Long's
quite different thoughts, or does Long's statement represent a tacit agreement
between two subtle individuals to whom language is a profoundly useful and
flexible instrument?

These scenes reveal little about a putative set of character relationships;
alternatively (and it comes to almost the same thing), the scene reveals a
tremendous amount about a nearly infinite series of relationships. While it is
possible that some later solution will organize these incompleted questions into
a coherent and stable pattern, later evidence – and the evidence of wildly
different critical readings – suggests otherwise. This first conversation partakes of
a larger structure of unanswered questions in the novel, by means of which final
judgment, and, indeed, the possibility of final meanings, are constantly deferred.

From fragmented questions such as these, the narrator's words weave plots that changing circumstances and competing theories of character development persistently unravel. Questions that receive partial or inconclusive answers sabotage the linearity of "story line," instigating instead a constant referring-back to the mysterious questions that set the narrator's fantasy plots in motion. Alternative interpretations of the initial questions, to which the narrator's shifting plots are answers, force us to hesitate over each hypothetical reading. Early in the novel, for instance, the narrator remarks on Grace Brissenden's new-found beauty to Gilbert Long and asks "Why else shouldn't we have recognised her?" Gilbert Long (typically capping the narrator's question with a "Why indeed?" of his own) actually refuses the narrator's analysis, arguing instead that "Her clock has simply stopped. She looks no older – that's all" (6). Long's comment strikes at the heart of the narrator's theories, which are based on relationships that must either increase or diminish (older, younger, more intelligent, more stupid) rather than remain static. In other words, Long's "Why indeed?" broaches a wholly different train of thought that is, subsequently, neither debated nor rejected. His observation remains an unanswered and unanswerable objection, a constant reminder of how easily the narrator's edifice might be demolished. Endless labyrinths of meaning or of nonmeaning? In terms of the perverse dynamic of energy-exchange expounded by the narrator, we hesitate, while reading *The Sacred Fount,* between seeing it as plenitude or blank.

My point in constructing this long introduction to *The Sacred Fount* is not to extend the kind of poststructuralist readings already produced by John Carlos Rowe and Susan Kappeler, but to clear the ground for the larger question, which goes begging in their work, about the historical and cultural preconditions for the kind of (in Roland Barthes' terms) writerly "jeu d'esprit" (Edel 1979, xxx) we find in this text. Kappeler is not wrong to describe the work of this text as an "infinite production" where "perceptions are perceived, interpreted, reproduced in discourse, reinterpreted, and where palace is built upon palace, with none at the bottom built upon rock" (1980, 173). But neither does her statement account for the historically embedded notion of an infinitely productive text whose esotericism creates its cultural and canonical authority. We need to see the indeterminacy of James's text as a strategy designed to accomplish certain cultural functions rather than to see his text as a function of the indeterminacy of writing. And *The Sacred Fount* functions as a cultural and critical icon extraordinarily well. If acts of writing and reading take place within discursive formations that privilege certain modes of understanding (as Michel Foucault and others argue), *The Sacred Fount* may be said to direct our attention to the modes of constitution of the modernist text in unparalleled fashion. Anomalous as this novel seems to be (James's only first-person narration, excluded by the author from the New York Edition), Perosa correctly argues for its "crucial position at the very center of our twentieth-century *querelle* over the possibilities, the nature, and the fate of novel writing" (74–5).

As many critics have noted, the novel advertises itself as an allegory of reading and interpretation. Acts of reading in *The Sacred Fount* constitute the action of the novel as surely as they do in *The Reverberator,* even though the earlier constellation of characters around the hidden text of the newspaper article now gives way to character-as-text. The narrator's discrimination of verbal and gestural nuance, together with his eloquent readings of relationships, points to his superiority over the bad readers of the Dossons family. While the bookless reading room of *The Reverberator* appropriately counterpointed sterile readers of character, the haven of Newmarch makes possible a "charmed communion" between the "wonderful" (1979b, 208) bookshelves and readers (of character) there. As E. C. Curtsinger writes, the wonderful bookshelves at Newmarch create a "demesne of the imagination" (1982, 119), unobtrusively reflecting the hermeneutic act of "reading in" carried out by the narrator and the other characters. And there is no George Flack to threaten Newmarch's well-stocked bookshelves: The novel lacks the overt conflict between bad readers (within the text) and the culturally privileged reader (outside the text) characteristic of *The Reverberator.*

James has stocked the libraries at Newmarch with books and *The Sacred Fount* itself with infinite readings. After the bookless reading room of *The Reverberator,* the later novel seems some "fantasia of the library" (to use Foucault's term) in which event becomes plot and identity becomes character to the narrator's critical eye. "[W]e were in a beautiful old tale" (130), remarks the narrator about himself and May Server – a tale soon to be reenacted within a burgeoning library of commentaries on the novel. But in one sense *The Sacred Fount* turns the cultural vision of *The Reverberator* on its head. The narrator of *The Reverberator* functioned as a guardian of literary privilege, creating restrictive reading codes comprehensible only to readers of a certain competence. The inordinate complexity of *The Sacred Fount* further curtails a potential audience, yet seems so far from privileging its readership that one critic, Charles Baxter, has argued that the novel is "a structural attack upon James's audience, those shadowy tormentors who had jeered at him when George Alexander brought him on stage after the first night's performance of *Guy Domville* (1895) and who after 1886 had been denying him the consistent critical and popular success he craved" (1981, 327). *The Sacred Fount* fits beautifully into the most common description of James's career, which has him shifting from the social novel of the 1880s and the public stage of the 1890s to the intensely private world of his late work.

But if *The Sacred Fount* threatens the concept of audience as a community of readers linked by shared expectations and responses to the text, it is only to reshape that concept in a different guise. The novel does not attack the concept of audience so much as question received notions of what constitutes an audience and, as a corollary, of how a narrative shapes and defines an audience. We have already seen James debating questions of accessibility, literature, and literature for the billions in "The Question of the Opportunities" ([1898]

1984); and similar debates were continued everywhere at this time, from commentators in and about the new mass media to the near-invisible but profoundly important discursive practices emerging from the growing university system. Obsessed as James is in *The Sacred Fount* with the construction of a labyrinthine textual world, the novel is quintessentially of its time. It reintroduces in fictional form the kind of questions raised in "The Question of the Opportunities" about the relationship between audience and the constitution of a literary text within a burgeoning (and fragmenting) mass market. The novel reintroduces as well that complex relationship I began to describe in Chapter 1 between writing and the enterprise of literary criticism forming within the new institutions of the university. Most commentators on *The Sacred Fount* have recognized that the narrator, possessed of an "artistic glow" (104) through much of his reconstellating of narrative possibilities, is or at least would like to be an artist figure (see Curtsinger 1982; Rowe 1977, 223). More recently, Kappeler has written that "critics are ready to read the novel as a parable or allegory of almost anything except themselves, and to perceive analogies between the narrator and James, the writer in general, or 'any man', except, again, the critic" (1980, 202). In response to a more general understanding of the critical act as the precondition for interpreting any text, that omission has been amply redressed. But no one has addressed the pressing issues of what the narrator-as-critic has to do with the formation of a critical reading elite in the twentieth century, and what the narrator's power struggles have to do with the struggles of many writers around the turn of the century for cultural hegemony. The implications of these questions for reading James and for interpreting our own institutions of criticism are, to use a Jamesian phrase, immense, especially when we turn to consider that most scorned of all figures, kicked out from serious consideration in almost every critical encounter with *The Sacred Fount:* the newspaperman.

I

The first quoted conversation of the novel, we saw, provides at least two potential interpretations of Newmarch-style dialogue. On the one hand, characters talk past each other in a space filled with dashes, hiatuses, interruptions, and appropriations while, on the other, a discontinuous dialogue suggests the enormously complex ability of a small and tightly-knit linguistic community to forgo otherwise laborious processes of communication. The silences, as it were, signify in the latter case. But there are other options. If – one interpretation the novel makes possible – Mrs. Brissenden is having an affair with Long, the first conversation between the pair reads very differently. The first questions ("Didn't you really know?" "Why in the world *should* I know?") then register a necessary pretense of ignorance performed for the benefit of the narrator, while her rejoinder ("Oh, it's only that I thought you always did!") might signify an in-joke based on, presumably, long acquaintance. As readers we are mystified, angered, or entertained by such obscurities. But this conversation resonates for the narrator out of all proportion to its apparent weight in the novel; it is the only recorded conversation taking place, after all, before his anecdote truly begins (5). At the moment in the long final conversation with Mrs. Brissenden when the narrator's plots begin to fall apart, Mrs. Brissenden's claim to "know" (304) (about a liaison between Long and Lady John) causes him to murmur "What if she *should* be right?" and think back to that early conversation: "She had for these seconds the advantage of stirring within me the memory of her having indeed, the day previous, at Paddington, 'known' as I hadn't" (305).[1] Now the conversation has been reframed: knowing, in retrospect, represents holding an advantage. It is less a question of epistemology (how or what one knows) than a question of power (what one can do with what one knows). This new frame of reference displaces the interpretive problems broached in the first pages of this essay, replacing them with more radical questions: What are the different forms of knowledge inscribed in the novel and in what ways do they lead to or deny authority on the part of their possessors?

Let us return to Ford Obert's bemused, but precisely worded, question to the narrator: "How on earth can I tell what you're talking about?" Interestingly, Obert does not ask for information (as in the question "what are you talking about?") but for an enabling frame of reference that is constitutive of the meaning of any particular utterance by the narrator. Obert puts us in mind of one of the major thrusts of twentieth-century linguistics which, from Wittgenstein to Bakhtin to Searle and Austin, has been to explore the ways in which utterances signify within a social, metalinguistic context. Mikhail Bakhtin, for instance, writing in 1926, commented that the "*extraverbal context*" of a spoken utterance is comprised of three factors: "(1) the *common spatial purview* of the interlocutors . . . (2) the interlocutors' *common knowledge and understanding of the situation,* and (3) their *common evaluation* of that situation" (100). The precondition for comprehension, then, is not only real people speaking in real situations that afford the possibility of communication (a commonality of language and cultural context), but a willingness to speak and evaluate in common. Communicative codes must not only function; speakers must seek to use them in functional ways.

Dialogue in *The Sacred Fount* constantly evokes the possibility of the kind of shared codes Bakhtin indicates here. Just before Obert's question, for instance, there is the following exchange (the narrator has just asked whether all the ladies have left):

> "Save, it struck me, so far as they may have left some 'black plume as a token' – " "Not, I trust," I returned, "of any 'lie' their 'soul hath spoken'!" (204)

Although the narrator appropriates the conclusion of Obert's thought (completing line 99 of Edgar Allan Poe's "The Raven"), his interrruption in this case serves to establish a referential code. By completing the verse, the narrator gestures toward a community of interpreters bonded by a shared education, language, and culture – a community enhanced, moreover, by the narrator's eager participation. The exchange places the two speakers in dialogue with a transpersonal agent of communication as much as with each other. Like a choric refrain (say within a call-and-response structure), the narrator's remark ritualistically embeds both speakers within a preexisting cultural frame of reference that is at once communal and community-forming. The narrator's rejoinder, by bringing to closure this moment of dialogue, potentially stabilizes a complex set of personal and cultural relationships within the social bonds of language.

Yet the rhetorical appropriation structuring this exchange, whereby the completion of the verse signals the reorientation of meaning on the narrator's own terms, is far more characteristic of his mode of procedure. He subverts the communal possibilities of language by manipulating it in order to disguise his frames of reference, thus transforming dialogue into dialogues with himself. As Brissenden complains (observantly, the narrator adds), he has "not a notion of" what the narrator knows, for "you know *how* you know" (124) – and it is precisely the masking of *how* he knows that constitutes, at least provisionally, the narrator's authority. Immediately after Obert's "How on earth can I tell what you're talking about?" for instance, the narrator waits a moment before asking: "Did you happen to count them?" (205). This cues the predictable response of "Count whom?" for the narrator is referring back over some ten paragraphs to the vanished "ladies." Yet, within his own frame of reference, the narrator's ostensible non sequitur responds appropriately to Obert's "How on earth can I tell what you're talking about?" That bewildering "them" is, to the narrator, perfectly comprehensible; more importantly, however, the response gives him the advantage in a rhetorical game whose goal is overtly stated and which structures scene after scene: "intellectual mastery" (214).

A more extended rhetorical ruse by the narrator, of which the victim is Ford Obert again, suggests how profoundly a strategy of concealment bestows authority upon him. Just before meeting Mrs. Brissenden for a final time, a game of "cross purposes" with Obert brings to a triumphant conclusion an encounter that commences badly. Obert's conviction that May Server is now, after all, "all there" (232), initially confuses the narrator. "Things *had,* from step to step, to hang together, and just here they seemed . . . to hang a little apart" (230). And the narrator's assured "I see – I see" masks a deeper uncertainty: "Yet I really didn't see enough not to have for an instant to turn away." He regains the upper hand, however, by the simple trick of obscuring which woman he is to meet that night. Using a pronoun instead of Mrs. Brissenden's name, he causes Obert to assume – naturally – that the referent, the subject of their previous conversation, is May Server. The switch so baffles Obert (he repeats the by now familiar question "But what in the world – ?") that he acquiesces in the narrator's superiority: "'You do,' [Obert] sighed with an effort at resignation, 'know more than I!'" His sense of intellectual balance restored, the narrator now ends by reminding himself triumphantly of "the innumerable steps [Obert] had necessarily missed"; Obert is naturally "vague" and in the "darkness."

A vital distinction needs to be made here. The narrator insists that a methodological application of language and thought to "making all this out" (125) will bring about the intellectual mastery he desires by revealing objective truth unavailable to other characters: "*I* alone," he says at one point, "was magnificently and absurdly aware" (177). I have already suggested that the narrator's logic is at once undemonstrable and indisputable, given that none of his observations, let alone his conclusions, can be confirmed, and in this sense the whole novel forces us to confront what poststructuralist critics are fond of calling the "*mise en abyme*" of interpretation. The narrator's moment of absolute knowing is always deferred. Yet we need not therefore take Obert's "You do know more than I!" as James's final exquisite touch to his self-obscuring artifact. Obert merely assumes he has been masterfully out-interpreted. Whatever the content of the narrator's speech, in other words, its very significance as language within a social context endows it with an authority that Obert can sense and acknowledge.

The narrator's substitution of Mrs. Brissenden for May Server in the pronoun "she," for instance, exploits a semantic confusion inherent in the structure of the English language. But he displays that confusion to his advantage only because "she" is situated within certain socially stable rules of discourse that promise, when obeyed, to offer up a conventional signification. It is not that he plays the anarchic potential of language against narrowly conceived social forms, but that his linguistic freeplay depends upon the immanently social properties of language. Obert's mystification arises out of his perception that the referent of "she" can and should be determinable. The narrator's authority depends on presenting private knowledge as determinable, a strategy that in turn requires us to see that the narrator can only demonstrate his possession of secret knowledge by placing it in relationship to that which is public and consensual. The shameless trick of the mistaken pronoun is effective not because of the protean freeplay of language the trick liberates, but because of Obert's double assumption that, first, context determines meaning and, second, that only one context is operative. The first assumption happens to be true: We comprehend Obert's mystification because we know, as he does not, that the narrator will soon meet Mrs. Brissenden. It is the narrator's covert awareness of other contexts that baffles Obert, which is to say that the narrator skilfully employs and controls the capacity of language to signify within a specific social context in order to crow, at the end of Chapter XI, "I left him under this simple and secure impression that my appointment was with Mrs. Server."

There is more to be said about this relationship between language and power. The mastery over language evinced by the narrator (and later Mrs. Brissenden) depends upon forcing their victims to become aware of two aspects of linguistic ability that are so securely anchored in social discourse that their conventionality generally goes unrecognized: first, the contractual basis of dialogue, presupposing an obligation or willingness to communicate and, second, linguistic competence, presupposing a socially formed skill in manipulating and comprehending utterances. Each aspect implies the other to the extent that the dialogic contract requires competent speakers, while competence demands a thorough investiture in the contractual and structural formations of language. The narrator and Mrs. Brissenden call both into question in such a way as to place a character's competence at issue. In his long encounter with May Server, for instance, the narrator conceals the name of the man he alleges is looking for her, causing her to stutter "Do you mean − a − do you mean − ? . . . There are so many gentlemen!" (143). Like Obert, who fails to discover the referent of "she," May Server suffers from the narrator's imputed confidence in her ability to figure out the referent of "he." The narrator's little game works because one of its covert rules requires that its ludic context shall remain hidden. Mrs. Server and the narrator work on the assumption that a statement like "He wanted to find you" (142) refers to a character known to them both; "He" could refer to God, but contractually and contextually such a reading would be nonsensical. It is only because the narrator is socially bound to mean someone (and not a cat or God), and only because the number of candidates for "he" (and later "she") is small, that May Server (and Obert) feel obligated, by virtue of their competence in social conversations of this sort, to perceive the name implied by the narrator. Having accepted the narrator's hints as information, Obert and Server are doomed to admit their incompetence by guessing wildly at the narrator's referent, by asking an obvious question ("Who do you mean?"), or − as it actually turns out − to flounder miserably.

The pronoun "she" thus functions in several ways. It persuades Obert that the narrator's speech is meaningful (that is, grammatically and contextually it satisfies normative preconditions for making sense); it conceals the narrator's true frame of reference, all the more effectively for appearing to function normatively. And it reveals yet another frame of reference that this time Obert sees with utter clarity: that the narrator does "know more than I!" Throughout the novel, the narrator employs oblique references, sentence fragments, masking pronouns, questions that are parried but never answered − in short, the entire verbal arsenal of the late James − in order that his deferred or obscured meanings should clearly communicate his personal authority. Deferral, above all, affords the narrator rhetorical advantage, prompting a whole litany of questions from the mystified Obert: "And − a − where is it then you meet?" "The household sits up for you?" "Do you mean you propose to discuss with her − ?" "But what in the world − ?" (233). In now familiar fashion, the narrator brusquely refers Obert to "*she,*" "*her*" for answer; Obert's questions might as well be rhetorical. We need not take this fact of obscurity as a metaphysical loss of value or even as a social statement about a breakdown of communication. Nor, for that matter, need we salute the narrator's creative ability to generate pages of dialogue out of a simple pronoun switch while the academician Obert flounders benightedly.[2] The fact that delights the narrator most is that his discourse functions; its obscurity maintains its efficacy and, at their most despairing, his interlocutors are ready to acknowledge that.

The narrator's "intellectual mastery" rests on a strategic appropriation of linguistic and cultural codes, which creates the appearance of superior knowledge. At its peak, this knowledge bestows on him (he claims) an almost divine prerogative, an intensity of consciousness in which "*I* alone was magnificently and absurdly aware — everyone else was benightedly out of it" (177). The true challenge to his "personal privilege" (183), the narrator believes, arises out of his sudden thought, while talking to Lady John, that he has penetrated the stupidity of Long and Mrs. Brissenden only to illuminate for them their roles at the sacred fount: "I was responsible perhaps for having, in a mood practically much stupider than the stupidest of theirs, put them gratuitously and helplessly *on* it" (183). The narrator's dismay arises, in a satisfyingly ironic twist, out of the confirmation of his own theories of energy exchange; the rhetorical strategy designed to ensure secrecy seems to have created, against the grain, a community of readers. In fact, it is precisely the social nature of his "personal privilege" (183) that I want to emphasize. His knowledge subsists throughout on others' statements, ideas, and perceptions; plots formulated in private enter the public sphere in order to be fleshed out or transformed. Other voices constantly invade his ruminations. The beginning of his anecdote, he claims, was "a word dropped by Long" (5), a word augmented thereafter by Mrs. Brissenden (9, 71–88), Obert (66–8), and by many other encounters and dialogues that force him to keep his theories in a state of flux, until Mrs. Brissenden utters the "word that put me altogether nowhere" (319) to close his ruminations.

The relational nature of his theory of relations means that the narrator must constantly negotiate the paradox that knowledge conceived and held secretly confers an authority that becomes functional only within a social discourse. Intellectual mastery ultimately depends on forging a consensus, as when, in the final scene, he is forced to ask Mrs. Brissenden to reestablish the connection he initially made (that a "clever woman" has drained her own wit to service Long's). His excitement before and during his final meeting with Mrs. Brissenden, indeed, arises from his sense that she will verify his reading of the situation at Newmarch. "Hadn't I possibly burrowed the deeper — to come out in some uncalculated place behind her back?" (243), wonders the narrator, and the final scene is intended to turn that "possibly" into actual superiority by having Mrs. Brissenden admire his incalculable knowledge. But Mrs. Brissenden's attack, carried out on two fronts, is perfectly calculated to demonstrate the weak points of the narrator's tactics. By arguing that Long is after all "perfectly stupid" (294) and that May Server is "awfully sharp" (317), she overturns the narrator's first premise but agrees with his publicly held position about May. For the narrator to dispute the first claim is to inquire into the basis of her knowledge and thus to posit a relationship between Mrs. Brissenden and Long that the former has already denied (265); to dispute the second claim is to compromise May Server and himself by reversing his previously stated position. Mrs. Brissenden, who neatly maneuvers the narrator into an ethical dilemma before seizing the "last word" (318), thus brings the narrator to his moment of aporia. The narrator cannot with propriety inquire further into her arguments, but neither can he feel that the "personal privilege . . . of understanding" (273) is enough. With good cause he finds himself thinking "with a kind of horror of any accident by which I might have to expose to the world, to defend against the world, to share with the world, that now so complex tangle of hypotheses that I have had for convenience to speak of as my theory" (173–4). The horror lies not so much in exposure as in the need for exposure, and not so much in the fact of sharing as in the fact that the authority of "my" theory is predicated upon the moment of consensus.

The act of publicly displaying theories secretly held thus requires a consummate act of rhetorical negotiation. The novel suggests, by way of justifying the narrator's final statement, that he was methodologically superior to Mrs. Brissenden but lacked her tone, that tone (rhetorical power) rather than method (insight, accuracy) best characterizes the socially powerful figure. Put differently, the narrator is most successful when his rhetorical maneuvering is tricked out as "method" and when his play with linguistic and social conventions erases from his speech the aspect of (power) play. Mrs. Brissenden merely outplays the narrator at his own game. At one of the crucial moments of the final encounter, Mrs. Brissenden promises to reveal the "truth" (302) about the characters under discussion, drawing from the narrator this bleak statement: "I wanted my personal confidence, but I wanted nobody's confession. . . . Without the personal confidence, moreover, where was the personal honour? That would be really the single thing to which I could attach authority, for a confession might, after all, be itself a lie" (302). The narrator is correct: Mrs. Brissenden's confession might be a lie. But the point is that, in the absence of any invalidating context, a statement like Mrs. Brissenden's thrice-repeated "Lady John *is* the woman" (303) carries with it the illocutionary force accorded confessional statements. Neither narrator nor reader can really determine whether "Lady John *is* the woman" signifies a constative or performative utterance. The statement's self-affirming truthfulness may mask other reasons for making Lady John out to be Gilbert Long's lover, but these must remain speculative. Determining the truthfulness of "Lady John *is* the woman" depends on context; but the only available context (beyond the narrator's own doubt) is that confessional "Lady John *is* the woman."

The first conversation in the novel, we found, registered a similar interpretive impasse, but now we are able to supplement that first reading with the fact that such impasses function in specific ways to empower their creators. The narrator's claim that personal confidence would be "the single thing to which I could attach authority" is thus shown to be false. Authority attaches instead to Mrs.

Brissenden's confident and public assertion of a fact that can be neither proved nor disproved; it gathers authority because it evades (or simply assimilates) any context we or the narrator may adduce. Most readers assume that the narrator's theory of energy exchange, in which one element is augmented at the expense of another, governs the narrative logic of *The Sacred Fount*. The narrator does indeed seem to grow in power as he masters the likes of May Server, Ford Obert, and Lady John, and to deflate as he capitulates to Mrs. Brissenden's superior tone. Yet intellectual mastery, I have suggested, derives from a dynamic *interchange* between public and private. The moments of aporia to which these characters inevitably tend thus indicate a function of language manipulated by characters within the context of a specific social setting, and whose consequence is the advantage in an ever-present power game.

Perhaps because language in *The Sacred Fount* is immanently social, intimately bound up with a character's struggle to accrue social authority, the novel frequently associates characters with public figures: the artist, the critic, the public speaker, the detective, the actor, and the reporter, among others. Lady John, for instance, reminds the narrator of a "clown bounding into the ring" (18) and of a "celebrity at a public dinner" (17), too much aware, according to the narrator, of her "'speech' – of how soon it would have to come." Quite the opposite is true of the inarticulate May Server who, constantly staging herself before the Newmarch crowd, requires a "frantic art . . . to make her pretty silences pass, from one crisis to another, for pretty speeches" (139). For each woman, governing public speech enables her to become "mistress" (17) of a limited domain. The narrator, to match the crudely efficacious figures associated with May Server and Lady John, characterizes his own performance in terms of the "uninvited reporter" and the "newspaper-man kicked out" (156–7). The novel invites the correlation of this figure to the "public ugliness" (174) born of the narrator's prying, especially in the light of George Flack's role in *The Reverberator,* where the "great public questions" (1979a, 25) on his mind allow him to transgress the established propriety (and privacy) of the Proberts. The narrator clearly foresees the possibility of scandal, of the sort Flack inspires, arising from a too-crude publicizing of his alleged information, and it is on this terrain of decorum, I have suggested, that Mrs. Brissenden finally manoeuvres him out of the game. The narrator is at his most un-Flacklike, indeed, in choosing to work within the codes of conduct established by this traditional society.

Yet James uses the reporter figure to do more than suggest the possible impropriety of the narrator's discussions. In context, that figure doubles for the role of the artist. In Newmarch's "halls of art and fortune," claims the narrator, "the imagination . . . was almost inevitably accounted a poor matter," and continues:

> Even the sense most finely poetic, aspiring to extract the moral, could scarce have helped feeling itself treated to something of the snub that

affects – when it does affect – the uninvited reporter in whose face a door is closed. I said to myself during dinner that these were scenes in which a transcendent intelligence had after all no application, and that, in short, any preposterous acuteness might easily suffer among them such a loss of dignity as overtakes the newspaper-man kicked out. (156–7)

Even allowing for his inflation of his own acumen, the narrator makes grandiose claims for Newmarch, depicting it as a palace of the imagination too fantastic for any human imagination to gild. His use of the reporter figure runs counter to expectation. In an odd conflation of images, the "transcendental intelligence" suffers the snub accorded the despised reporter, while the lost dignity of the "newspaper-man kicked out" stands in for the artist's. I am not suggesting that, as George Flack took on artistic attributes, so the artist-narrator of *The Sacred Fount* demeans himself and his vocation by dabbling in unhallowed pursuits.[3] Rather, James forces an acknowledgment of the shared function of artist, reporter, and narrator. Flack, like the narrator "professionally so occupied with other people's affairs," considers that "it's about played out, any way, the idea of sticking up a sign of 'private' and thinking you can keep the place to yourself" (1979a, 27, 61). Flack presides over the world of public speech, unfolding the "*chronique intime*" (61) of Europe's elite for the mass readership of the *Reverberator,* and acquiring the authority that places him (covertly, to be sure) at the narrative center of that novel. The narrator of *The Sacred Fount,* whose impulse toward secrecy seems diametrically opposed to Flack's, in fact constantly suggests that the play of the "transcendent intelligence" and the joy of "intellectual mastery" rest upon language as a socially constituted and socially empowering agent. Once revealed to the public gaze, the narrator's "palace of thought," crumbles to (in Mrs. Brissenden's contemptuous image) "houses of cards" (262). But if the narrator ends in silence, it is not because of his failure to preserve intact codes and interpretations formulated in silence. Rather, it is because he misjudges the power of language to protect him from the public arena where he is outperformed by Mrs. Brissenden.

II

In glancing at the textual labyrinths of *The Sacred Fount,* we have seen that language functions in ways unrelated to its actual content, so that, for instance, a rhetorical strategy that reveals nothing of the narrator's actual intent calls from Ford Obert an awed tribute: "You do know more than I!" The narrator's labyrinthine performances threaten other characters, stimulate inquiry, evoke responses and counterattacks, draw admiration and hostility. It is thus scarcely enough to observe only that this text is a "self-conscious narrative that reveals its own fictive moves" or that James is concerned with "the ways in which authorial identity is made possible within the system of language" (Rowe, 225,

229). The "content" of the narrator's speeches may be the play of language itself as it supplements, enriches, and overburdens determinate significance; yet indeterminacy creates an objectively real social effect. As the narrator appropriates language, answers question with question, masks contexts and, at his crudest, pleads with Obert "You tell me . . . first!" (223), his words communicate a rhetorical mastery that Obert, at least, understands as the narrator's cognitive superiority. These strategies signify because other characters accept that this kind of linguistic game-playing establishes a signifying framework – a way of knowing about knowledge. More precisely, perhaps, they tend to accept linguistic play as though it were itself a way of knowing about the world – until, by way of demolishing the constitutive grounds of the narrator's discursive strategies, Mrs. Brissenden's linguistic performance in the final scenes of the novel replaces the esoteric with the pointedly crude: "It's nonsense. I've nothing to tell you" (250), "I think you're crazy" (278).[4]

Even this incomplete analysis of *The Sacred Fount* indicates why the novel has steadily moved from a somewhat peripheral status to interest literary theorists as well as critics of Henry James. Perhaps it would be fairer to say that the novel, with its constant attention to language, reading, interpetation, interpretive communities, and private significance, forces any Jamesian critic to become a theorist. The novel is structured in such a way that almost any investigation into the narrator's role quickly becomes an allegory of one's own process of reading, and in this sense Kappeler is surely right to call attention to the narrator's role as critic. But we need to ask some clarifying questions that impinge directly on the iconic status of this text. To what extent is the narrator's rhetorical mastery commensurate with the effect of this text as a production of the "Master"? Why and how does a text by Henry James accrue authority? In what sense does the narrator's audience represent James's? What are the historical forces that allow James to construct such an anomalous text (which we might nonetheless assimilate as a normative example of literary modernism) and allow us to enter into a specific critical discourse about it? One thing is sure: Like the narrator's linguistic games, the discourse of *The Sacred Fount* possesses an authoritative effect that is not merely adumbrated by its content. The novel asks something of us, does something to us; by the very act of reading it we are cast in a certain role unavailable to those who would or could not read it. Like the narrator-newspaperman, we are forced to negotiate the boundary between "private" discourse and public codes. We need to ask, then, how James's writing strategies locate and legitimate his text with regard to the reader, the canon, communities of readers, and our culture.[5]

Critical responses to *The Sacred Fount* have described an odd trajectory whereby first reactions have been recently reintroduced with far different significance. Bliss Perry, on first reading the novel, remarked that it "makes me feel insufferably stupid."[6] Some, like Joseph Warren Beach (1918) and Alwyn Berland (1981, 44), have called the novel a failure; others, assuming that James, as it were, does not play dice, have placed the responsibility on the reader for decoding a difficult but ultimately decodable work.[7] Two works, Susanne Kappeler's *Writing and Reading in Henry James* (1980) and Charles Baxter's "Wanting in Taste: *The Sacred Fount* and the Morality of Reading" (1981), deserve to be studied more closely because they address most thoroughly this issue of audience response. Both begin by positing the maddening complexity of James's text, but their interpretations thereafter diverge. For Baxter, the novel is "an act of language deliberately intended to call forth a disorganized and frustrated response from the reader" (315), situating the reader in the spaces between normal reading conventions: "The 'naive' reader who wants to become involved in character and plotting finds that all his interests are moved aside for analysis. At the same time, the reader who attempts exegesis, interpretation, and explication discovers that data in the book are contradictory. The narrative seems designed to please no one" (325). For Kappeler, the novel marks the end of the "*bona fide* confidence between writer and reader of the Realist novel*" (52) and the beginning of the modernist game text where "the pleasure lies in the playing, which is a matter of skill and technique, both of one's own and one's partner" (73). Baxter considers James's novel "a game that any reader is bound to lose as long as that reader assumes that there is something to be seen through the keyhole" (320), while Kappeler argues that "with Henry James [the reader] is invited to join the game – he is honoured by the challenge" (53).

The work of these two writers, in its own right, provides a fascinating glimpse into our contemporary critical establishment – especially when we consider that their perspectives are closer than they seem. Baxter's reader can be equated with Kappeler's "reader of the Realist novel," desiring, whether interested in character or explication, only the "Realist guarantee of Truth" (52). On the other hand, Baxter's characterization of the game novel as one that the reader is bound to lose "as long as the reader assumes that there is something to be seen through the keyhole" opens a space for the introduction of a reader like Kappeler, whose only commitment is to the game itself, not to the solving of an unsolvable riddle. Whereas Baxter all but refuses to posit the kind of poststructuralist reading Kappeler delights in, Kappeler sees James as educating readers to move beyond the limited realist text and to revel in just this kind of sophisticated game.

Both works are notable for the issues they foreclose. Their notion of "reader," for instance, elides the problem of historicity. History figures in these works insofar as the modernist game text appeared at the turn of the century, not because James's writing was historically shaped and produced within the context of a specific audience and marketplace. Their work is compromised to the extent that it implies a reader (real or ideal), timeless, transcendent, and unitary. Kappeler takes on this issue obliquely:

> The effect of the aestheticist's decision to abstain from a consciousness-raising for the masses and to presuppose an audience only of fellow artists

and equally cultivated sensibilities necessarily turns out more flattering for the reader. . . . The reproach of elitism is the result of a confusion over the classification of the elite and of who does the classifying: it is entirely up to the reader to join the illustrious audience and take on the reader's share, while the elite artists have no power whatever to exclude anyone. (53)

Actually, as I have argued in the first chapter, the playful, self-reflexive, esoteric writing strategies characteristic of a modernist text function precisely through an exclusionary process that, by rewriting and defamiliarizing the texts and language of mass culture, achieves a narrow but real authority in our society. The "elite artists" not only had power to exclude, but used that power to maintain hegemony. Kappeler elevates exclusivity into a principle of good reading on the one hand – it forms, for one thing, an "illustrious audience" in contrast to the "masses" – while disclaiming its priority for her on the other. Thus the statement that "it is entirely up to the reader to join the illustrious audience" invites the reproach that, historically speaking, the actual audience for this kind of game text has remained small but stable, largely because of the institutionalizing power of the university. It would be more accurate to say that an existing readership, in the process of educating an individual to comprehend certain otherwise obscure game texts, actually selects the reader. Reading a James text, as Kappeler admits, is a learned skill; Kappeler, however, assumes that the "Master's" texts are accessible without the thoroughgoing mediation of an educational and critical apparatus. Her construct of an educated, subtle reader – already conversant with the kinds of texts she privileges – merely disguises the structuring presence of an interpretive community that underwrites her argument. This is, again, not to say that Kappeler is wrong; but we need to situate her ideal reader historically and to see that her ostensibly unproblematic act of reading ignores the actual differentiation of reading groups based on class, education, or interpretive community.

Henry James, in constrast, showed himself to be keenly aware of the historical preconditions for writing in a series of articles published in the 1890s; as he said in "The Future of the Novel" (but everywhere understood), "the future of fiction is intimately bound up with the future of the society that produces and consumes it" ([1899] 1986b, 247). James's essays in the 1890s frequently place the desire for an ideal collective readership against a more practical call for a small, highly trained cadre of critics, so that, by "The Question of the Opportunities" ([1898] 1984), we find James beginning to think about discourse in a way that will lead to *The Sacred Fount* and the other late novels. "Criticism," first published in 1891 and revised in 1893, marks a distinct change from the conciliatory and optimistic tone of "The Art of Fiction" (1884). James's theme, to begin with, is the "huge, open mouth" of the periodicals, which demand a copious "free expenditure of ink" ([1893] 1986a, 232–3). James's own rhetoric responds, swamping his text with commercial images: "commodity," "affluence," "economy of production," "expenditure," "business of reviewing." The question James poses about this "periodicity of platitude and irrelevance" is a common one for the time: "how literature resists it; whether, indeed, literature does resist it and is not speedily going down beneath it." "We are paying a tremendous price," argues James, "for the diffusion of penmanship and opportunity." Seven years later, however, "The Question of the Opportunities," while accepting the leveling effect of the "great common-schooled and newspapered democracy" of America, drastically revised this pessimism. As I argued in Chapter I, James saw that the diverse constitution of a "mass" public might guarantee at least the survival of a literary art differentiated from other productions of mass culture. The tremendous price for the "diffusion of penmanship and opportunity" might be precisely the opportunity to maneuver on the new "chess-board" of the mass public, where "each little square confess[es] only to its own *kind* of accessibility." Having invoked the problem of the "fast-arriving billion," moreover, James adds in startling fashion that "all this depends on what we may take it into our heads to *call* literature." "It truly does much depend on that," he continues, "But that, in its order, depends on new light – on the new light struck out by the material itself, the distinguishable symptoms of which are the justification for what I have called the critic's happy release from the cramped posture of foregone conclusions and narrow rules" (232–3). The "happy release," profoundly important in its implications, occasioned by the arrival of new markets and audiences, is that the sign "literature" has been emptied of traditional significance – set adrift, as it were, to reformulate its sources of authority or to be assimilated to a literature of mass culture.

"The Future of the Novel" (1899) retains this new spirit of opportunity, even though it begins with another disquisition on the flood of new writing "threatening the whole field of letters, as would often seem, with submersion." A lament over the "indifferent and the alienated" who no longer read novels transforms easily to a recognition that "The high prosperity of fiction has marched, very directly, with another 'sign of the times,' the demoralisation, the vulgarisation of literature in general" (1986b, 245). And, after a long consideration of the regenerative possibilities latent in the novel, James reintroduces the value of criticism to literary culture: "In a world in which criticism is acute and mature such talent [that is, literary talent] will find itself trained, in order successfully to assert itself, to many more kinds of precautionary expertness than in a society in which the art I have named holds an inferior place" (247). James gestures, in a passage like this, toward the kind of attitude that has led to his canonization as the "Master." A mature criticism, trained in the subtleties of fiction writing, might elevate cultural production to new heights; James has already introduced into the essay the figure of a "life-giving master" whose messianic advent might revive literary art (246). It is easy to see why, in the hagiography of the twentieth-century canon, James has always figured highly; his work provides not only material for complex critical systems, but makes that call for "expertness" in reading everywhere apparent. What James did not foresee is the remarkable expansion of criticism within the university which was to take place within a few decades, in great measure under the example and tutelage of his own writings. The dilemma that informs all three of the above essays – that contemporary criticism reveals itself to be merely "the practice of 'reviewing'" (1986a, 232) within mass market publications – soon becomes supererogatory upon the separation of the review (in any publication) from the literary critique or analysis (appearing only in specialized, esoteric journals). James predicted and, in his own work, helped to create, the "precautionary expertness" and "chessboard" public in answer to the questions he himself raised; the more complete implementation of his ideas lay in the departments of literary studies that were organizing as he wrote.

Keeping James's comments in mind, we need now to return to *The Sacred Fount,* published just two years after "The Future of the Novel," and inquire further about this novel's kind of accessibility by looking once again at our two model critics. Kappeler's and Baxter's concepts of "reader" appear, on the surface, to oppose each other. Baxter's putative reader expects realism, conclusiveness, plot, and continuity, and is shocked when they fail to materialize. Kappeler posits a reader who dismisses such interpretive strategies as products of a dated worldview and who would be shocked only if, in some reversion to realism at the end of *The Sacred Fount,* James "gave the game away." (If, for example, an omniscient narrator stepped in to remove the incumbent narrator to an asylum.) We can resolve that conflict, however, once we restore the context of an interpretive community that underwrites their assumptions. That context need not determine every word the critic writes, but it must situate the new work within a referential network of canonical works, critics, readings, and protocols in such a way as to allow a critical dialogue to take place. For Baxter and Kappeler imply much more about James's text than they state overtly, and it is in this covert content where we find these critics finally sharing common ground. Both perceive *The Sacred Fount* as in some way iconic, possessing a cultural authority that overrides (for Baxter) the problems it poses to naive readers and that constitutes (for Kappeler) the near-religious aura of the text. Indeed, Baxter quietly disassociates himself from his postulated reader; whatever the novel's effect on that reader, for Baxter it at least "has a place in discussions of critical theory, reader-response, and the institutionalization of criticism" (316). As a reader of the text himself, Baxter demonstrates his expertise – his right to speak about the text – by constantly situating his postulated reader within critical constructs that allow for the possibility of different (and more sophisticated) readings. "Wanting in Taste" is not so much a reading of *The Sacred Fount* as an exercise in and analysis of reader response criticism. For that reason the novel signifies, to Baxter, not merely a bewildering and intransigent game text, but a specific kind of game text, authored by the "Master," anchored within the canon, and surrounded by a small library of commentaries that all agree on the cultural value of reading James, even if *The Sacred Fount* itself seems somewhat an aberration. In other words, Baxter's critical model, which overtly argues that *The Sacred Fount* represents an attack on its audience, readily accepts that the novel possesses status and value to an audience (a professional, competent one) in such a way as to make it, a priori, worthy of the attention bestowed on it. The fact that both Kappeler and Baxter detail negative critiques of the novel is something of a red herring. Those critics who label the novel a failure, an anomaly, or unimportant merely testify to the potential for analysis vested in any novel by James. These critics might not agree with Kappeler that this novel belongs in the Jamesian canon, but all would agree that the work belongs in a literary canon if we choose by way of contrast, say, George du Maurier's novel *Trilby* (1884), which James mentions at the beginning of "The Question of the Opportunities."

I have dealt with the provocative work of Baxter and Kappeler at such length because, by looking at writing strategies and audience response, they encounter head-on the question of how this text might take on an authority that has little to do with the truth, universality, or wisdom of its narrative content. These critics reveal not what the text means but some of the ways in which it might signify within specific institutionally valid reading models; they begin to reveal, unintentionally to be sure, the power of institutionalized readings, verdicts, and appraisals. Critics do not bestow authority on *The Sacred Fount* in the process of writing about it; its authority preexists and in a sense preempts whatever the critic might say. Its authority, evolving out of the incredibly complex constellation of values, canonical judgments, and institutions that make authorititative meanings possible, has already occurred, is already in place, in such a way as to structure the possibilities of speaking about the text. This is not to say that all historically formed reputations and judgments are inalienable; but it does suggest that shifts in reputation and judgment happen slowly and tend to come about after or during major changes in critical charters. Certainly Baxter's essay can only enhance James's reputation. To say that one does not "like" *The Sacred Fount* is in one sense irrelevant: James's canonical importance alone negates the notion that taste is a sufficient criterion of judgment. We need only know that the novel is "important."

Thus, although it is scarcely unusual to consider what the narrator calls his "apologue or . . . parable" (29) as a parable about fiction-making, writers, critics, or readers, the narrator's fate needs to be carefully distinguished from the novel's. The narrator ends self-confessedly "altogether nowhere" (319) and certain that he should never again "quite hang together"; but the certitude and mastery thereby dispersed is not necessarily lost by the text. Those who see the narrator's final failure as a questioning of the fictional process might remind themselves that Mrs. Brissenden beats the narrator at his own game. The text, as textual labyrinth, thrives on the moments of aporia that lead to his undoing. The narrator, uncertain about the certainty of Mrs. Brissenden's confession, can only end in silence; but it is that silence that opens up the polysemic potential of the text. The novel's lack of closure makes endlessly generative a moment like Mrs. Brissenden's early appraisal of Gilbert Long, "Oh, it's only that I thought you always did [know]!" (4), which she subsequently seems to retract in claiming that Long is "perfectly stupid" (294). It might bespeak long acquaintance, which she later tries to disguise. Or it might be the demonstration of what she later asserts; that is, she knows all along that Long, never knowing, will not know that she is being sarcastic. We can read Mrs. Brissenden each way or both ways (or still another way), but neither choosing one of these alternatives, nor choosing to accept the impossibility of choosing, empties the text of its potential for endlessly eluding any categorical statement about it. The text, in other words, functions like the narrator at his rhetorically sharpest, making meaningful statements like "What in the world does she mean?" that turn out to signify only in the context of specific – and variable – frames of reference. And, like the narrator, the text does not invite just any interpretation; rather, it sets in motion (and describes) a struggle for control of interpretive contexts within a community of observers.

Earlier I argued that the narrator's strategies of deferral, concealment, and foreclosure were irredeemably social to the extent that their effects presupposed a general acknowledgment of language's contractual basis, and to the extent that the breaking of that contract brought into question the character's linguistic competence. The subversion of that contract and the questioning of a character's competence must take place before a public that underwrites, as it were, the legitimacy of the original contract. The narrator engages constantly with the socially rooted nature of his meditations and conversations. His rhetorical strategies cannot enforce his "personal confidence" until they become materially present in the public arena – until, that is, they are capable of functioning as discourse. As a material and marketable text, published, read, reviewed, and written about within specific historical institutions, *The Sacred Fount* has achieved a more authoritative position than was ever possible for the narrator – but achieved it in ways that are discursively similar. The novel reflects on the relationship between discourse and power. It describes a quest for power within a linguistic community that, once read (or for that matter left unfinished), begins to organize and objectify reading communities, thus refocusing the same issues of power on the relationship between text and society. Most importantly, the novel reveals that questions of linguistic and literary competence concern, at root, power relationships among reader, text, interpretive community, and culture. Bliss Perry's response to the novel ("[it] makes me feel insufferably stupid") recognizes instantly what Baxter implies but most other critics evade entirely: that the discourse of *The Sacred Fount* – obscure, intransigent, and elusive – constitutes its authority.

Saying that one does not like *The Sacred Fount,* then, demonstrates the real power of this kind of writing. By not liking, understanding, or reading the novel, one confesses, by reducing its potential audience still further, to its "*kind of* accessibility" – as long as one perceives, at the same time, its accessibility to a diminishing audience of others. And professional discourse is constituted in such a way that it encodes its forms and practices while broadcasting to the uninitiated its possession of modes of accessibility. It is in this sense that Baxter's essay duplicates the object of its critique, whereas Kappeler's essay denies its own statements about James's anti-elitism: Both essays, in other words, depend for their authority on the approval granted by small but highly expert cadres of readers. It is in this sense, too, that these critics both emulate and outshine the narrator of *The Sacred Fount.* Their texts, like the narrator's plots, function to make exclusion a principle of authority. More precisely, exclusivity accrues authority not in itself but when it is seen to be, and agreed to be, the privileged possession of a small group of people. The question of audience cannot be separated from an exclusion of some audiences. But exclusivity cannot be considered secret. Even the most abstruse critical document is therefore inherently social, for otherwise that critic would be left with nothing but his or her "private confidence." Henry James understood much more clearly than his narrator (and Baxter and Kappeler) that true authority lies in the constitution of a particular kind of audience – even if its members all appear to disagree – than in the privileging of any individual's interpretation, whether it be the radical certainty desired by Baxter or the radical uncertainty desired by Kappeler. Both critics' arguments would allow any individual access to the text; in so arguing, both critics fail to understand the authority of their own critical practices.

We can answer Ford Obert's resonant question "How on earth can I tell what you're talking about?" in numerous ways. We may assume, with Jean Frantz Blackall, that the novel is an "intellectual detective story" (1965, 37) notable for the lengths to which the decoding reader must go in order to solve the mystery. Or we may assume, with John Carlos Rowe, that the novel negotiates its own perpetual slippage of meaning, recognizing "the incompletion on which both meaning and identity depend" (1977, 238). Blackall's positivist assumptions promise to establish consensual, verifiable meanings – at least if one happens to be a "discerning reader" (7), already capable, through some mysterious process, of an "objective estimate" (39) of James's writing. Rowe offers only the vertiginous prospect of a critical commentary enmeshed in its own frames of reference, dealing obsessively with incomplete statements about incomplete texts, and therefore precluding a consensus which could anyway only be expressed in terms of another appropriation, another incompletion. Actually, the stated positions of these critics mask large areas of covert agreement. Blackall's consensus can only arise within an interpretive community that posits as a precondition of meaning the possibility of a "discerning reader" who is limited only by a neutral set of cognitive abilities rather than by historical variables such as education or class. Rowe's essay similarly shows in its vocabulary and citations a great debt to European poststructuralism. The critical activity, he says, "involves the continual reprieve of the subject from its loss in the totality of language"

(239), an influential perspective that in itself arose not within "language," as some neutral medium of discourse, but within a network of debates, conferences, and readings.[8] If Blackall's communal meanings are far from all-inclusive, Rowe's own strategy of interpretive indeterminacy is far from denying its own historicity.

Historically speaking, then, the most exclusive and esoteric discourse is deeply social in the sense that our twentieth-century society accords it a near-automatic priority and respect. In the arena of writing, where principles of clarity, accessibility, and intelligibility are associated with mass-market productions, literary writing defines itself as "other" and, by virtue of its greater truth, complexity, or ability to accommodate the expressive forms of mass culture, more important. The question of the opportunities for James was to distinguish one mode of accessibility from another and then to make the distinction signify to those readers most likely and able to assign the work value. James found his key – and not by chance – in the authority of the obscure. Yet if literature thus inscribes its own marginality within its texts, those texts are themselves written into the margins of the more prolix text of mass culture. In *The Sacred Fount,* the newspaperman, symbolically speaking, is not kicked out; more precisely, the newspaperman is kicked out only to be smuggled in via the back door. The discourse of transparency and easy accessibility for which the newspaperman stands haunts the magisterial complexity of the narrative and language of the "palace of thought." As the "newspaper-man kicked out" forms an integral part of the text, doubling for the narrator's artistic pretensions, so does the novel's bewildering play of language presuppose and invoke, to its own ends, the voice of mass culture.

4

The Plots of Murder

Un/Original Stories in Theodore Dreiser's An American Tragedy

The word reproduction means what it says....
Theodore Dreiser in a letter quoted by H. S. Kraft in
"Dreiser's War in Hollywood"

In the 1930s, Dorothy Parker wrote to Alexander Woollcott that the "Kiss of Death has come" (Fine 1985, 99–100). She was referring, in her inimitably morbid way, to a contract from the Paramount film corporation, and in so doing became one of a long line of writers to establish themselves as different than, superior to, the Hollywood script factories, while welcoming that vampirish – but lucrative – kiss of death. Behind Parker's remark lies an already long history of writers struggling to reconceive their social function, their professional standing, and the nature of their literary work in an age of mass culture. And one of the most remarkable moments in that struggle was Theodore Dreiser's suit in 1931 against Paramount-Publix corporation, which was brought in at attempt to halt the release of an allegedly "inartistic" version of his *An American Tragedy* (1925). His goal was not merely to preserve his literary character but to subject a new and, to him, ominous cultural power to the scrutiny of the court – and thus to legitimate the traditional authority of the author, despite the fact that the image of the writer he defended had begun to assume a new form and to exercise a new kind of prerogative.

As a prelude to my discussion of *An American Tragedy,* I want to describe how Dreiser used the furor surrounding the movie version of the novel to formulate a new sense of professionalism. We shall see that Dreiser's battle for literary authority in the Paramount case is presaged by the novel, albeit more obscurely. The novel, for instance, broaches questions of originality well before Dreiser raises them polemically for the benefit of the court. And novel and suit both focus our attention on the cultural authority of the writer. As H. S. Kraft has put it, the court case featured a power struggle between "two Goliaths" (1946, 10), but the struggle nevertheless masked a prior complicity whereby an acknowledged champion of literature contracted with a giant of the movie industry to

84

supply a literary product for mass consumption. But if Dreiser found Paramount's reworking of his novel a problem, we cannot help but recognize a similar problematic in Dreiser's reworking in *An American Tragedy* of the voices, expressive forms, and documents of mass culture. To the extent that the accommodatory tactics of a Henry James tend in this novel toward downright plagiarism, questions of cultural interpenetration become of crucial importance. Un/originality, writing that appears to be mere rewriting, literary narrative that appears indistinguishable from mass cultural expression, and (worst of all) critics forced to negotiate unfamiliar reading strategies out of mass culture – *An American Tragedy* confronts these issues in complex and paradoxical ways before Dreiser ever raises them in the open forum of the court.

The events leading up to the Paramount trial are worth reviewing quickly here. Dreiser sold the book rights to Paramount for the sum of $135,000; the contract stipulated that the seller (that is, Dreiser) should have the right to suggest changes to the "motion picture photoplay" before filming began, while quite clearly reserving to the film company the right to refuse those changes. After seeing Samuel Hoffenstein's shooting script, Dreiser proclaimed in a letter that it would result in a "cheap, tawdry, tabloid confession story" (1959, 522) and threatened legal action under what he called a "new principle in equity."[1] He argued:

> Even though they buy the right of reproduction, they don't buy the right to change it into anything they please. The word reproduction means what it says.
>
> They can't make a piece of work that is inimical to my standards, and picture me as writing something I never in the world would have written.
> (Kraft 12)

Dreiser's brief was, to say the least, audacious: His notion was that imaginative work remained the writer's property even when transformed into a different medium and even when received within a different cultural milieu. One sees that Dreiser has in mind a film audience extrapolating back from the movie to the original text; nevertheless, his conflation of picturing and writing posits an oddly serene and uncomplicated transposition of structure, information, and artistic essence from one medium to another. With these arguments in mind, Dreiser actually flew to Hollywood to work on additional scenes for the film, some of which were later added. When the film was completed under the direction of Joseph von Sternberg, Paramount offered Dreiser a preview in New York. At this point, Dreiser assembled a group of literary friends and acquaintances into what he called a "jury" of "critics and authorities," to sit in judgment on the preview with him. His viewers were to comprise a main jury of eighteen, including Carl Van Doren and Floyd Dell among other critics, publishers, and writers, and a sub-jury of twenty, Alexander Woollcott among them (1959, 530; Swanberg 1965, 368–78). His letter to the members of the "jury" asked for their comments on "whether or not in your opinion the picture sufficiently carries out the ideology of the book as to hold me free from any personal or artistic harm before the world" (1959, 530). Having seen the film, Dreiser's jury (for the most part) agreed with him that the picture was an inferior version of the novel, and he sued to have an injunction placed on the film's release.

Dreiser lost the case but gained the pleasure, as he said, of Judge Witschief's "priceless" comments. The judge, in fact, disallowed Dreiser's submission that the movie failed to portray Clyde as a victim of circumstances beyond his control, and went on to represent the very position that Dreiser worked so hard against throughout his career, and which the novel itself clearly rejects: "In the preparation of the picture," the judge stated, "the producer must give consideration to the fact that the great majority of people composing the audience before which the picture will be presented will be more interested that justice prevail over wrongdoing than that the inevitability of Clyde's end clearly appear" (1959, 562). Social justice, in the judge's view, wins out over the exigencies of the determinist vision. And more: The judge quite casually certifies the mass audience, the "great majority of people," as arbiters of taste – a particularly galling move in light of Dreiser's avowed intent that the trial should extend the writer's control over his or her imaginative work. The judge was of course outlining the prerogatives of the film audience rather than identifying Dreiser's reader's expectations, and Dreiser might easily have rhetorically maneuvered the judge's comments, which seemed to confirm the adaptability of cinematic productions to mass taste, into a critique of the compromised art of film producers. Nevertheless, it is easy to see how the judge's statement, with its tacit appeal to a kind of ethical determinism (that justice, in other words, should always prevail) might have seemed to Dreiser to present the artist as secondary, dependent, and subservient to the dictates of mass taste. Indeed, the judge assumed a situation in which taste alone might engender artistic principles and then allow a mass audience to hand down decisions on an artist's performance of them.

Dreiser's own carefully selected elite jury of cultural authorities refocused the question of taste on professional standing, training, practice, and experience. At the heart of Dreiser's argument was not his authority as creator or manufacturer but the special authority of his empanelled "jury" of "critics and authorities," whom Dreiser expected (and he was right) to hand down a different decision on the movie than that supplied by mass taste. He required a double trial and a double sentencing: a consensus between judge and "jury" that would affirm the judgments of a literary community by means of the legal, all of which would point up the power of expert opinion. This strategy had an unexpected consequence. Charged with critiquing the movie and buttressing Dreiser's case, the "jury" in important ways displaced his authority as creator and arbiter of his own work. Among this group, Dreiser could only match opinions with other experts, submerging his authorial privilege into the role of professional critic. To mandate a jury of "critics and authorities" clearly challenged the self-sufficiency and autonomy of Dreiser's judgment of his novel and the film version of it. His jury, however, was a crucial step in achieving a new and powerful identity for the writer. The jury was to be heard, not because it claimed a moral right, or because it claimed to speak for society, but because of its expertise in literary matters. And it would abrogate a special kind of expertise. Dreiser's "jury" was not to be consultant to the process, as would a handwriting or ballistics expert at a murder trial, but a final authority. Indeed, we might argue that Dreiser intended the judge to legitimate not only the jury's judgment but its competence to make that judgment. The court was to rubber-stamp the jury's opinion and simultaneously grant its accreditation.

Most commentators argue that if Dreiser was victorious at all, it was on the pragmatic grounds of gaining more recognition for writers in Hollywood.[2] But Dreiser's suit tells us a good deal more about a writer's opportunities for legitimation in an age of mass culture. Though he ran the risk of ceding to a judge and his "jury" traditional prerogatives of the literary writer over the status, value, and meaning of the work of art, he was successful in shaping a literary community bonded by its common opposition to mass culture. And, though he was forced to adopt an ambivalent position toward his own novel by taking the issue to court, arguing on the one hand that his work was superior to the commodifying forces of the marketplace but also, as the product of a professional writer, subject to laws regulating private property, he was successful in establishing that link between the individual professional's right to speak and a supporting community of competent inquirers. The "jury's" skillful evaluation and expert reading of the movie, rather than Dreiser's attempted defense of his property, establishes the terms of his victory. In particular, Dreiser's "jury" anticipates the power of professional critics within the university system to legitimate opinions about literature – opinions that can never be legally verified or stabilized, but which nevertheless possess an objective authority as they are institutionalized within the critical profession.

During Dreiser's trial of Paramount, the film company's attorney condemned the novelist's use of newspaper reports in *An American Tragedy* as "cold-blooded plagiarism" (Swanberg, 377). This accusation proved to be one of the more startling reversals of the case. The attorney was implying that he – or any literate person – could read the novel expertly and deliver an opinion on its (in)adequacy; insofar as Dreiser had merely plagiarized from texts that any person could comprehend one did not need to belong to Dreiser's panel of experts to recognize the novel's failings. More important, the attorney was setting out to subvert Dreiser's position by way of Dreiser's own criteria; crucially, his attack put Dreiser's conflation of origins and originality into question. In terms of chronology, Dreiser had insisted on the film version's *un*originality. As producer of the novel, he could argue for his prior ownership of copyrighted and contractually bound material. As creative author, he could argue that the novel's prior existence as art bestowed on it an originality and priority lacking in the reproduction. These puns on origin/originality and prior/priority are at once inevitable and illuminating. Chronological advantage, in effect, gave Dreiser a metaphoric purchase on the problem of his authority as writer: His novel had to come first because it was original; its coming first testified to its originality. By the same token, the novel's originality meant that the movie version could only be a mere copy, and this was so even though Dreiser appeared to grant the movie the originality possessed by the novel. If "reproduction means what it says," Dreiser's efforts to have Paramount's moviemakers copy his novel should have done them the favor of forcing them willy-nilly into creative work. Certainly Dreiser implied this throughout. He would be glad to cooperate, he said at one point, if the studio would "seriously agree to work along the lines I know to be most valuable" (Swanberg, 371). Whatever Dreiser consciously intended, this argument by its own criteria could only have resulted in diminishing Paramount's work and aggrandizing Dreiser's own. For originality (to borrow Dreiser's words) means what it says. His case was built around the supposition that the artistic originality and uniqueness of *An American Tragedy* was worth a great deal in terms of money and prestige. Which is to say that if *An American Tragedy* were one more formulaic version of a dozen other such novels, the novel would be worth little in terms of prestige and nothing to Paramount, who would not have handed over $135,000 to one author for a story already wholly in the public domain.[3] It is precisely this uniqueness, this difference from other narratives, that Dreiser thought he was selling. To argue, then, that the movie version's only possible originality arises from its reproduction of another original work amounts to a contradiction in terms. Since there could be only one original, Dreiser's argument must force the filmmakers to consult the novel for guidance, thus forestalling the creative possibilities of the film medium and preventing the exercise of their own imaginations – preventing, that is, the emergence of anything original.

The attorney's counterstroke was to cut through Dreiser's pretensions to originality by labeling him a plagiarist. How could Dreiser accuse Paramount of destroying his novel's artistic integrity, the attorney implied, when the writer had merely reproduced some sensational newspaper coverage of murder trials? The novelist assailed the filmmakers' inartistic representation of his novel; Paramount's reply, in what amounted to a duplication of Dreiser's attack, was that the novelist had not created literature and thus lacked any authority to pronounce judgment on the domain of culture. Two aspects of the attorney's accusation are worth pointing out. First, Paramount had paid Dreiser astonishingly well for plagiarized work; money, if not critical judgment, appeared to speak for the novel's value. Even interpreted as a sign of the novel's commodity status, that payment bespoke the novel's unlikeness to most other commodities – even if that difference was measured by its best-sellerdom. Second, the attorney introduced the possibility (unseen by Judge Witschief) of judging works by aesthetic criteria. How, after all, could plagiarism become a sign of worthlessness without presupposing, in reciprocal relationship, original forms of artistry?

But the attorney's attack was acutely directed. He probably had in mind the events of March 19, 1931, four months before the Paramount trial, when at a party in honor of Sinclair Lewis's Nobel prize Lewis had accused Dreiser of plagiarizing several thousand words of Dorothy Thompson's work; the resulting assault on Lewis (her husband) by Dreiser had made headlines. And the attorney's characterization of the novel may well have drawn on contemporary reviews, for many, as Robert Shafer reported, dismissed the novel on publication as "Eight hundred and forty pages devoted to the unconscionable prolongation of a mere sensational newspaper story" (1971, 33).[4] To many readers, and doubtless to Paramount's delight, the novel seemed to arise out of a nonliterary discourse composed of the voices and texts of popular novels, the movies, newspapers, and "society-column and advertising cliches" (Moers 1969, 299). According to Paramount's line of reasoning, Dreiser's utilization of mass culture placed him in an untenable position. If reproduction means what it says, condemning mass culture could only mean condemning his own work; likewise, to praise his own work must signify holding in high esteem the newspaper reports he had consulted, reproduced – or stolen.

For two centuries, originality has been a precondition for the acceptance of authentic literary writing, while formulaic repetition has usually signified its absence (critics have tended to distinguish between the formulas of epic or folk art and those of, say, the dime store western). Different fields of art have variously articulated the terms of that originality.[5] In art, Walter Benjamin argues, authority can attach to the original artwork by virtue of its ability to exist singly. "Even the most perfect reproduction of a work of art," as he says, lacks "its presence in time and space, its unique existence at the place where it happens to be" ([1936] 1969, 220). This authority of uniqueness, this testimony of subsequent ages to uniqueness – this aura – is what "withers in the age of mechanical reproduction" (221). In fact, the history of art institutions in the twentieth century has consistently demonstrated the reverse: that the aura of an original work of art has dramatically increased in a culture where the possibilities of mass reproduction place an ever greater emphasis on the values of singleness and rarity. This is true, at least, in financial terms, and we might argue that works of art have also regained some of the mystical and ritual significance that Benjamin claimed mechanical reproduction would destroy, as individual works are enshrined in the hushed semisacred spaces of museums that frequently limit access and that offer written or recorded guides to its arcana. In writing, where few books (except in limited editions or as signed copies) can lay claim to an aura, it is the name of the author that promises to deliver authenticity and originality (as the increased value of a mass-produced book when autographed by the author suggests). Michel Foucault writes that from the eighteenth century onward, literary discourse, as opposed to scientific texts, "was acceptable only if it carried an author's name; every text of poetry or fiction was obliged to state its author and the date, place, and circumstance of its writing" (1977, 126). In Foucault's very interesting discussion of the author or, as he prefers, the "author-function" in Western culture, it is the author's name that

> characterizes a particular manner of existence of discourse. Discourse that possesses an author's name is not to be immediately consumed and forgotten; neither is it accorded the momentary attention given to ordinary, fleeting words. Rather, its status and its manner of reception are regulated by the culture in which it circulates. . . . [T]he name of the author remains at the contours of texts – separating one from the other, defining their form, and characterizing their mode of existence. It points to the existence of certain groups of discourse and refers to the status of this discourse within a society and culture. (123)

Foucault's point does not appear to allow us to distinguish between elite and mass fiction. The name "Ian Fleming" marks out a certain manner of discourse – a highly recognizable kind of spy fiction – in the same way that "Dreiser" stood in the 1920s and 1930s for naturalism, or realism, or great American writing, and it is always possible to argue that Fleming's work is as original as Dreiser's, or is original in different ways, or possesses a different kind of originality. The name on any fiction, however abjectly that fiction appears to rely on stereotypical formulae, promises something new and thus authentic.

Nonetheless, there are observable differences in the ways a discourse's "status and its manner of reception" are regulated by our cultural institutions. Canons within the university or a review in the *New York Review of Books*, for instance, guarantee that prestige will attach to the author and the discourse the name represents, and by the same token ignore whatever originality the latest Gothic romance possesses. Indeed, for the purposes of making canons and assigning meanings to literature, critics and reviewers will tend not to register that originality as meaningfully original. The predictability of the man and woman falling in love, or of the first kiss occurring on schedule in the third chapter, automatically excludes such works from the category of originality – despite the fact that the pleasures of expectations fulfilled play an important role in most literary fiction. The point is that a main premise of literary originality in the twentieth century is not just difference but *difference from mass culture.* Any new Gothic romance assimilated by academia must (as a precondition of its assimilation) be perceived as marking its difference from comparable works. Its similarity must be somehow dismissed or, what comes to the same thing, emphasized in such a way (perhaps by means of parody, perhaps by means of its allusiveness to earlier canonical Gothic romances like Charlotte Brontë's *Jane Eyre*) that it becomes the condition of its perceived difference.

What this suggests is not the impossibility of judging work on the basis of originality but the power of institutional systems and cultural norms to allow certain names, and certain modes of writing, to represent authentic writing while allowing others to be ranked (or dismissed) by reference to them. Dreiser was well aware that the suit against Paramount represented an opportunity not only to clear his name but in some sense to clear a space for literary discourse to exist. As he said at one point, "I have a literary character to maintain" (Kraft 12), a statement that emphasizes the interdependence of his literary character and the character of literariness. Dreiser's "name stood for something," agreed Kraft, "whether it appeared on a book, a picture, a pamphlet, or on a committee. Integrity is indivisible" (12). By taking Paramount to court, Dreiser cleared the integrity of his name and the integrity – the uniqueness, the authenticity – of *An American Tragedy.* He lost the case but proved that the insertion of a prestigious name-brand author into the gaps between mass and high culture could successfully separate authentic work from the inauthentic and legitimate the cultural norms that gave such an assertion authority.

I

Crude as the attorney's judgment of Dreiser's novel may seem, his comment raises a significant question: How does Dreiser in fact distinguish his text from the "crime sensation of the first magnitude" that forms around Clyde Griffiths and features all the attributes of Dreiser's novel – "love, romance, wealth, poverty, death" ([1925] 1948, 577)? And to what extent does he succeed? Many critics have considered *An American Tragedy* in the light of Dreiser's firsthand knowledge of the newspaper business (Fishkin 1985, 90–130; Moers, 1969, 15–42; Kwiat 1953). His newspaper apprenticeship, which formed the basis of one autobiographical work (*A Book About Myself* [1922], republished as *Newspaper Days* [1931]), occupied Dreiser as journalist and editor in the 1890s and first decade of the twentieth century. And in the composition of *An American Tragedy* Dreiser used newspaper accounts of murders committed by young men dissatisfied with their lowly social status and trapped by a relationship with a poor girl. Commenting on Chester Gillette's murder of Grace Brown, the case that bears the closest resemblances to Clyde's story, Dreiser admitted "I drew not only from the testimony introduced at the trial but from newspaper investigations and information which preceded and accompanied the trial" ([1935] 1977, 293). Donald Pizer has shown that much if not all of Dreiser's information was actually taken from the reports in the *New York World* and a pamphlet of Grace Brown's letters, some of which Dreiser quotes almost verbatim during his account of Clyde's trial. Other similar murders – committed by Carlyle Harris, Theodore Durant, Roland Molineux, Harry New, and more – all stand behind this one (see Pizer 1976; Fishkin 112–21; Lehan, 1971, 142–51). Dreiser seems less the documentor of social realities than the mediator of public documents, and the novel less Dreiser's invention than one constructed by texts, stories, plots, and languages already existing within the realm of mass culture. In this respect, the novel's origins lie within mass culture, its originality suspect to the degree that those origins are not disguised. In another sense, the novel has no identifiable or traceable origins. The plots of murder related in newspapers have simply been appearing without any particular point of origin; their value as social documents has to do precisely with their repetitive and thus typical nature.

Critics have refuted such concerns by emphasizing authorial intercession and ironic intention displayed in the work of transformation Dreiser carried out on inherited material. Donald Pizer and Shelley Fisher Fishkin, examining the trial transcripts and newspaper reports of murders employed by Dreiser, have sought to show that by a process of reworking, Dreiser extended and changed the significance of prior material.[6] Pizer, for instance, concludes that Dreiser's transformations were meant to "shift the unavoidable impression of the documentary evidence that Gillette was a shallow-minded murderer to the impression that Clyde might be any one of us" (217). These critics depict Dreiser as the exact antithesis of his creation, Clyde Griffiths. Whereas Clyde is determined by an inescapable concatenation of social forces that exist as shaping agents prior to his birth, Dreiser reshapes preexisting texts in a way that affirms his control over them. That there is some question about Dreiser's success, however, may be inferred from the urgency (and similarity) of these attempts to rescue him from possible misinterpretations of his own tactics – that is, that a reader might feel that Dreiser fails to transform the material of mass culture. My position in this chapter is to assume, at least to begin with, that the possibility of misinterpretation opens up a legitimate interpretation of the novel, and one that forces us to see the attorney's charge and the problems of contemporary reviewers as credible and illuminating. I argue, in other words, that Dreiser in *An American Tragedy* seriously offends the decorum of originality and that this, rather than his authorial and original acts, constitutes both the problematic of the novel and, paradoxically, its originality. The fact that I do not conclude by accepting my "misreading" of Dreiser's novel should neither come as a surprise nor be taken as a denial of that earlier reading, but rather as one more instance of the exclusory and self-justifying nature of critical readings. Those critics, teachers, and readers who do perceive *An American Tragedy* as a prolonged "mere sensational newspaper story" could derive little interest and professional benefit from writing about, thinking about, or teaching that which belongs to the realm of the nonliterary; to write about *An American Tragedy* as a modernist text is already to have foreclosed that issue. Reading the novel as nothing more than the material it incorporates will convince no one; but such a reading possesses the hermeneutic value of questioning the critical strategies by which this material is "written off."

From the beginning of *An American Tragedy*, Dreiser quietly forces us to occupy – though not necessarily to recognize – certain cultural positions on the status of his text. Traditionally, for instance, one of the major problems in Dreiser studies has been the inadequacy of his writing style. Lionel Trilling put the case most famously, and for the most part his characterization of Dreiser and his critics still holds: "Everyone is aware that Dreiser's prose style is full of roughness

and ungainliness, and the critics who admire Dreiser tell us it does not matter"
([1968] 1971, 90). Trilling does not specify the ungainliness of mass culture,
though there are numerous moments in the novel, as we shall see, when Clyde's
mind registers crudely the matter of newspapers or popular novels. Should we
then take the position of condemning that ungainliness or recognize it (like
Moers) as a deliberate strategy designed to illuminate the inanities of American
mass culture and its vehicle, Clyde's mind? Should we admire that roughness as
somehow authentic when set side by side with the manufactured, polished, clear
writing of newspapers, in the same way that the crude wrenching apart of
mass-produced commodities in Cubist collage or Kurt Schwitters's *Merz* may be
held to recuperate possibilities of form lost in the objects' smooth, machinemade perfection? Saul Bellow claims as much when he contrasts Dreiser's
"clumsiness in composition" with the "terrible hunger for conformity and
uniformity" in the *New Yorker*'s "'good' writing" (Bellow, as quoted in Kazin
[1955] 1971, 17). But there are still more difficult questions, such as whether
we can tell when Dreiser's ungainly writing "works" as a strategy and when it is
simply bad writing. A similar case may be made about Dreiser's borrowings of
newspaper documents. We may argue (along with Pizer and Fishkin) that Dreiser
transforms those documents into something more profound, more authentic,
and thus more literary; or we might legitimately claim that his overprolonged
elaboration of these reports fails on any number of counts, resulting in boredom,
unoriginality, pretentiousness, overkill, and so on.

Or we may take up another position, which is to argue that Dreiser's
extensive borrowings underpin the determinist logic of the novel insofar as they
affirm the relevance of his subject matter and title, whose claim to represent a
typically American experience is sustained by the enduring popularity of the
story in the press. They testify to the generality of Clyde's predicament and
guarantee the certainty of his fate, which has been written and plotted many
times before the novel begins. His actions, as repetitive instances of Chester
Gillette's murder, are twice plotted and twice written. And more than twice, for
the newspaper accounts Dreiser consulted were themselves, as he knew, a reprise
of still other accounts of murders – by Carlyle Harris in 1893 and Clarence
Richesen in 1911, among others. As Lee Clark Mitchell (1985) has noted,
narrative patterns of repetition and doubling, which silently transform autonomous action into recapitulations of previous events, are fundamental to Dreiser's determinist vision. The newspaper accounts Dreiser adapted function in a
similar manner. For those readers who know these accounts, the novel acquires
a profound sense of fatality as the narrative of Clyde's actions converges with
archival material.

But if prior plots of murder silently inform crucial moments of the narrative,
so do newspaper stories within the novel inform the construction of Clyde's
character. Thus the killing of Roberta is suggested to Clyde by a newspaper
account of a double drowning, which itself recalls the Gillette murder in which

Grace Brown was drowned. During the trial, newspaper reports constantly appropriate Clyde. From his obscure beginnings, he becomes a public figure written into and known through public texts, and it is in this role that his character converges with the persona of Chester Gillette. Clyde's "self" is not integral or original, but emerges from a matrix of superimposed texts. His character is constantly being rewritten: as a repetition of the youth in the drowning at Pass Lake, as a simulacrum of Chester Gillette, and even as a repetition of himself, rewritten through a multitude of stories told through and for the mass media. Clyde, articulated from the beginning within a discourse of mass culture that shapes and binds every facet of his personality, emerges even more distinctly as a construct of proliferating newspaper stories by the end of the novel.

As Dreiser demonstrates the power of mass culture to shape character to its discursive structure, however, so does the novel's narrative voice increasingly draw attention to the principles of textual and linguistic construction by which it operates. Dreiser constantly refers, for instance, to the plottedness of this most laboriously plotted of novels. Clyde's plot of murder, the plot of Dreiser's narrative (itself shaped by preexisting plots of murder), and new plots constructed at the trial featuring Clyde as villain or victim, all function to expose the articulation of text and character within a matrix of discursive practices. But unexpectedly, the narrative strategies that evoke Clyde's entrapment take on another function: They force readers to account for a narrative voice whose manipulations of plot obtrude more persistently as the novel progresses and thus highlight the act of plot- and fiction-making. By reconstructing Dreiser's transformations of extant newspaper articles, critics have restored to him authorial control. But Dreiser's work of authoring is always more than just a matter of transformation, for it bears many resemblances to the narrative of Clyde's development within a pervasive media culture. The story of Clyde being authored by mass culture constantly weaves into and iterates the story – authored by Dreiser – of Dreiser's loss of authorship and authority. As the voices of mass culture intrude ever more deeply into the novel's formal and narrative strategies, and as what exists of Clyde's individuality is submerged within the stories that constitute mass culture, *An American Tragedy* reveals both its origins and its originality, both its adherence to preexisting texts and its persistent invocation of its own textuality.

Dreiser's reliance on narratives and rhetorical strategies that may be traced to mass culture has always fragmented his readership into those who would admire the novel in spite of its poor writing; those who reinterpret "poor" writing as a cunning strategy; those who separate the novel from its sources; those who do not recognize the sources at all; and those who view the novel as too reliant on or not sufficiently distinguished from its sources, and who have thus begun the process of marginalizing the novel. In the discussion that follows I try to argue from the interstices among these various positions while recognizing that this is possible only in a limited sense. The interstices themselves are situated within a critical discourse that enforces a certain jargon, a particular kind of audience, and predictable critical practices. My stance as a critic and the very premise of this book prevents me from claiming that *An American Tragedy* is nothing more than a "mere" sensational novel, though the readings that follow attempt to explore just that possibility. These readings of Dreiser's kinship to mass culture, however, resolve themselves into indeterminacy at the scene of Roberta's death. This scene becomes both a metaphor and the narrative focus of the impossibility of finally establishing the difference between Dreiser's novel and the documents he consults and inscribes – even as it does so. It is this indeterminacy that ultimately becomes the strongest argument in favor of the novel's literary status. What it reveals is precisely the novel's capacity to acknowledge its debt to mass culture while questioning both the nature of that debt and all critical readings of it. We accept the questioning of difference as a token of difference. This is to say, again, that we as critics can never conclusively define yet always recognize the fluid forms of literary writing. The proof of the literariness of Dreiser's novel occurs only, but then with great finality, at the moment we apprehend it as such. That proof occurs not in our subsequent explanations of the novel's literary quality but in our condition of always and already having known about the limited possibilities of mass culture and about the literary work's transcendence of them.

II

From the beginning of *An American Tragedy,* Clyde's world emerges out of the authority of what is written. Faith, says the narrator of Mrs. Griffiths, "was written in her every feature and gesture." Mr. Griffiths speaks only in "hack-neyed descriptions" quoted entirely from inherited texts: "a Bible and several hymn books," some "tracts describing the mission rescue work," and the religious mottoes on the windows of the Bickel Street mission (17–21). Clyde's parents are not merely identified with the communal texts they promote, for they quite consciously submit their identities to the exigencies of a divine language – the Word of God, to which earthly texts refer and by which they are controlled. Mr. and Mrs. Griffiths, spoken through rather than speaking, disappear into a building bearing inside and out the textual evidence of that submission; their characters approach the fixity of the characters of the words "God Is Love" and "How Long Since You Wrote to Mother?" printed in the mission windows. Written texts fix truth and character and lead to an eternal recurrence of action. Hence the last chapter of *An American Tragedy* repeats the mottoes in the windows and recapitulates parts of the first chapter's description of the Griffiths family (minus Clyde) almost word for word, so that the conclusion illuminates most obviously the novel's iterative design.

The ensuing narrative reveals the illusory nature of the "collective voice" (16) shared by the Griffiths family but substantiates the essential "writtenness" of character. Clyde, "only half singing," soon dissociates himself from his family, only to be attracted and shaped by a more compelling discourse: the dreams, stories, languages, and texts arising within a pervasive mass culture. At the age of thirteen he begins "looking in the papers" for a "start" (26) in life. What this search reveals characterizes him throughout the novel. On the one hand, the newspapers represent access to the worldly life excluded from his home; on the other, they promote his aspirations to rise above "all the commonplace things" (26) of a laborer's life. And the nature of this "start" – his origin – is ironic in more ways than one. We must wait until the trial to hear about Clyde's birth; but this moment in the text suggests that the fact of his biological origins is immaterial. His "start," like his end, can plausibly be said to lie within the newspapers. And we should be aware of a deeper resonance, for Clyde Griffiths's "start" as a character also lay in Dreiser's compiled newspaper reports. In consulting the papers Clyde fails to recognize his fictional genesis in the newspaper stories of murderers like Chester Gillette and Harry New. We recognize the connection and understand that his "start" is derived from stories of endings: murderers caught, tried, and executed.

Looking in the papers makes available to him a language that invests his thinking throughout the novel. Clyde's aspirations, as many commentators have recognized, are conveyed through a narrative voice that draws heavily on the stockpiled clichés of popular fictions. Clyde is less a "self" than a composite of previously written texts, less individual voice than voiced by mass culture, as the following passage, occurring a few pages before Clyde's fateful encounter with his uncle, illustrates:

> When he was within the precincts of the club itself, he felt himself different from what he really was – more subdued, less romantic, more practical, certain that if he tried now, imitated the soberer people of the world, and those only, that some day he might succeed, if not greatly, at least much better than he had thus far. And who knows? What if he worked very steadily and made only the right sort of contacts and conducted himself with the greatest care here, one of these very remarkable men whom he saw entering or departing from here might take a fancy to him and offer him a connection with something important somewhere, such as he had never known before, and that might lift him into a world such as he had never known. (189)

The scene might have been lifted out of a Horatio Alger novel; more precisely, perhaps, the scene compresses all of Alger's novels into a series of clichés. Clyde's dreams compose a litany of catchphrases counterpointed by deadening superlatives: "very steadily," "very remarkable," "greatest care." His first perception, that he has become "less romantic, more practical," vanishes with his flight into a fantasy marked less by imagination than vagueness: "something important somewhere," "such as he had never known," and then, rather remarkably, a repetition of "such as he had never known." With that repetition Dreiser emphasizes both the sterility and the facile optimism of Clyde's dreams.

Dreiser's language is constantly alive to the effect of flat clichés, rendering delicately the movement of Clyde's thought as he negotiates between present realities and an inherited plot of success. The sudden "And who knows?" intrudes inconsistently, under the shock of excitement, into the passage's free indirect discourse. And the next sentence, beginning "What if," is transformed midway from the expected question to a statement, as if this evocation of popular fantasies is to lead to unquestioned success. Ignoring consequence and continuity, Clyde's language and syntax recreate the illogic of the fictional legacy on which he unconsciously draws. Moreover, the ideas and the expression of ideas such as "some day he might succeed," "worked very steadily," and even "offer him a connection" strike us too readily as borrowed wholesale from fantasies of upward mobility to suggest the existence of an integral, differentiated self. Like his mother and father, Clyde thinks by appropriating thoughts, words, and narratives embedded within a discourse that has become, in contemporary jargon, "naturalized": They permeate consciousness too thoroughly to be seen as anything but reality. Newspapers and Horatio Alger novels do not actively manipulate Clyde; their formulaic plots compose the horizon of his knowledge and imagination, and articulate the enduring plots that define success and failure in American life. He is identified primarily by a unique relationship to formulas that revoke his autonomy and integrity, and they do so most persuasively because their effect is unseen and unvoiced.

Once Clyde lives in Lycurgus, the newspapers' plots of success invest his imaginative life still more thoroughly. Newspapers constitute a (limited) source of information about the world to which he aspires, provide him with a language, and function as a tacit reminder of social difference. As the narrator remarks:

> Yet so far as the movements of the Griffiths family and their social peers outside Lycurgus were concerned, he knew little other than that which from time to time he had read in the society columns of the two local papers which almost obsequiously pictured the comings and goings of all those who were connected with the more important families of the city. At times, after reading these accounts he had pictured to himself, even when he was off somewhere with Roberta at some unheralded resort, Gilbert Griffiths racing in his big car, Bella, Bertine and Sondra dancing, canoeing in the moonlight, playing tennis, riding at some of the smart resorts where they were reported to be. The thing had a bite and ache for him that was almost unendurable and had lit up for him at times and with overwhelming clarity this connection of his with Roberta. (330)

The society columns define two worlds, contrasting "all those who were connected" with "this connection of his" with Roberta. Because the columns offer a narrowly exclusive source of information, beyond which Clyde knows "little other," they enforce a relationship to privilege characterized by obsessiveness and ignorance. The reports encourage him and allow him to live out vicariously an elite existence. Yet his "pictured" scenes (borrowed wholesale from what the newspapers "obsequiously pictured") scarcely show Clyde thinking with "overwhelming clarity." His actual images, "dancing, canoeing in the moonlight, playing tennis, riding at some of the smart resorts," are absolutely ordinary: They are fantasies of the good life flatly reproduced in the language of newspapers and advertising. They are, as Ellen Moers puts it nicely, "highly tinted, patently fake images – the sort that appear on picture post cards" (1969, 229).

Newspaper columns detailing Sondra's activities keep his obsession with her constantly before his eyes (282, 330, 336, 355, 459). As Clyde says on the witness stand, "she dressed awfully well, and was very rich and in society and her name and pictures were always in the paper. I used to read about her every day when I didn't see her" (739). Clyde's compilation of Sondra's attributes, with its sprinkling of ubiquitous adjectives ("awfully well," "very rich"), proclaims its origins in the rhetoric of his earlier newspaper reveries ("more important," "big car," "smart resorts"). The connective "and," which allows Clyde to knead together separate aspects of his desire for Sondra paratactically, reveals much about distinctions he fails to see. For Clyde, so thoroughly does the paper articulate his perceptions of Sondra, that figuring heavily in the local papers, being very rich, and being in high society seem to hold equivalent value.

Indeed, Clyde's equation holds true insofar as the society column functions as an index of social position and identity. Sondra initially invites Clyde to join Lycurgus's high society, but thereafter the newspapers begin to promote his inclusion by printing his name as part of the "fast set." A particular article in the Lycurgus *Star,* mentioning his presence at a party attended by the town's elite, forces the Griffiths to welcome him more fully into their circles. The Griffiths ignore Clyde's early social successes, but "a society notice in *The Star* was different" (383); they, in fact, accord the act of publication quite as much authority as he does, accepting the newspaper's power to shape social rank. In a quite other context, however, the same article reveals to Roberta Clyde's duplicity, and enables her later to castigate him for lying to her. The article at once causes him to be invited to the Griffiths' Christmas dinner, elevates his sense of his own worth, and widens the rift between him and Roberta. Like George Flack's trivial columns in *The Reverberator,* this article carries a weight of plot developments quite out of proportion to its size.

The newspaper keys major elements of Clyde's psyche, shaping his character and opinions, magnifying and directing his desire for Sondra, and ultimately inspiring his grim solution to his predicament, for his murder plot arises from an article about an "ACCIDENTAL DOUBLE TRAGEDY AT PASS LAKE" (474) reported in the *Times-Union.* From a piece that "interested Clyde only slightly" (476), it soon becomes a "terrible item" (482) that is constantly in his mind, "born of his own turbulent, eager and disappointed seeking" (501). He fashions his own plot of murder to be congruent with the "ACCIDENTAL DOUBLE TRAGEDY" report because it offers a conveniently reproducible plot, one that is "commonplace enough in the usual grist of summer incidents" (476). Indeed, Dreiser's text relates that this incident has other fictional antecedents; the *Times-Union* reporter mentions a "similar accident" that had taken place fifteen years earlier. The *Times-Union* plot constructs yet another scenario of success for Clyde, describing a sequence of events that, if duplicated exactly by a deliberate recreation of accidental events, would bring about his relationship with Sondra. The report shapes action within a constraining story that only seems, as it effectively plots Clyde's future course, to offer him liberation and freedom of choice. His supreme act of volition – choosing to instigate the plan of action suggested by the *Times-Union* – suggests instead the limitations imposed on his options and opportunities as he chooses to act according to the dictates of a preexisting script. Clyde, as Belknap later (quite delicately) describes this existential quandary, "accepted *The Times-Union* plot and proceeded to act on it" (649). The article spurs action, allowing Clyde to proceed out of a dilemma that has threatened to incapacitate him completely. Yet "accepted" connotes a prior surrendering of volition; as so often during Clyde's first months at Lycurgus, the parameters of his possible actions are set by the mass media.

In *An American Tragedy,* repetitious stories, formulaic plots, and the insistent eulogies of society columns surround Clyde with a sense of inflexible realities. This is nowhere clearer than during the trial, in which public stories that weave scattered facts of his past life into new fictions reconstruct his identity. Born from the media, Clyde is finally taken as the genesis of innumerable other articles about him. Clyde, in fact, is constantly "writ small" as the complexities of his life are translated into a "crime sensation of the first magnitude, with all of those intriguingly colorful, and yet morally and spiritually atrocious, elements – love, romance, wealth, poverty, death" (623). Blaring headlines purvey a diminutive Clyde, condensed to a "BOY SLAYER OF WORKING-GIRL SWEETHEART" (670). By contrast, newspapers amplify Mason who, once the "Cataraqui County correspondent of such papers as the Albany *Times-Union* and the Utica *Star*" (547), is already adept at purveying fictions through the mass media. "It was," as the narrator remarks of Mason's performance, "as if some one had suddenly exclaimed: 'Lights! Camera!'" (689). He masterminds the rewriting of Clyde's self by playing to the audience in courtroom and media, and "directing" (638) Clyde's actions, and is rewarded for his performance by his apotheosis in the media's "sprawling headlines": "PROSECUTION IN GRIFFITHS' CASE CLOSES WITH IMPRESSIVE DELUGE OF TESTIMONY" (716). Ironically enough, Belknap and Jephson use similar tactics: Their first action after drafting the story Clyde uses at the trial is to publish statements to the press opposing Mason's stories.

Clyde's appropriation by the mass media at the trial is one of Dreiser's most compelling moves, for it restores Clyde openly to the discourse that has profoundly shaped him. The power of stories disseminated by the newspapers is demonstrated anew as their accounts now proliferate about him. And they continue to do so. His mother's attempts to raise money for an appeal are thwarted "because of what the newspapers had said" (822) about Clyde's conviction; the Reverend McMillan is satisfied by his reading that Clyde is guilty even before meeting him; and although Governor Waltham has read the official trial documents, the narrative makes clear that he is aware of the newspapers' (and thus the public's) conviction of Clyde's guilt (861). Yet Clyde spends his time in jail "reading and re-reading the newspapers" (678) – rereading, in oddly celebratory fashion, newly written stories about his life. Even more oddly, Clyde's reading anticipates the process we, as readers, undergo: As new plot developments impel him toward his foreordained end, the narrative itself is impeded by recurring stories that increasingly force us to read what has already been established. The constant rewriting of Clyde's life occasions, we shall see, his amnesia about his own story and his attempts to recall its original shape. Dreiser's narrative strategies place readers in a similar predicament as we strive to discover the shape of Clyde's plot of murder.

III

That subtle, pervasive, and banal inscription of mass narratives within Clyde's voice suggests a complex world of interrelationships in which each utterance, especially out of Clyde's mind, arrives resonant with the structure and idiom of mass society. Dreiser's vision of mass society, in fact, is fundamentally structuralist: The novel posits a network of relationships within which writing, culture, and self are constituted. Like the Lycurgus collar factory in which Clyde works, where male and female, managers and workers, workers and material all enter into a mutual relationship within the labyrinthine structures of the factory to produce identical bundles of collars, the sign systems and languages of mass society bind and shape Clyde in their collective image. But the absoluteness of this binding – to follow the structuralist paradigm a little further – imposes contingencies on the narrative strategies appropriate to this vision. For how can one describe and examine structure except by means of the terms it makes available? If insistent repetition organizes the material and symbolic economies of mass culture (mass production, endlessly repeated advertising ploys, formulaic plots), we should be prepared to look to strategies of replication and repetition as the mode of exploration.

But the dominant critical strategy for illuminating the "influence" of mass culture is to search for *singularities*. The point at which Henry James's "personal style" invests and refashions popular narrative (William Veeder's argument), for example, or the point at which Dreiser transforms the limited perspective of newspaper reports into the universal and profound. What some early reviewers of the novel (as reported by Robert Shafer) saw as unconscionable prolongation, Pizer and Fishkin recognize as conscious exploration. And these critics are undoubtedly correct to point to Dreiser's important revisions of borrowed material; the Gillette story does not constrain Dreiser's in the sense that the author literally reproduced the murderer's story. But in emphasizing Dreiser's revisions of preexisting plots of murder, critics have not recognized the extent to which his dependency on unoriginal stories might prove a precondition to constructing the novel's originality. This is a crucial shift of critical stance. To suggest that the novel resists the very operations of transmutation on which its originality is purportedly built, and then to rediscover the novel's originality in the act of resistance, is to step away, at least, from the assumption that disrupting inherited material must be a premise of the novel's value. It is to accept the novel's origins as a token – provisional, perhaps, but nonetheless real – of its necessary unoriginality. The key to the problematic in Dreiser's text is that the formal strategies that promise to unfold and disrupt the patterns of mass society duplicate those patterns so thoroughly. Something of this problematic can be seen in the critical debate over whether Clyde possesses a self apart from the articulation of mass narratives within him.[7] Should we read endless clichés and disjointed syntax as a recreation or as a subtle exposure of characterlessness? To what extent do we read this prolonged narrative about Clyde Griffiths different-ly than an equal number of pages of the journalism of Dreiser's youth, which "loved long-winded yarns upon almost any topic" (Dreiser [1931] 1974, 65)?

Clearly, the inscription of mass narratives must be viewed not only in psychological but in narratological terms. As Clyde's character unfolds within mass narratives that invade his voice and then, by story's end, assimilate him completely, Dreiser's narrative increasingly bears the traces of that mass voicing and plotting. Dreiser constantly draws attention to questions of narrative and psychological construction by broaching the issue of plot in its double sense of "illegal plan" and "narrative structure" – the first a function of conscious scheming, the second the narrative shape of that scheming and the actions resulting from it. The *Times-Union* article suggests a new plot to Clyde; both remind the reader of Chester Gillette's plot (as told in the New York *World*); and the ensuing narrative of Clyde's demise exactly duplicates none of them. His plot, moreover, is replotted by Jephson and Belknap following his capture. As Clyde emerges more fully into the public world, and as newspaper stories assert their prerogative over his identity and story, Dreiser's strategy of repeated stories obsessively characterizes the structural patterns of his text. For that principle of replication is embodied within the text in the form of retelling and replotting, in some cases by the obsessive doubling and repetition of characters, scenes, and events (some of which Lee Mitchell details), in other cases by word-for-word repetition of previously told episodes.

The novel's final chapter, "Souvenir," recalls (as its title implies) and reprints whole chunks of material from Chapter 1. Roberta's long letters to Clyde, read to such great effect by Mason during the trial, are largely reprinted from Grace Brown's letters, published in pamphlet form during the Chester Gillette case. But long before the trial, recurring stories characterize Clyde's schemes to release himself from Roberta. His implausible explanation of the discrepancies between his account of a party at the Steele residence and the *Star* account causes Roberta to cry: "Oh, Clyde, you don't have to story to me" (390). Despite his rejoinder, "But I'm not storying to you, Bert," his insistent "storying" begins to occupy significant portions of the text. Richard Lehan has rightly commented that *An American Tragedy* "employs the familiar block method with a great mass of accumulated material being arranged into blocks or units, each scene repeating and then anticipating another" (1963, 191). As striking as Dreiser's tendency to repeat action and character in a different guise, however, are those scenes composed of stories that are, like file material inserted in a newspaper article, merely retold, sometimes in precisely the same words. Redundancy, as Clyde struggles to "story" his way out of situations that have already been written – and have already written him off – has become an integral and perhaps inescapable part of Dreiser's narrative strategy. We cannot help but reread stories we thought had been told, as if the retelling fundamentally comprised the story's significance and originality.

Before the trip to Schenectady to purchase "medicine" for Roberta, for instance, Clyde pieces together a plausible story: "he might say . . . that he was a newly married man – why not? He was old enough to be one, and that his wife, and that in the face of inability to care for a child now, was 'past her time' (he recalled a phrase that he had once heard Higby use), and that he wanted something that would permit her to escape from that state" (409). In Schenectady, the story thus sketched, including the phrase remembered from Higby, is repeated in full: "I want to know something. I want to know if you know of anything – well, you see, it's this way – I'm just married and my wife is past her time and I can't afford to have any children now if I can help it. Is there anything a person can get that will get her out of it?" (410). After the treatment fails, Clyde's next plan is narrated in the same way. It "now came to him" that "if only he could get her to say that she had been deserted by some young man, whose name she would refuse to divulge, of course, well, what physician seeing a girl like her alone and in such a state – no one to look after her – would refuse her? It might even be that he would help her out for nothing" (419). He elaborates this story – which is itself a variant of his sister's experience in Kansas City – over the next two pages (419–422), and then repeats it as a pep talk to Roberta before she enters the doctor's house at Gloversville (430–431). Clyde maneuvers in the same way to gain information from Orrin Short. The "tale he had fixed upon to tell Short" (424), a modified version of the story he uses in Schenectady, is recounted in some detail before being narrated once again in his speech to Short. The stories first imagined by Clyde and then recounted to Roberta and Short are repeated yet again by Roberta. During the first visit to the doctor, Roberta employs Clyde's original tale (married but too poor to have children) before amending it to Clyde's second version (pregnant but deserted) when the doctor proves obstinate. Later, after both stories fail, Roberta narrates a series of future plans to Clyde, the burden of which is to "get married right away" and then find some way of "getting along" (450). Her vision of future happiness, in other words, virtually recapitulates – with changed emphasis – the story Clyde uses to persuade the druggist and Orrin Short of the necessity for abortion.

These instances prepare the way for the insistent retellings of Clyde's story in Part 3 of the novel. The narrative refers repeatedly to the plot exigencies under which Clyde labors: those that shape him anew and those he attempts to reconstruct. At the trial he claims "No! I never did! I never did plot to kill her" (745), although "in his heart and mind was the crying knowledge that he had so plotted." To counter "the true story of his plotting" (652) Jephson creates an alternative "plot" (661) that will at once construct a new narrative out of existing facts and dismiss the charge that Clyde schemed to commit murder; Jephson, that is, "stories" in such a way as to undo the criminality of Clyde's plot. In contrast, Mason's understanding of plot is straightforward: He charges during the trial that Clyde "plotted for weeks . . . with malice aforethought and in cold blood" (690) to kill Roberta. Each version of the "great plot," as a "penny-dreadful publisher" (679) puts it, constructs a narrative that drives Clyde toward the predetermined conclusion of his life and, increasingly, refers the reader back to the events that make such a conclusion inevitable. While still free, Clyde reads a long and incomplete version of Roberta's drowning in the Albany and Utica papers (588–9). During his imprisonment, plots are constantly refined, variants employed, and roles revised. He relates one version to Mason (609–11), another to Smillie (629–32), and yet another to Belknap (642–3); Belknap and Jephson then rehearse Clyde's story detail by detail while reworking it into a more satisfactory version (646–62). During the trial, other versions of his life are offered by Mason, Jephson, and Clyde himself on the witness stand. Even after the trial, when Clyde believes "All the long grim story had been told" (804), partial narratives are still retold in prison (845–6, 851–7).

The question is to what extent we can read these multiplying plots and obsessively reproduced stories – of which the reprinting of Grace Brown's letters is only the most obvious example – as signifying Dreiser's originality, and thus his priority over the texts of mass culture. How do we recognize originality in a text where the totalizing nature of mass society seems to preclude originality and where the text itself seems to partake of the formulaic and repetitive? It is as though Dreiser, far from seeking to disguise his novel's genesis in stories worn threadbare by their popularity within the media, has transformed his act of recuperation into the dynamic of the text. Nathanael West's *The Day of the*

Locust, as we shall see, displays a similar dynamic, whereby the fragmented modes of Hollywood film are appropriated, subverted, and then revalued within the meaningful fragmentation of the text. But Dreiser's novel is more perplexing. West (and John Dos Passos) decomposes that which lacks all coherence in order to construct a narrative about fragmentation possessing all the force of a coherent, organized, focused attack. To be likewise recognized as "other," Dreiser's strategy of repetition must somewhere mark its difference from the sterile reproductions of mass society; it must invoke the singular and by so doing separate out a transcendent position from which to observe the emerging patterns of reproduction; it must somehow disrupt its own tactic of reproduction. But Dreiser's strategy runs the risk of compromising the novel's very originality by its reinscription of stories from mass culture and by its seemingly banal iteration of them within the text. Dreiser forces his reader to undergo deliberately something of the incessant inscription of mass narratives within the psyche; for many readers, the novel manages only to parody its own methods of analysis, hardening into formula itself rather than exploring the condition of formula. In making repetition such an integral part of the text, Dreiser poses the question of whether genuine difference is likely or possible or even truthful to the pervasive formations of mass society. And in that repetition, the novel forces us to examine to just what extent the novel enters into complicity with the realm of the inauthentic it is supposed to counter.

IV

In Part 3 of the novel, a plethora of public stories usurps Clyde's private self in such a way as to dismiss the notion that a single narrative can ever uncover the logic behind his actions and motives. Clyde himself seems to recognize that possibility for, faced by a labyrinth of recurring stories after his capture, he manifests a near obsession with rediscovering the original scheme that gave rise to his murderous actions. Even before his capture, Clyde wonders whether he should "make a clean breast of . . . the original plot" (589). Once captured, he wonders again whether he should make "a true explanation as to his plot, his real original intent" (617). He fears, at the trial, that his erstwhile friends will believe him "as terrible as his original plot" (685). And while awaiting execution, in response to a progressive failure to recall and specify his original motives, he asks the Reverend McMillan whether he thought him guilty "because of the original plotting – and hence the original intent" (851). Clyde twice stumbles on a point that generations of readers have pondered: To argue (along with the coroner's jury) that he "devised and executed" (638) a murderous plot entails his voluntary and conscious control over a sequence of events – mastery over a "plot." Clyde seems intent upon confessing (but also confused about) his role in plots he believes originated within himself; he wishes to see himself as an original, despite the feelings of most readers who disregard his own silent admission that "he had so plotted" (745) to kill Roberta, preferring to read the scene of her death as placing in doubt the extent of his volition and agency.

To the extent that we seek to uncover the originality of Dreiser's text from what is so patently unoriginal and banal, Clyde's predicament corresponds to our own. His search for the "original plot" reminds us of the critics' searches for points of difference to which origins and originality might be traced – that is, for the points at which the novel's antecedent texts are finally displaced in a process whereby prior material resurfaces as original (authentic) material. It is as if we have not begun the authentic work until the inauthentic can be recognized, accounted for, and bracketed off; having done so, we become, as it were, amnesiacs, forgetting what ground must be traversed in order to arrive at that point of difference. Such tactics operate under the sign of what I earlier called assimilation, and can be identified virtually anywhere in today's academia, from Shakespeare studies to studies of Dreiser and James. The strategy typically follows two stages, from the identification in a particular text of legend, folk or mass cultural material to the demonstration of the author's manipulations. One cannot after all apprehend them as manipulations until a typical pattern has been established and literariness thus observed in the writer's ability to repattern and rewrite. Such readings place a heavy but usually covert emphasis on process. The process of repatterning is acknowledged as important but subordinated to the finished product, in which the traces of that work of refashioning are erased or viewed as inseparable from the work's literary functions. "Source study" in the case of a text's antecedents in, say, mass culture is characterized first by a denial of the value of that source and second by an inevitable teleology whereby process is considered only insofar as it contributes to a literary end that has been in sight from the beginning. An expectation of literariness precedes recognition of the strategic process by which the literary is allegedly attained. Paul Orlov (1982), in his discussion of Dreiser's rewriting of the typical Alger plot, must be convinced before elaborating on Dreiser's plot manipulations that rewriting is necessary (for Alger's plots are untrue, melodramatic, and so on) and that observed points of difference carry a literary value. Orlov is not wrong, but we should note that this discursive practice of using analyses of writing strategies to prove underlying assumptions about a text is itself a strategy – and a powerful one.[8]

Let us look at a longer example of how critical exegeses, however different they appear, seek to construct the originality of Dreiser's writing. The context is a well-known debate about *Sister Carrie* that began with Sandy Petrey's essay "The Language of Realism, The Language of False Consciousness: A Reading of *Sister Carrie*" (1977) and was pursued in a later printed discussion between Petrey and Ellen Moers (1977). Petrey's initial essay begins "Is there a way to appreciate *Sister Carrie* as a whole when things like this are in it?" and he goes on to quote a long passage of "rhetorical bungling" (101) ("make clear the rose's subtle alchemy evolving its ruddy lamp in light and rain," for instance). Petrey's point is that Dreiser's text constantly includes such sentimentalized, purple prose out of popular sentimental novels, popular songs, and melodramas in distinct contrast to the novel's dominant tone, which is dry, descriptive, and realistic. To Petrey this stylistic discontinuity suggests a thoroughgoing exposure of a false language and hence the false consciousness out of which it emerges. In a later issue of the same journal Ellen Moers responds by rejecting Petrey's argument: "I early learned in my years of work on Dreiser that it was perilous to read him sloppily," Moers writes, "for he was a serious thinker not a dealer in half-baked clichés" (Moers and Petrey 1977, 63). By reading the offending passage in the light of Dreiser's interest in Herbert Spencer, Moers manages to rescue a phrase like "evolving its ruddy lamp" – not on account of its fine language but on account of Dreiser's serious and sincere concern with contemporary science and philosophy. Indeed, far from falling into popular cliché at a point like this, Dreiser's interest in science enabled him to avoid the "slick platitudes of nineteenth-century literary and journalistic Naturalism" (65). "Dreiser's style always labored," Moers argues in final defense, "when he alluded to the cosmic unknowable."

We appear to have two combative readings of Dreiser's language and its relationship to mass culture. For Petrey, a strategy of discontinuity separates the novel from the sentimental ethos, bad language, and false consciousness of nineteenth-century popular culture; for Moers, in spite of frequent lapses in language, passages such as those Petrey dismisses are "full of Dreiser's wisdom" (63–4). My interest, however, lies not in defending Petrey or Moers but in observing some of the profound similarities between their critical positions. Petrey himself notes that Moers agrees with him about Dreiser's bungling language, disagreeing only about what that language then signifies. More importantly, both critics manage to view Dreiser and his work as legitimate and valuable by circumventing the problem of Dreiser's language. For Moers, content ("wisdom") assimilates poor style; for Petrey, who refuses to overlook poor style, stylistic discontinuity becomes the means by which bad writing can be directly confronted yet still be assimilated to a larger framework of meaning. Moers relies on Dreiser's wisdom, Petrey on a textual unlocking of society's pervasive false consciousness. Moers rests her case on an aware and fertile mind that is insensible (in this passage) to stylistic beauty; Petrey argues for formal and linguistic subtleties that Dreiser may never have intended. These strategies are mutually contradictory except as each attempts to recuperate a culturally powerful text from troubling and potentially dangerous material. In answer to Petrey's initial question "Is there a way to appreciate *Sister Carrie* as a whole when things like this are in it?" we must answer, "Of course." Both Moers and Petrey unwittingly demonstrate the power of critical discourse to find principles of reorganization with which to distinguish Dreiser from (in this case) popular, sentimentalized language. Petrey writes that "*Sister Carrie*'s stylistic play crushingly refutes the facile certainties of a self-satisfied age" (Moers and Petrey, 69) and if Moers could not agree here she surely would with Petrey's following remark, which ratifies pursuit of "the most majestic sense literature can make."

An American Tragedy, however, remains obstinately impenetrable to such common critical strategies. If, as I have suggested, Dreiser reproduces the banality, repetitiveness, and melodrama of the newspaper idiom so convincingly that we may become unsure about where the points of difference lie; if we respect fully Dreiser's tactic of replicating newspaper reports and view this material as intransigent and unassimilated; then the model I have outlined above collapses. Instead of finding Dreiser's originality in the rewriting of mass codes and idioms, we might conclude that his originality suffers from a too-great reliance on original (that is, prior or source) material. Instead of admiring Dreiser's appropriation of material from mass culture, we might lament mass culture's appropriation of him. Many criticisms of Dreiser's work – its length, tediousness, shabby style, melodrama – do indeed come to that conclusion. At that point, either we consign Dreiser to the ranks of the unreadable or search for compensatory approaches in which his failings are counterbalanced by his truth to life, universality, or elaborateness of vision.

Whether we conclude that Dreiser succeeds or fails to transform his originary material, the principle of literature-as-transformation remains undisturbed. The principle assumes in either case the scandal of unassimilated source material; and in either case a writer's literary qualities are held ransom to the previously ordained marginality of that source material. But one can imagine reading Dreiser differently. After all, until prior material and guiding plots are recognized as such one cannot help but read any text as unique. Any reader who comes to the genre of fantasy for the very first time, for instance, might well judge the most derivative work as fresh and exciting. Since, in the case of *An American Tragedy,* the murders Dreiser drew on are in themselves little known, it is logical to predict a rather different group of readers who learn of Dreiser's borrowings after reading the novel and who subsequently view it as less original or even merely derivative, just as that fantasy novel might come to seem less and less interesting with further exposure to the genre. This situation, to speculate further, might provide a truly radical reading of *An American Tragedy,* for it would reverse the trajectory we have noted in criticism of James and Dreiser (among many others) whereby an analogy between, say, the plots of mass-produced fiction and the plots of James and Dreiser leads to a recognition of uniqueness. But what if one's reading of the uniqueness of Dreiser' novel were compromised by a later discovery of his borrowings? And what if one's reading of uniqueness were compromised by the discovery of *difference,* the realization that the text is not, as it were, identical with itself, but contingent, relational, involved with the other of mass culture?

The point is not to confirm one of these reading experiences as more valid than another but to suggest that both are logical and possible. It is as logical, in other words, to hypothesize about reading a pristine, unique text as it is to hypothesize about reading a text that is, from the moment we begin it, fallen, marred, and colonized by sources that must somehow be redeemed. Critical discourse, however, privileges the second model, and for powerful reasons. By making the process of rewriting function within a literary teleology, a critic ensures that potentially disruptive source material is identified and controlled; consequently, he or she maintains the reciprocal but mutually exclusive relationship between literature and mass culture. To do otherwise would be to run the risk of confusing originality with source material and to be faced with the scandal of seeing the literary text converge with the texts from which it is supposed to have arisen and then displaced. At stake here is the legitimacy of critical strategies themselves. To read Dreiser's novel as "cold-blooded plagiarism," to read it as depending on that which remains crudely unassimilated, or even to read it as potentially pristine (that is, self-identical, sourceless, answerable only to itself) is at once possible and, for a critic, unlikely. The structure of critical discourse ensures that, in reading modernist fiction, we tend to use a paradigm whereby an expectation of originality guides the discovery of certain transformative patterns. Institutional pressures provide correlative support. There would be little use in setting out to prove, for instance, that Dreiser's text is sensationalistic and banal, though such a judgment might indeed be made in passing or as part of a different enterprise.

As I have suggested, our search for the sign of the authentic and original (in both senses) is figuratively embodied in Clyde Griffiths. Just as Clyde attempts but never manages to separate himself from the newspapers that give him his "start" in life, we find ourselves considering the authenticity of Dreiser's text on the basis of its incorporation of the inauthentic and at times unable to determine adequate categories. And Clyde also finds it impossible either to forget or to discover his own points of origin; each reading and rewriting of his relationship to those origins makes that relationship more obscure. Let us consider Clyde's appearance on the witness stand, where he undertakes, at the bidding of Jephson, to retell "the short but straitened story of his youth" (725). His tale of straitened circumstances is also a "straightened" one in the sense that chronology and syntax are reshaped in the time-honored fashion of nineteenth-century first-person narrators. We are reminded, for instance, of David Copperfield in the second sentence of Dickens's novel, stating "To begin my life with the beginning of my life, I record that I was born (as I have been informed and believe) on a Friday, at twelve o'clock at night." Here is Clyde's beginning: "I was born in Grand Rapids, Michigan. My parents were conducting a mission there at the time and used to hold open air meetings." "I was born" makes birth coterminous with the birth of self-awareness (the "I"). His retelling postulates the existence of a self that has form, significance, and autonomy prior to the shaping sequence of events unfolding from the moment of birth – an anachronism that Copperfield's parenthesis recognizes and accounts for. Clearly, one must read back from a knowledge of later events to construct an ego not (at the moment of birth) yet formed, and Copperfield's acknowledgment of a fictional design allows him to distinguish subtly the beginning of "my life" from the "beginning of my life" *story* while preserving the illusion of an immutable individuality. "I was born" is a fiction, buttressed by conventional props of time, place, and event, that nonetheless suggests the unassailability of self, which cannot be thought of as less than complete and in control.

Clyde's simple, declarative version blurs the import of Dreiser's first telling, which introduces an anonymous family enchained within the "tall walls of the commercial heart of an American city" (15) and already defined by its ad-herence to a preexisting set of divine dictates. We see Clyde on the point of self-awareness, but perhaps more in the sense of self-consciousness about his family's shortcomings than awareness of himself as a separate and autonomous individual. Clyde, in fact, is born into a configuration of forces – the downtown business district, his parents' rabid religiosity, the apathy of the passing people – within which the autonomy of self is radically curtailed. As if to disparage from the start Clyde's witness-stand attempt to tell his life story, the first sentence of the novel ("Dusk – of a summer night") presents a scene whose content seems divorced from the actions and identity of witnesses. It undermines Clyde's later attempt to stand witness for his *capacity* to witness: As he stands half-singing in the streets of Kansas City, Clyde still appears not to have been born as an identifiable and separable "I." Dreiser, concerned with the evolution of self within interrelated social systems, must begin in media res – not with an arbitrary point of origin such as an "I" who could not yet exist.

Clyde's story is in any case not "his": It is manufactured by Belknap and Jephson as the most appealing way to dismiss the charge that he schemed to commit murder. At the moment when Clyde steps forward to speak for himself (and as if he possessed the powerful and relatively unproblematic self of a nineteenth-century hero) we are aware that once again he is merely articulating others' words. Belknap and Jephson become the witting authors of a narrative mode Dreiser shows to be outmoded, and which bases Clyde's defense on the kind of autonomous self Dreiser's narrative brings into question. The defense's strategy can only play into Mason's hands. Clyde is thus in the contradictory position of believing that "he had so plotted" to murder without being able to reconstruct an "original plot" – a moment when he, as an active and controlling agent, first plotted a sequence of events that would be uniquely his. He is, in a sense, desperately seeking to fill the David Copperfield role Belknap and Jephson have mapped out for him – which happens to correspond to the autonomous and volitional self Mason argues he possesses. His inability to trace stories to their origins unmasks the illusion of a controlling self, which is enmeshed in a pervasive discourse composed of stories disseminated through the mass media. The *Times-Union* article is only one of numerous newspaper articles that shape Clyde's life, and thus can scarcely be said to have a unique impact on Clyde. His story is contingent upon preceding and more powerful stories that revoke the power of characters to "story" in original ways; indeed, within the seamless web of discourse Dreiser is intent on describing, it seems, there can be no original stories, only prior ones.

Such a categorical statement still does not do justice to the novel. We may find grounds for doubting the authenticity of Dreiser's text in Clyde Griffiths's questioning of his original plot; but does not his questioning support a reading of Clyde as more original than the murderers to whom he bears resemblance? May we not attribute to him the originality of one who cannot carry out the murder he intends? Clyde has often been defended on the grounds that he is not the murderer that Gillette clearly was; the marks on Roberta's face, for instance, are described as much less severe than those in the case of Grace Brown. And it should be noted that though Clyde derives his plot of murder from the "ACCIDENTAL DOUBLE TRAGEDY" reported in the *Times-Union,* he also fails to enact the narrative that inspires him. The events leading up to Roberta's death in many ways transform the "commonplace" story of the "ACCIDENTAL DOUBLE TRAGEDY" into the unique and particular. Even the headline's abbreviated phrasing mocks the lengthy and convoluted tale of Clyde's sufferings and, unlike Clyde and Roberta, the participants in the Pass Lake tragedy remain unidentified. They set forth, quite anonymously, "at a small lake anywhere" (476), whereas Clyde's efforts at anonymity result in two aliases beginning with the initials of his own name. Likewise, the convenient obscurity of "a small lake anywhere" becomes the precisely described environment of Big Bittern lake; at the trial, in fact, Mason uses a map of the area to trap Clyde. Given the number of missteps Clyde takes while unfolding his plot of murder, it is not surprising that the outcome of Roberta's death fails to reproduce the drowning as described in the *Times-Union.* Nor is it particularly surprising, given Clyde's relationship with newspapers, that he continues to identify his situation with the Pass Lake tragedy long after all correspondence seems to have vanished. At the Cranston Lodge following Roberta's death, for instance, Clyde yearns for information about "that drowned couple" (583; also 585) – referring to Roberta and himself! – quite forgetting that he is not the man in the *Times-Union* report. But the narrative has foreclosed Clyde's wishfulness: Preceding chapters already show Clyde identified and under strong suspicion.

The Pass Lake drownings, it seems, provide a narrative upon which Clyde increasingly fails to model his actions; in contrast to drownings that are (by implication) accidental and innocent, the unique catastrophe of Roberta's death and the botched cover-up point to his difference and to his extraordinary status. Clyde often invokes the commonplace nature of such drownings (476; 497; 503) and his desire to reproduce them, but we see the flaws in Clyde's logic. He might hope, by deliberately reproducing a series of accidental events, to commit murder, but not at the same time to pass off those deliberations as accidental and commonplace. That drowned couple, without malice aforethought, must have had events happen to them; circumstances rather than sentient beings initiated a sequence of tragic actions. Their story therefore provides a narrative (series of events) that has occurred without a plot (scheme); put differently, it provides a plot that has not been plotted. In order to reproduce that narrative Clyde must consciously shape potentially random events by way of a preconceived plot and thus add the one element whose lack made the Pass Lake drownings so attractive to him. Each of Clyde's attempted reenactments transforms the constellation of events and ironically bestows on him a name, history, and even fame, all of which are specifically absent in the Pass Lake story. Events and Clyde's desires conspire to make every attempted step toward anonymity an actual step toward his extraordinary end.

But we are not yet done with entangling newspaper narratives, for this way of arguing Clyde's differences from the Pass Lake story has the effect of weaving him into a narrative that is, for the reader, ever more reminiscent of Chester Gillette's. His attempts to re-create the *accidental* double tragedy, in other words, keep turning out suspiciously like attempted murder; each failure of Clyde's to duplicate an accidental tragedy identifies him further with the silent but guiding story of Gillette's murder. Indeed, that story's control over Clyde's is all the greater for appearing to play no part in his fictional world; it functions like the deep structure of myth, silently plotting the script of Clyde's identity and story. Chester Gillette, after all – so the jury believed, and so the critics who wish to see Clyde as distinct from Gillette argue – did plot Grace Brown's death and did execute it at Moose Lake. And as many critics have noted, the traces of Gillette's narrative are inscribed everywhere in Clyde's. The latter's unthinking use of his initials during the journey to Big Bittern Lake (Clifford Golden, Carl Graham), for instance, quickly leads his pursuers to an identification. Just as quickly, it leads us to identify Clyde with Chester Gillette, who also used his initials (as Carl Graham and Charles Gordon) to similar effect during his murder of Grace Brown. And although Clyde strikes with a camera rather than the tennis racket used by Gillette, we know that Clyde carries a tennis racket strapped to his case during the journey to Big Bittern (514). A trial witness's fuzzy recollection of what Clyde carries– "an umbrella it might have been" (705) – is the only other reference to this forgotten item. More than a quiet joke on Dreiser's part, the tennis racket functions like an obscure allusion out of Ezra Pound's *The Cantos*. Once the allusion is recognized as such it becomes suddenly multivalent, resonant, persuading us of a significance that is all the more authoritative because of its sudden limpidity.

Clyde and our interpretations of him seem caught, as ever, between conflicting but entangling narratives: on the one hand, the *Times-Union* report, which he consciously tries to follow, but may fail to reproduce, and on the other, the Gillette trial reports, of which he could not be aware, but which, if Roberta's death is not accidental, his story may profoundly resemble. How then do we situate Clyde within the traces and echoes of prior narrative structures and establish, once and for all, his difference? The key is that scene to which all of

Dreiser's critics sooner or later turn their attention: Roberta's death. The scene of her death has become one of the classic moments of plotlessness in American fiction, though, oddly, the scene is packed with specific detail; the camera, we know, strikes Roberta's "lips and nose and chin" (531), while her head, we note, does not strike but is struck by the "left wale of the boat as it turned." But we lack a larger framework within which each detail might take on a cumulative value. At a few crucial moments the narrative enforces no single reading of what "really happened" or of what Clyde was really thinking, a lack that is actually surprising given the detail and vitality of Dreiser's description. After the blow, for instance, we follow Roberta down into the water in a kind of slow-motion choreography whose every gesture and every pause seems precisely plotted. But those pauses – floating participles, disjointed phrases, weird syntax – are crucial. The narrative's hesitations are registered in phrasing like "he flinging out at her," "the camera still unconsciously held tight," and "the blow he had so accidentally and all but unconsciously administered" (531). Specificity of action and motivation vanish beneath the amorphousness of that "all but unconsciously" – as though "unconsciously" alone were still too determinate. As Clyde contemplates Roberta's veil clinging to a rowlock, his negative question articulates the doubt all readers must feel at this moment: "Will it not show that this was an accident?"

The scene focuses attention directly on the double sense of plot as a series of narrative actions and as a scheme motivated by criminal impulses, leading us to question the pertinence of either as a way of determining what really happened. Each different reading of motive, in fact, transforms our reading of plot. Judging the criminality of Clyde's scheme rests on our interpretation of the blow (did he strike out at Roberta?), while our interpretation of the blow rests on our apprehension of Clyde's motives (did he intend to strike her?). The scene at once foregrounds questions of plot (what really happened? did Clyde, at the end, intend to execute his plot of murder?) and holds each solution in abeyance, despite the fact that Clyde clearly did plot to kill Roberta. The death scene governs the unfolding of the subsequent text insofar as ensuing narratives about Clyde's plot constantly refer the reader to this moment as the gauge of their adequacy. Yet the scene does not authoritatively constrain future plots. It unplots subsequent versions, as it were, by refusing to authorize them, and thus allows for a proliferation of later narratives, each seeking to replot, comprehend (and sometimes obscure) the perceived events of Roberta's death.

Clyde's relationship to preceding narratives is correspondingly equivocal. For if a definitive description of how Clyde strikes Roberta with the camera is missing, we cannot definitively ascertain the nature of the resemblances between Clyde's plot and the *Times-Union* and Chester Gillette plots. In connection with the latter set of correspondences, Clyde senses that he is not as guilty as others suppose, but he cannot, in his final agonized meditations on his guilt, substantiate his suspicions. Clyde strikes Roberta with a camera; Gillette battered Grace Brown with a tennis racket; but beyond the difference in the implements of death lies only conjecture about the identity between Clyde and Gillette. That "all but unconsciously" does not preclude the possibility of lingering conscious intent by which to condemn him for executing the plan he has plotted all along. Despite the fact that Roberta's wounds seem less severe than those incurred by Grace Brown, the narrative leaves room for interpreting Clyde as every bit as much a murderer as Chester Gillette.

Thinking of the *Times-Union* report, conversely, Clyde ponders a "smooth, seemingly blameless, if dreadful, blotting out of two lives at Pass Lake" (479). I have suggested that Clyde could not knowingly reproduce a "plotless" and blameless accident; yet, remarkably, the scene of Roberta's death seems to afford just that possibility of a plot finally executed by circumstances standing in for an "all but unconscious" Clyde. "Yet," observes the narrator, "(the camera still unconsciously held tight) pushing at her with so much vehemence" – a fragment that foregrounds the camera as the object and somehow the agent of striking. We must read Clyde back into this scene, first as the one who holds the camera tight and then as the one "pushing" it at Roberta, but syntactically the camera has eclipsed its putative holder. In one sense, we must read the death scene as we and Clyde read the *Times-Union* report, which is to say by way of registering lacunae and then in some way negotiating them into significance. The *Times-Union* report, after all, provides an unexpectedly wide range of interpretations. As Clyde quickly realizes, the Pass Lake drownings may have been murder – "might it not be possible that that man had gone there with that girl in order to get rid of her?" (479). Or might the man have survived after a pure accident and run from the suspicion of murder? Because the newspaper report, for all its specificity about the discovery of the body and about the couple's appearance, lacks crucial evidence about motive and action, it is just as logical to assume that the man murders as that he dies along with the woman. In that case we cannot confirm the correspondences between the Pass Lake accident/murder and the Big Bittern Lake accident/murder. Nor, and for the same reasons, can we ever deny them.

Dreiser constantly invites us to distinguish (in Lehan's term) a "sentimentalized" (1971, 149) Clyde from preceding plotters of murder while refusing to guarantee the legitimacy of those distinctions. What we do know is that the three drownings at Pass Lake, Big Bittern, and Moose Lake are homologous, bound by a correspondence of event if not motive: the apparent death of both occupants of the boat, the straw hat floating on the water, the upturned rowboat. Actions undertaken by Clyde (such as the choice of a camera to strike Roberta) merely assume a new place within that familiar narrative structure; each original event of Clyde's life reveals an ever-shifting relationship to patterns already played out and, it seems, infinitely renewable. Prior narratives establish contingencies, if not the shape of those contingencies. Even if we were to establish some unique act of Clyde's, that is, it could only be in the context of the recurring narratives of commonplace murders already committed. Striking Roberta with the camera only becomes a unique detail, worthy of distinguishing Clyde from Chester Gillette, once we have invoked the Gillette murder and made sense of it as a model Dreiser investigated and then put behind him. Whether we accuse Dreiser of "cold-blooded plagiarism" or insist on his work of refashioning, we must somewhere figure in that un/original material and view it not as compromising but as uncompromisingly present, intransigent, and pervasive.

V

Clyde Griffiths's story, then, is neither Chester Gillette's nor that of the man at Pass Lake nor that of the unspecified people in the "similar accident" which took place fifteen years before. Nor is it *not* those stories. Clyde possesses, as it were, an interstitial existence and interwoven voice. He is born out of the newspapers, speaks in their voices and refashions their plots, is rewritten by the mass media during the trial, yet remains weakly aware of an appropriation he can never articulate and of a plot of which he is captive rather than author. That process by which the structures of mass society shape and colonize Clyde, casting into doubt the extent of his private voice, autonomous self, and unique actions, represents figuratively the reading of *An American Tragedy* I have outlined here. The contingencies and constraints Clyde experiences are inscribed into this text as a repertoire of strategies for betraying its dependency on the formulaic and repetitive: that which is always being spoken rather than that which pretends to be unique. Writing that cannot be assimilated to any standard of good style; a derivative plot; a sensationalistic story that unconscionably prolongs its newspaper antecedents; and, as the most dramatic sign of inauthenticity, material cold-bloodedly plagiarized from newspaper reports – all of these possible readings of the novel mark the points at which Dreiser's text refuses to be quietly assimilated to familiar strategies of literature making. The novel, in other words, goes further than most canonical texts toward immersing itself within the world it purportedly examines; at best we view the novel as a thoroughgoing disruption of incorporated material; at worst, we hover on the brink of writing off the story as a mere reproduction.

But it is precisely Dreiser's brinkmanship that lies at the heart of my reading of the novel. His tactics suggest the problematic of human identity and the dilemma of the writer working within a mass society. Dreiser's accommodatory tactics, pushed to the limit, flesh out a strategy necessary to his depiction of an identity thoroughly invested and characterized by the voices of mass society. And that strategy leads to the inwoven, relational, contingent, inclusive text of which Clyde's narrative voice is only one part. The kind of deliberate framing we saw in Henry James's *The Reverberator* (whereby certain modes of understanding were bracketed off as inferior) is in this novel discontinuous, fuzzy, and perplexing. Reading *An American Tragedy* thus becomes a process of being confronted with unassimilated, inchoate material out of mass culture and sensing the difficulty of framing and rewriting it to make it appear manifestly "other"; we hesitate, while experiencing how mass idioms relentlessly appropriate the field of discourse, to recognize too easily and thus hypostatize Dreiser's contextualizing frames. To read the novel is to enter a border region between the already shifting and hazy categories of literature and mass culture. It involves a process of negotiation with the text and its fragile, uneasy fashioning of differences, a process that resists easy and premature closure.

To read *An American Tragedy* is to experience the constraining power of stories that constantly affirm their contingency on prior stories, yet also to experience an often baffling indeterminacy about the nature of that contingency. The novel calls attention to its determining narratives in a process that liberates where we might expect constraint (because prior stories do not explain Roberta's death), yet constrains where we might expect liberation (because of the impossibility of stabilizing differences from prior stories). The problem with those studies that seek to set Dreiser free from his scandalous reliance on mass culture is that they move too far toward making the novel determinate. Pointing to the clear distinctions between the category of media stories and Dreiser's (superior) fiction, they determine, as it were, the shape of his plot of murder. Yet Dreiser's narrative is never determinate. Its dependence on mass media fictions compromises its difference from them, and the nonplot of Clyde's plot at the moment of Roberta's death convinces us that the actual extent of that compromise cannot be accurately ascertained. Imprisoned in a world of texts, Clyde's habit in prison of "reading and re-reading the newspapers" seems illustrative of his plight, as if he is less in search of his self than his self's story – yet never, in his rereading, finding the true shape of that story. Clyde's experience, as so often in *An American Tragedy,* is pertinent to our own.

That problematization of the frame – that persistent uncertainty about just where Dreiser begins that process of transforming source material into the unique and original – ultimately enforces a reexamination of our own critical strategies, of which critics tend to be as unconscious as Clyde of his sources. All kinds of criticisms may be, and have been, leveled at *An American Tragedy* and all kinds of (often mutually contradictory) defenses aimed at restoring or defending the text's value may be, and have been, employed. Jurnak and Davidson, Pizer, Fishkin, and Moers all recognize certain similarities between Dreiser's work and mass culture in order to assimilate them into a larger framework of critique which has the effect of subjugating that source material. Readings of Dreiser that seek to interfere in these patterns of similarity are not neutral but critical and cultural strategies for bestowing authority on Dreiser's text; they achieve this effect by employing a powerful structural dynamic within the adjudicating and legitimating bodies of the university. *An American Tragedy,* I have suggested, questions and puts in doubt the certainty of assimilative readings; it represents a rough-edged accommodation rather than an assimilation of mass culture. But that is not to deny the power of assimilative readings. The ones I have mentioned are intellectually honest and cogent studies that feed off and consolidate a crucial premise of critical discourse. By perpetuating the authoritative name of Dreiser as an institution within the academic institution, they clear the way for the kind of reading I follow here. Indeed, in a sense I have arrived at as unsurprising a conclusion as the rest; far from overturning conventional wisdom about Theodore Dreiser I have merely increased that store. Invoking the indeterminacy of Dreiser's work, after all, is to rescue it from its source material just as effectively as those who assume that the presence of that material can be gracefully argued away – and perhaps more effectively, since the principle of indeterminacy opens a space between Dreiser's work and mass culture which, if it can now never be guaranteed, can also never be finally closed.

This chapter began with Dreiser's attempt to consolidate the writer's professional standing and ends with professional critics reading the novel that gave rise to the suit. In a sense we have come full circle – from the shuffling of professional identities that characterized Dreiser's suit to the powerful but still relatively unconscious critical strategies promulgated within the academy. We no longer need to go to court to defend the artistic integrity of *An American Tragedy;* that happens in critical debates carried forward in specialized circles within the university, invisible and silent to the majority of the population. The mechanisms and apparatuses that allow this process of literature fashioning, however, are nascent in Dreiser's suit. The formation of communities of competence and expertise, present in Dreiser's "jury," come to be developed most powerfully within the academy. And his attempt to identify Von Sternberg's movie with crass trivialization (or perhaps to disallow its dynamic, creative potential) in favor of his own original and authentic work comes to find new life in our strategies of "writing off" mass cultural material. In a sense, Dreiser's overt tactics for legitimating literature have gone underground, disseminated among a multiplicity of texts, few of which agree on how to read Dreiser but all of which form part of a textual body whose aim is to legitimate certain texts, exclude others, and moreover inscribe those exclusions and legitimations into discursive practices. In the case of *An American Tragedy,* simply because its immersion in those obtrusively nonliterary sources, we see the full force of critical mechanisms on display. The accusation by Paramount's attorney that Dreiser cold-bloodedly plagiarized material from mass culture is one professional's piece of sophistry and it provides us with an intriguing thesis. But his condemnation of the novel seems too decided and inflexible. In the highly organized but also highly negotiable territory of critical discourse one can always enter a surreptitious wedge to recuperate the literary and thus assimilate and silence that which is other, even though the shape of that other changes radically in the give and take of critical negotiations.

5

Reading John Dos Passos Reading Mass Culture in U.S.A.

*"It's not the name you give things, it's who's getting
theirs underneath that counts. . . ."*

Edgar Robbins in *1919*

In the same year that Theodore Dreiser took Paramount to trial (1931), Dreiser and John Dos Passos met up to promote the cause of Harlan County miners during their bloody and ultimately futile strike against the mine owners. Neither writer placed any great significance on their meeting, though its aftermath was oddly typical of their characters. Dreiser just escaped standing trial for adultery, while Dos Passos was asked by the Communist Party leadership to stand trial in Harlan County to test the free speech laws – and refused (Ludington 1980, 297–300). But though Dreiser and Dos Passos avoided the courtroom on this occasion, other inevitable courtroom dramas can be traced within the history and the narrative composition of their novels *An American Tragedy* and *U.S.A.*. For murderous plots lie at the inception of both Dreiser's and John Dos Passos's narratives. The trial of Chester Gillette, as we have seen, sparked Dreiser's exploration of recursive narrative structures. In Dos Passos's case, the Sacco and Vanzetti murders – or rather the state's murder of the innocent anarchists – prompted his analysis of a nation torn by political and economic strife. Both Dreiser and Dos Passos were familiar with the pertinent trial documents. Dos Passos thoroughly researched the murder trial, taking the trouble to talk to Sacco and Vanzetti and other key witnesses before adding material of his own to the case, most notably a monograph-length pamphlet entitled *Facing the Chair* (1927) and several articles. Their publication occurred as the first jotted ideas for *The 42nd Parallel* appear in his private notes. Nearly ten years later, the anarchists face the chair once again in the final Camera Eye sections of *The Big Money*. As Clyde Griffiths's trial and execution situate him within the anterior press reports of Gillette's celebrated case, so do the anarchists reappear, near the conclusion of *The Big Money,* within the trilogy their deaths inspired.

As thoroughly as newspaper reports invest the character of Clyde Griffiths, the Sacco and Vanzetti trials identify and expose a logocentric and text-pervaded society. In Dos Passos's article "The Pit and the Pendulum," written after visiting Sacco and Vanzetti in 1926, he notes that the "real world has gone":

> We have no more grasp of our world of rain and streets and trolleycars and cucumbervines and girls and gardenplots. This is a world of phrases, *prosecution, defence, evidence, motion, irrelevant, incompetent* and *immaterial*. For six years this man has lived in the law, tied tighter and tighter in the sticky filaments of law-words like a fly in a spiderweb. And the wrong set of words means the Chair. All the moves in the game are made for him, all he can do is sit helpless and wait, fastening his hopes on one set of phrases after another. (1988a, 89)

In "The Pit and the Pendulum" world Dos Passos depicts there appears to be no "real world" apart from language: no cucumbers apart from that neologism "cucumbervines" and no existence for Sacco and Vanzetti apart from "law-words," "lawbooks," and "one set of phrases after another." Living "in the law" sounds ironic, to be sure, but the phrase embodies a profound insight: It is to survive (or to live a living death) within a lexicon; and that lexicon penetrates out beyond the jail walls. Systems of words signifying systems of power infiltrate every aspect of this society, forming interlocking hierarchies of wealth and class: an Anglo-Saxon supremacy whose members enunciate with a "broad A" lest they lose their status to "men who spoke broken English" (88); anarchists who lie losing out to the police who lie about them more powerfully; witnesses who swear they saw Vanzetti elsewhere at the time of the robbery but whose testimony is discounted by the judge because of their alien culture and language; and those "law-words" that subordinate "literature that might be interpreted as subversive" (86). Language, as much as people, must be annexed, regulated, and controlled according to the "lexicon" by those in power. Thus "people had even been arrested for distributing the Declaration of Independence" (86); Andrea Salsedo, an anarchist printer, was arrested and tortured for eight weeks before jumping (or being pushed) to his death, causing radical friends like Sacco and Vanzetti "to hide pamphlets and newspapers"; and the pair are arrested with handbills on them announcing a protest meeting for Salsedo. Vanzetti, who was to be a speaker at that meeting, is "grilled" and effectively silenced, his speech supplanted by Boston laywer William G. Thompson, who in turn "wishes he were well out of it" (91). Later, according to Dos Passos's account, due process of law somehow excludes the words of a gang member named Madeiros, who confessed from his jail cell to the murders for which Sacco and Vanzetti are to be executed. Everywhere words are constrained and enmeshed within a thorough and arbitrary seeming seizure of language. Signifiers are separated from their signifieds: "guilty" attaches to the innocent, and "the wrong set of words means the Chair." The anarchists are manipulated by incomprehensible latinate law words and subjected by way of euphemism: "grilled," the "third degree," "the Chair." In a world of floating signifiers, the emptying of language signifies the presence of power systems working anarchically (as it were) to disrupt certainties, to enforce the hiding of radical literature, to force the speakers from their podiums. And yet, because these systems split the true anarchists from their freedom – Sacco from his finely worked garden, Vanzetti from his fish cart – they make suddenly visible the relationships of power that presumably were there all along. In prison, Dos Passos relates, Sacco "has learned to speak and to write English, has read many books" (89). Sacco learns English living "in the law" – the living embodiment of a grammar, syntax, and vocabulary composed and sedimented by the regulatory mechanisms of American society.

When Dos Passos returns to Sacco and Vanzetti's deaths near the end of *The Big Money,* it is to affirm the inextricability of power and speech, but also to reach an unexpected conclusion. Camera Eyes (49) and (50) register a series of grim appropriations by "strangers who have turned our language inside out who have taken the clean words our fathers spoke and made them slimy and foul." These strangers are quickly identified as Americans – "lawyers districtattorneys collegepresidents judges" – and the ensuing Biography of William Randolph Hearst ("Poor Little Rich Boy") demonstrates the complicity of the mass media in this fouling of language. But in the process of defining this linguistic appropriation, Dos Passos manages to reclaim the territory thought lost and to suggest the possibility of redefining the relationship between language and power. Crucially, he restores in very un-Dreiserian fashion a sense of linguistic and ideological origins. Whereas Dreiser's novel referred back through a pattern of recurring stories to obscure, and in any case irretrievable, origins, rewriting in *U.S.A.* functions to put readers in the presence of an original "speech" against which other utterances must be measured. In Camera Eye (50), for instance, the imminent deaths of Sacco and Vanzetti call forth the "old American speech of the haters of oppression," which is made "new tonight in the mouth of an old woman from Pittsburgh . . . in the mouth of a Back Bay socialworker in the mouth of an Italian Printer of a hobo from Arkansas." Speaking in tongues, hobo, printer, old woman, and social worker become mediums for a speech that transcends both individuality and the limited historical moment. It is not that their speech possesses a firsthand originality but that they subsume – rather like Dreiser's desire that Von Sternberg subsume the original text of *An American Tragedy* – the conditions, the frames of reference, the self-identical meanings of the first founders of the United States written into the Declaration of Independence and the Constitution. Their speech is truly original insofar as it puts them in touch with a true starting point at which an infinitely renewable political entity and defining discourse was created.

It would not be difficult to read in the trajectory between "The Pit and the Pendulum" and the conclusion of *The Big Money* a familiar narrative of Dos Passos's career, signalled in the images used by many critics to describe his "path," his "odyssey," his "search" for U.S.A. as both nation and novel (Landsberg 1972; Ludington 1980; Wagner 1979). Their narrative of Dos Passos's involvement with radical politics between about 1927 and 1932, his growing disenchantment with those politics (and the Communist Party in particular), and his gradual shift to the values and ideals of Jeffersonian democracy by the end of the 1930s is a compelling one. Camera Eyes (49) and (50), for instance – grim as they are – may be read as a fundamental rejection of the vision embodied in "The Pit and the Pendulum," whereby a free play of signifiers allowed certain structures of power to lawfully regulate every aspect of society. So "the wrong set of words means the Chair" but "the right move ... the right words" (89) are *also* a function of the "sticky filaments" of this spiderweb, yet another move in a Kafkaesque game. By the end of *The Big Money,* the game has become a function of an original speech; that speech has taken priority. America has been beaten by "strangers who have turned our language inside out," yet Sacco and Vanzetti's deaths turn it outside in; the "clean words our fathers spoke" are not diminished but renewed in a moment of transcendence for the hobo, printer, and social worker. It is no longer a question of living "in the law" that works its way into every word and moment of perception, coopting wrong words and right words alike, but of being able to perceive the lawless operations of those who exercise power. Indeed, the very exercise of power seems to have revealed the process by which the clean words were besmirched and the old words ruined, and that revelation in turn seems to have closed down the machinery that operates the process. The rulers (rather than the foreigners of "The Pit and the Pendulum") have become *other* ("strangers") and their laws have become in one sense marginal, supererogatory and, above all, suspect. Their laws turn out to be misreadings of Law, which they may appropriate (as they appropriate the law words and law books that bind Sacco "like a fly in a spiderweb") but never fully coopt.

In this respect, Dos Passos's vision of the anarchists is telling. "The Pit and the Pendulum" situated them as anarchists within a specific historical context; indeed, Dos Passos insisted that a prime condition of their wrongful arrest was a blind misunderstanding of what their anarchic beliefs really signified. Dos Passos attempted to describe some of that historical and cultural context, from their antiwar protests to the mundane facts of their culture. Hence the "fact that so many people testified to having bought eels [from Vanzetti] was considered very suspicious by the court that did not know that the eating of eels on the last day before Christmas is an Italian custom of long standing" (87). But Camera Eyes (49) and (50) transform Sacco and Vanzetti into contemporary Christ figures: The narrator's search for truth reminds him of Pontius Pilate, Sacco he significantly calls a "fishpeddler," and he describes both Sacco and Vanzetti as betrayed, falsely accused, and executed. As Christ figures they transcend history; their deaths return speech and consciousness to the "beaten nation." And if it is true that "without the old words the immigrants haters of oppression brought to

Plymouth how can you know who are your betrayers America" it could no longer be said that their deaths were even unnecessary. Their new status thus reverses the earlier vision of a body politic thoroughly invested with legality and reveals a new horizon of significance. Far from living "in the law," the law must have always lived in them; far from being the victim of others' secret moves, they were the master strategists. The erstwhile anarchists, like the "old words" their deaths renew, are finally restored to a place outside history and culture, but from which history and culture might be built anew.

Persuasive as this reading of a gradual orientation to an immutable Law may sound in the light of the familiar view of Dos Passos's growing conservatism, it is a fragmentary and partial one that does scant justice to the shape of Dos Passos's career or to the complex discursive operations within which Dos Passos's work was written, received, and is now read anew. In fact this reading seems at odds with, or does not fully explicate, key features of the trilogy. First, Dos Passos's observations about the totalizing nature of mass communications, the mass media, and other systems of consciousness control strongly suggest that there is – or should be – no transcendent, nonmanipulated, free perspective from which to make such observations. Questions of Dos Passos's reading of mass culture, his analysis of its power, and our reading of his analysis thus become crucial. Second, given that the *U.S.A.* trilogy seems to document the increasing powerlessness of the writer, we must ask what forms of authority Dos Passos's text asks for, activates in its readers, and achieves. Once again, this will involve not only a reading of Dos Passos's accommodatory tactics but of critics reading Dos Passos's text. How, in other words, have critics recognized and lent the support of their rhetoric and their institutions to the literary qualities of *U.S.A.?* How have they participated in shaping those qualities and what forms does that shaping consistently take? The title of this chapter places emphasis on just that operation of recognizing and abstracting what is legitimate and meaningful from Dos Passos's own readings of mass society; it indicates a complicity of methodology and intent that critics rarely confront. Such a double reading is particularly rewarding in the case of Dos Passos. It enables us to focus again on the question of interpretive perspectives. Most importantly, it enables us to scrutinize the nature of the professional ties that bind his novel to our critical and institutional perspectives. Out of this discussion a wholly new configuration of Dos Passos's career emerges, one that rests on the professional ethos that informs so much of his writing but that is so often subordinated to discussions of his liberalism or his radical politics. I will suggest, in fact, that we tend to miss the profound significance of Dos Passos's professionalism precisely – though paradoxically – because our own professional affiliations allow us to read his work *too easily.* We share enough discursive premises with Dos Passos that key structural identities to do with the legitimation of the individual voice within a mass society are routinely ignored. Thus, although I question what has always appeared unquestionable in Dos Passos's narrative strategies, particularly his use of irony and the meaning of the Newsreel sections, I conclude this chapter by returning to some of the secret bonds between professional writer and professional critic. That discussion, of course, will not become public but – like Dos Passos's trilogy – reinvested as "symbolic capital" within a closed professional field.

I

Early in *The 42nd Parallel* Mac's Uncle Tim, a printer, purchases a new linotype machine, an event that causes a temporary stoppage of work, speeds up the work of printing, and then indirectly leads to the eventual closure of Uncle Tim's business. The new press possesses an undeniable power. "For a whole day there was no work done," the narrator remarks. "Everyone stood around looking at the tall black intricate machine that stood there like an organ in a church. When the machine was working and the printshop filled with the hot smell of molten metal, everybody's eyes followed the quivering inquisitive arm that darted and flexed above the keyboard" ([1938] 1978, 31).[1] The linotype seems to focus the accumulated values of more than a century of a revolutionary democracy built on the constitutional guarantee of free speech, rational inquiry into the nature and abuses of political systems, and the free dissemination of printed knowledge. It allows Uncle Tim to articulate his beliefs and distribute them in the shape of a handbill entitled "An Ernest Protest" and signed "A Citizen." It seems the apogee of the Enlightenment. Yet the small printing press, even as the workers stare at it in awe, has already become an anachronism, more suitable for some museum charting the transformations of American industry – as the workers' first awestruck response perhaps suggests. For during a strike in the printing trades the master printers of Chicago buy out Uncle Tim's outstanding paper and force him into bankruptcy. And that silencing is foreshadowed by Mac's failure to distribute Uncle Tim's handbills when a cop asks to see the permit Mac does not possess.[2] By the end of the trilogy that printing press seems as ancient as a Gothic cathedral, its intricacy supplanted by massive electronic systems of communication and the even more intricate systems of corporate capital that support them.

Taken as a whole, the *U.S.A.* trilogy documents in unprecedented detail the formation of interlocking structures of power at the turn of the century. As the preface (added after Dos Passos completed the trilogy) suggests, U.S.A. is "a group of holding companies, some aggregations of trade unions, a set of laws bound in calf, a radio network, a chain of moving picture theatres, a column of stockquotations." No one person masterminds this process of progressive ag-glomeration; no one person is truly responsible for locating and defining centers of power, arranging relays, and overseeing the entire system. In this respect Dos Passos's understanding of power is structuralist and close to Michel Foucault's sense of power as invisible, pervasive, secret, and autonomous. The consecutive biographies of Thomas Edison ("The Electrical Wizard") and Charles Proteus

Steinmetz ("Proteus") in *The 42nd Parallel* are crucial to this vision. In "Proteus," Steinmetz's mathematical equations make possible "all the transformers that crouch in little boxes and gableroofed houses in all the hightension lines all over everywhere. The mathematical symbols of Steinmetz's law are the patterns of all transformers everywhere." Presumably, those electrical transformers also represent the human transformers of American society. Steinmetz, as his middle name and Dos Passos's title for the biography suggests, is one such transformer, imbued with the power to change the face of America "all over everywhere." Thomas Edison, who brings invention to bear on Steinmetz's formulas in order to produce "systems of generation, distribution, regulation and measurement of electric current, sockets, switches, insulators," is described as another such magician in "The Electrical Wizard." His seminal work on the movie camera sets up the Hollywood dream merchants, who would within a few years work their own protean transformations on the American imagination.

By the end of *The Big Money,* abstract systems of mathematical representation transformed into material systems for generating and distributing power are transformed back into the abstract systems of capital. In "Power Superpower," Samuel Insull's equally intricate and equally baffling regulation of capital operates by similarly delicate mechanisms. "It has been figured out," the narrator tells us, "that one dollar in Middle West Utilities controlled seventeen hundred and fifty dollars invested by the public in the subsidiary companies that actually did the work of producing electricity. With the delicate lever of a voting trust controlling the stock of the two top holdingcompanies he controlled a twelfth of the power output of America." As Dos Passos puts it nicely in the biography of "The House of Morgan," this architecture of power operates on "the cantilever principle, through interlocking directorates." Insull called it "superpower"; yet "superpower," Insull's biography makes abundantly clear, controls him. At one point Insull panics for fear of losing his delicate leverage; after the stock market crash he becomes a "tottering czar," his power dissolving into the confusion of his business affairs. "Insull's companies," despite his vaunted sense of control, "were intertwined in a tangle that no bookkeeper has ever been able to unravel." The invisible structures that make possible his extravagant thieving, however, outlast him. Samuel Insull, far from being the great villain of "Power Superpower," seems its last great human architect; he seems the last human sign of the presence of power. In its protracted and comic account of Insull's attempts to escape justice, the biography hovers between satirizing Insull and presenting him as larger than life; it traces a trajectory from "superpower" to the tale of a rascally but charismatic "deposed monarch." As if in tacit recognition of the all-pervading invisibility of "superpower," the biography's colorful finale silences it. Superpower is not removed with the person of Insull; it continues on to invest the vacancy his removal creates.

But if the biography depicts an architect progressively overwhelmed by the cantilever structures he has never quite controlled, it is perhaps surprising that

Insull masterfully interacts with the news media. This is nowhere more apparent than during his trial which, as the narrator remarks with a touch of dry Hemingwayesque humor, "was very beautiful." Unlike the grim story of Sacco and Vanzetti's trials and executions, partially played out in the accompanying Camera Eye sections, the Insulls "stole the show." They "smiled at reporters, they posed for photographers" and are eulogized by the newspapers; in a final lugubrious analogy to the Sacco-Vanzetti case, thousands of ruined investors supposedly sit "crying over the home editions at the thought of how Mr. Insull had suffered." Interestingly, Insull's career change from manipulator to "deposed monarch" is accomplished without direct manipulation on his part. "When the handouts stopped" directly after Insull's resignation, the narrator tells us, the "newspapers and politicians turned on him." But the newspapers, it seems, are not bound in any conspiracy at the trial. They offer aid gratis; they participate in the creation of a grand pseudoevent – all the more dramatic after the odyssey of Insull's Mediterranean escape from justice was played out before the news media; and they do so out of consent rather than coercion. Like William Randolph Hearst, whose biography precedes Insull's, Insull understands how to cash in on "geewhizz emotion" (1112). The narrator portrays his Horatio Alger tale of his "struggle to make good, his love for his home and the kiddies," the fiction of his "honest errors," his strategy of becoming just "folks," as more than just lying of Odyssean proportions. The newspapers' unwitting complicity with ideologies that underpin American middle-class consciousness – father, big man, poor boy made good, the underdog – plays a major role in Insull's show. Dos Passos's rather Gramscian insight is that consent of such a wide-ranging and spectacular nature cannot be merely bought or engineered; it must in some fashion already exist, woven inextricably into the nation's psychosocial fabric.

Mass communication in America does not simply function by way of conspiracy; the conspirators themselves participate in an interlocked system of power "all over everywhere" that is not only too complex to be grasped by any individual but is fundamentally structural: Any individual seeking to understand it is always in the position of having been constituted and embedded within it. Dos Passos's trilogy thus concerns the largely silent functioning of the unconscious "transparent" domain of ideology, to which the mass of Americans consent as inalienably true and real. For every hired newspaper editor there is one (such as the one who fires Mary French) who just dislikes foreign-born strikers; for all the power of Hearst's empire of print, there are movie actresses and political careers (his own) he cannot launch and wars he cannot initiate (1116). Unexpected resistances arise out of a mass mind whose dynamic its would-be manipulators do not clearly understand. Nevertheless, Dos Passos is acutely aware that technicians of mass consciousness work most powerfully and completely at the unconscious level. The biography of Steinmetz provides an early analysis of this issue. The biography appraises Steinmetz's role in the formation of vast industrial systems depending on a ubiquitous power grid; but is is General Electric that at once makes his discoveries significant and makes significance of his discoveries. "General Electric humored him, let him be a Socialist . . . and the publicity department talked up the wizard, the medicine man who knew the symbols that opened up the doors of Ali Baba's cave . . . the publicity department poured oily stories into the ears of the American public every Sunday and Steinmetz became the little parlor magician." He "became" the little parlor magician, that is, to the serpent-tongued PR men and to the deceived public. "Became" attributes to him a presence and solidity he does not possess (for he does not really become a magician) but also, oddly enough, underplays his far-reaching significance to General Electric as "the most valuable piece of apparatus" they had. Among varied representations of him (little parlor magician, Socialist, wizard, medicine man), Steinmetz disappears as a human being to emerge as the linking apparatus between the power grid and structures of ideological manipulation. It is with some irony, then, that the "mathematical symbols of Steinmetz's law are the patterns of all transformers everywhere," for the publicity department transforms his abstract mathematical symbols into a world of symbolic representations, and the wizardry of technology into a magical hocus-pocus.

This leads to a double consequence. Neither Steinmetz nor (presumably) the publicity department's public recognizes this radical disembodying of significance, this gradual warping of incalculable technological changes into a weightless rhetoric suitable for fairy tales. The PR man's "open sesame" to Ali Baba's cave of riches depends on foreclosing precisely that relationship between Steinmetz's abstract symbols and the power grab it occasioned. To extend Dos Passos's own figure of speech, talking up Steinmetz as magician is also to "talk around" him. And it has the further advantage, no doubt, of disguising the whereabouts of the forty (or more) thieves, who hide now behind "oily stories" rather than in empty jars of oil. But though the PR rhetoric masks from the public all knowledge of a crystallizing structure of power, that rhetoric, we should note, also creates a rich, dense, symbolic language to which *The Thousand and One Nights* may after all be an appropriate analogy. The publicity department, like Scheherazade, spins out stories to stave off the moment of death (or discovery); more importantly, their stories possess the kind of imaginative power most readers do associate with literature. In this sense, Dos Passos grants mass communication the kind of totalizing power we saw in Dreiser's *An American Tragedy* while posing the possibility that its idiom might be dramatic and entertaining rather than banal. Although the primary goal of the PR department is to work by way of a series of disengagements to pry apart language and its underlying formation of power, it captures Steinmetz in a free play of signifiers that is all the more dazzling for an ostensible plenitude of meaning. Steinmetz's menagerie of gila monsters and alligators plays off his physical deformity and oddly intensifies his charisma, while his "greenhouseful of cactuses lit up by mercury lights" pays homage to his own power of genesis and (electrical) generation; at the same time, the very extravagance of these hobbies suggests their essential triviality. The publicity department engineers him and language alike. Its signifiers lead to hidden signifieds: wizard (protean transformations, authority); gila monsters (an alien power, yet also perhaps dangerous, needing to be leashed); talking crows (Steinmetz was a Socialist who made "speeches that nobody understood"). The PR men brilliantly dramatize him as wizard yet diminish him as a little parlor magician firmly under the company's control.

In *U.S.A.*, the fictional J. Ward Moorehouse, counterpart to real-life publicity departments and Hearstian appropriations of the press, and based on the real PR man Ivy Lee, is the arbiter of this world of sliding, disembodied, yet powerful images and meanings. Class orator and essayist, book distributor, reporter and erstwhile songwriter, Moorehouse is responsible for the "molding of the public mind" (1145) and for nothing less than a new poetics of history, politics, and technology. Early in his career, for instance, we find Moorehouse puzzling "over what kind of literature from a factory would be appealing to him." He

> would see long processions of andirons, grates, furnaces, fittings, pumps, sausage-grinders, drills, calipers, vises, casters, drawerpulls pass between his face and the mirror and wonder how they could be made attractive to the retail trade. He was shaving himself with a Gillette; why was he shaving with a Gillette instead of some other kind of razor? 'Bessemer' was a good name, smelt of money and mighty rolling mills and great executives stepping out of limousines. (214)

Moorehouse neatly characterizes a number of advertising strategies. Not surprisingly, he associates products with concepts, seizing on archetypal images from the mass psychology of capitalism to spark a relationship made and apprehended, on the whole, unconsciously. Thus Moorehouse "smells" the value of Bessemer as a good name rather than intellectually defining its appeal. Images of the status to which Americans aspire, or should aspire, invest Moorehouse's lively dramas: tools in celebratory procession, almost as if cast in a Disney cartoon, and great executives stepping out of limousines. Moorehouse's colorfully spliced fragments of action – name, money, mills, executives, cars – suggests his intuitive grasp of a covert and interior relationship to power. And the very crudity of his imagination points, paradoxically, to a formal sophistication he does not know he possesses. One thinks of Dada, cubist collage, surrealism: arts of disruption, eschewing traditional logics of perspective, connectivity, and narrative for the immediacy of upwelling fantasies and the vibrant interval between juxtaposed images. One thinks of that modernist predilection for the primitive and of the Poundian "vortex," functioning, like Moorehouse's hard, concrete images, to create whirlpools of associative imagery. And one thinks of Dos Passos's own writing strategies, to which Moorehouse's intuitive mythmaking bears a curious affinity. Moorehouse carries other poetic credentials, too. A little later, on a train bound for Chicago, he eulogizes American industry like some latter-day Whitman or Shelley, his words coming in a spontaneous eruption as though he were more medium than orator:

> The rumble of the train made the cords of his voice vibrate. He forgot everything in his own words . . . American industry like a steamengine, like a highpower locomotive on a great express train charging through the night of the old individualistic methods . . . What does a steamengine require? Co-operation, co-ordination of the inventor's brain, the pro-moter's brain that made the development of these highpower products possible . . . Co-ordination of capital, the storedup energy of the race in the form of credit intelligently directed. (227; Dos Passos's ellipses)

These passages, the first in which Moorehouse meditates seriously on his PR work, initiates an increasing uncertainty about just how nonliterary his "litera-ture from a factory" really is, and just how much to scorn his secretary, Janey, who admires the office's "literature about bathsalts and chemicals and the employees' baseball team" (279). Dos Passos defines much more clearly than James or Dreiser a new visionary company whose tactics really do draw on the stock of imaginings, images, and formal strategies thought to be the preserve of literary work. That debased sense of literature as "written material" quickly becomes subject to revision as we see Moorehouse's tactics colliding with and overlapping Dos Passos's at every step. Dos Passos's concern is U.S.A., "the speech of the people" (7); Moorehouse's is to use words as a form of capital, vast systems mediating the "storedup energy of the race" (227) and tapping energy from the main conduits of the American psyche. Moorehouse also imaginatively invests language with powerful symbolic meanings; indeed, those meanings must already and always have invested him. Moorehouse puts us in mind of William Randolph Hearst at Manila Bay, who "brandishing a sixshooter went in with the longboat through the surf and captured twentysix unarmed halfdrowned Spanish sailors on the beach and forced them to kneel and kiss the American flag/in front of the camera" (1113). The point is not that Hearst's cowboy heroics and the resulting dramatic tableau before the recording camera are false, for powerful collective emotions like patriotism and a desire for military power here find appropriate expression.

That process of capitalizing on language works, not because of the manipula-tions necessary to disguise the appropriation of language and the usurping of its true functions, but because of what is genuine and (as George Flack put it in *The Reverberator*) "straight from the tap." At the level at which images and words flow unbidden from a reservoir of largely unconscious impulses, desires, and beliefs, public relations and Flack's journalism become commanding idioms. Thus Manila Bay is not a "pseudo-event" in Daniel Boorstin's sense of the term as a spectacle staged for the benefit of the media, and therefore incomplete, false, empty. The staging does not invalidate the spectacle; like Moorehouse's fantasies of mighty rolling mills and limousines, these formal strategies of association, juxtaposition, and dramatic "retailing" of images (to use the pun Dos Passos often employs on retail/retell) are evocative and powerful. To call Manila Bay a pseudo-event is to ignore a new poetics that does not record history but imaginatively refashions it. Indeed, this form of historiography, whereby the recording eye is not viewed as trans- or ahistorical but itself part of the onrush of events has become increasingly common in the twentieth century, Dos Passos's own Camera Eye sections being the obvious analogy. This is not to say that Moorehouse and Hearst cannot be attacked, but that the hollowness we attribute to them should not be confused with the dramatic power of their fiction making. Put simply, the problem we face in uncovering the hollowness of Hearst at Manila Bay is not that the event is banal but *that it is dramatic.*

II

Moorehouse and company thus overlap what we might conceive of as Dos Passos's own imaginative terrain. But we have yet to define the nature and extent of the accommodatory strategies that frame and rewrite the ostensibly unassailable voices of mass culture and thus compel us to transform a series of correspondences into relationships of difference. Because of that omission, the preceding discussion has emphasized the totalizing nature of mass communications at the expense of their limitations. This seems a paradox, for a language, perspective, or system cannot be said to be total if it allows the presence of alternative or transcendent points of view. But a version of this paradox does present itself in *U.S.A.* We have seen that the trilogy presents the mass media and J. Ward Moorehouse's public relations work as though they exercised the insistent, totalizing effect of Dreiser's *An American Tragedy* or the pervasive "living in the law" of Dos Passos's essay "The Pit and the Pendulum." As Dos Passos writes of the movies in "Poor Little Rich Boy," "the empire of the printed word continues powerful by the inertia of bigness; but this power over the dreams/of the adolescents of the world/grows and poisons like a cancer"; the "warmedover daydreams" of the masses are churned out in a blinding "opiate haze." J. Ward Moorehouse's task is to disseminate those opiates; he constructs systems of (mis)communication, elaborates protocols, controls and regulates the distribution of words. And he does so, failed songwriter though he is, by assimilating techniques that would normally be considered literary. Because this coopting of language, images, and dreams seems so complete and seamless, the irruption of "old words," transcendent and still-governing, might (or should) take us by surprise.

   I want now to raise the question of why so few critics exhibit any sense of surprise and, as a corollary, I want to reexamine the ways in which Dos Passos's strategies invite and legitimate certain critical perspectives, particularly those that note his satiric and ironic intent. My point is not to ask whether Dos Passos ironizes mass communications and its ties to corporate power but to inquire under what conditions such a reading could be made at all. The following discussion thus treats Dos Passos's attack on mass communications as problematic rather than as a given. More precisely it suggests that what is most problematic about the novel is that its attack on mass communications is a given and thus not problematic at all. What is most striking about criticism of Dos Passos, in fact, is the way in which writers insist on his vision of a totalizing and invisible structuring of mass consciousness yet go on to occlude or dismiss the importance of that insight. F. R. Leavis, to take an early instance, wrote in an article significantly entitled "A Serious Artist" that Moorehouse embodies the "power that, in the general disintegration, in the default of religion, art and traditional forms and sanctions, holds society together – the Power of the Word, or let us say, Advertising" ([1932] 1974, 72). There are grounds for admitting the pertinence of Leavis's point. No religious leaders or artists figure prominently in the novel, and writers like Randolph Bourne, Jack Reed, and Thorstein Veblen scarcely provide visions of sufficient complexity to hold society together. At the same time, Moorehouse confidently and explicitly puts forward an agenda whereby a new, PR-led manipulation of language will direct labor and capital toward a unified America. But if Advertising really does hold society together, granting it structure and meaning, investing it with an ill-defined yet obviously immense power, what room would be left for a serious artist or for Leavis's critical comments? What meaning, indeed, would the term "serious" even possess? At best, we might envisage a situation in which the Power of the Word is incomplete and serious art less in default than marginalized. In any case, sanctions against the very power Leavis supposes to have replaced traditional sanctions fill his essay. Leavis, Dos Passos (as serious artist), and presumably the readers of Leavis's critical audience participate together in creating a community (the "us," for instance, of "let us say") that should not exist. Leavis grants Advertising a serious power but not serious legitimacy; an audience but not "us."

This may seem a trivial attack on Leavis; but elsewhere this dynamic of attributing to mass culture a consensual or disintegrative power that is simultaneously rescinded occurs much more subtly and persuasively. As another example, let us take Charles Marz's two fine essays on the Newsreels, "Dos Passos's Newsreels: The Noise of History" (1979) and "U.S.A.: Chronicle and Performance" (1980). The public world Marz depicts in the former article is a grim one indeed, a "speakerless world," a "constantly eroding world," a world in which "private voices give way to the public noise." All that remains in the Newsreels, Marz argues, is "the residue of voice, the debris of character, action, and experience." And, though in the Camera Eye sections there is a "refusal to abdicate personal control," even that pocket of resistance seems to dissolve finally as the Newsreels "invade the text" and "collide with the Camera Eye" so that "the wreckage of public voices buries the individual and silences him" (196–9). Except, one must add, individuals like Charles Marz and his students and readers, or journals like *Studies in the Novel* in which this article appeared –

in short, the writings and the whole supporting system of methodologies and apparatuses whose business it is to fence off and write off the silencing, wrecking, overwhelming world of mass communication. Indeed, the latter (and later) article specifically exempts the author and reader, and this despite the fact that, in a moment that strongly suggests the impossibility of escaping interlocked systems of speech and power, Marz tells us that Dos Passos, "his characters, and his readers are linked in their susceptibility to reduction and anonymity. All are embedded in the echoing public space – in the space of the text and the world" (1980, 414). U.S.A. is a "continent and a composition ruled by crisis and collision; it is fragmented, radically incomplete." For all that, "neither the composition nor the country disintegrates" for the "performing voice of the novelist-historian, and his accomplice, the reader, survive the tale" (399).

Both essays reveal a great deal about reading Dos Passos, as much for what they say covertly as for what they speak "up front." While emphasizing the threatening power of the "echoing public space" to shatter and colonize in-dividual minds, these essays quietly marshal their strategies of resistance. But these strategies *need never be spoken*. Marz designates the reader as "accomplice" to the author's performance but never considers under what circumstances such a formidable feat of coherence could be possible. Nor does he need to. He defines the form of Dos Passos's saboteur tactics as ironic (403, 407) but never explains how a disparity between, say, word and deed might even be recognized in this "fragmented, radically incomplete" world. Nor does he need to. Even as he despairingly invokes the power of consumerism, the media liars, and the forces of history, Marz talks up the authority of author and critic. The over-whelming power of consumer capitalism registered in novel and essays is transformed ultimately into the symbolic capital arising out of the joint par-ticipation of reader, author, and academic institution. The problem, in other words, is a thoroughly rhetorical one that is exposed as such by the clarity and confidence of its ensuing exegesis. The engagement of this professional critic and his never-invoked but always-present community of professional readers show the premise of "the extinction of the private voice" to be merely hypothetical. Marz is correct to point to the complicity of author and reader, but – because the reader is not *any* reader – misleading when he emphasizes the desperate and marginal nature of that engagement. Far from chronicling the hopelessness of Dos Passos's task, Marz unwittingly demonstrates why his and Dos Passos's task is so easy.

Marz's unspoken assumption, like Leavis's, is that the effects Dos Passos describes are not totalizing and invisible; they must leave spaces in which a critic (not wholly overwhelmed by the voices of mass culture) may insert his or her critical intelligence. But Dos Passos exerts a great deal of pressure on the need to perform critical acts of recuperation and transformation. He does so most strongly by his wholesale incorporation of raw material from mass culture. Headlines, fragments of newspaper text, advertisements, and snatches of popular song completely invest the Newsreels, often appear in the other sections and, as in the case of Clyde Griffiths, seize the imagination of the characters. Janey, for instance, in Moorehouse's office, feels "right in the midst of headlines" (279); Eleanor, thinking she might inherit a fortune, imagines that she "could see it in headlines – MARSHALL FIELD EMPLOYEE INHERITS MILLION" (196); later, she begins to meet all the "names she had heard or read of in the bookcolumn of the *Daily News*" (234). But Dos Passos's narrative strategies place this material in a different context. Reading Dreiser's *An American Tragedy,* we saw, became in part a question of discovering disruptive frameworks; plagiarizing mass culture can only be unfolded as critique if we identify some singular perspective in the representation of that raw material. That originary material must be framed in some way to make it appear subordinate to the real work of genesis performed by the artist. My reading of *An American Tragedy* hinged on the difficulty (but ultimately the assured ease) of locating and stabilizing such frames. There appears to be no such difficulty in *U.S.A.* The four primary techniques (narrative, Camera Eye, Newsreel, biography) plus preface ("U.S.A.") and epilogue ("Vag") offer multiple frames in a kaleidoscope of shifting styles, typographical conventions, perspectives, and voices. And a discontinuous style is found within sections, particularly in the Camera Eye and Newsreels. *U.S.A.* compels us to confront a strategy of framing and to formulate appropriate reading strategies.

Reading Dos Passos's frames leads to two surprises. The first is how easily critics, in the absence of definitive instructions from Dos Passos about how to juxtapose frames, manage to read across discontinuities to produce stable and determinate interpretations – testimony to how well the academy has adapted to modernist writing strategies. The second surprise is how difficult it becomes to stabilize Dos Passos's meanings once we forgo some presuppositions about how to read discontinuity – presuppositions that are most deeply lodged and invisible when the frame is the Newsreel and the content is the mass media. Let us then look more closely at Dos Passos's style, beginning with an analogy to film practice that is often invoked as a way of comprehending Dos Passos's tactics. The rapid crosscutting, editing, and montage techniques of *U.S.A.* have reminded many readers of the work of early film directors. We might trace Dos Passos's techniques back to the innovations of D. W. Griffith, but Carol Shloss (1987) is probably correct to point to Dos Passos's contemporary, the Soviet film maker Sergei Eisenstein, as the most profound influence.[3] Shloss's intriguing point is that

> the Soviet example gave Dos Passos a way to use the fragment, the small structural unit that was already his preferred narrative mode, and to activate it for the audience. From Vertov he took the idea of the interval, the thought that the space between fragments could invite participation, that the film-maker/ writer/technician's job was to edit, to provide the juxtaposition of information that, when assembled in the viewing/reading, would lead to a recognition of the importance of each unit within the whole. (158–9)

In particular, Shloss argues, the theories and practice of Soviet directors offered Dos Passos a way of reimagining the relationship of the individual, as a tiny fragment, to history and thus to discover a "larger coherence" (157) unavailable to the single perspective.[4] Shloss clarifies two points that inform the work of virtually all critics. First, there is the sense that *U.S.A.*'s style alone, in the absence of an explicit political agenda, carries a profound weight of meaning.[5] Camera Eye (49) lends support to such readings in its representation of the veracity of certain forms of writing: "pencil scrawls in my notebook the scraps of recollection the broken halfphrases the effort to intersect word with word to dovetail clause with clause to rebuild out of mangled memories unshakably (Old Pontius Pilate) the truth." This strategy of dovetailed "broken halfphrases," captured nicely in this line with its gradual rise through nouns to verbs to a climactic and unshakable truth, certainly bestows a weighty potential on the text's formal properties – almost as if form were incidental to any political position, or as if it might somehow incorporate all principled positions.[6] Shloss manages to close that gap by exploring the social theory embodied in the technical innovations of Eisenstein and Vertov. The fragment functions serially to link each part to a whole but also functions allegorically to link artistic form to social form.

Second, Shloss puts forward a theory of the "interval" that is crucial to critical interpretations of Dos Passos's work. Or, rather, she suggests a pertinent historical context that might lead toward a theory of the interval. She emphasizes that in *U.S.A.* Dos Passos, following Vertov's lead, saw the fragment as the "prelude to synthesis, to construction of the historical world" (158). The emphasis is an important one because a clear danger with montage is that the relationship of one individual fragment to another, or to a pattern of others, or to the whole, will not become evident. One fragment alone does not begin to carry meaning until it has been juxtaposed with another, a recognizable series or group begun, and thus a principle of selection ascertained; the individual fragment must somehow bespeak its relationship to a larger pattern or whole. At least three interrelated processes appear necessary to circumvent a possible failure of recognition. First, montage must be created and activated within a communal context in which any particular fragment will be expected to perform dialogically; the fragment, that is, enters into relationships with something outside itself, and those relationships can be understood because of the larger, homogeneous context within which they occur. Second, there must not only be an expectation that a fragment will perform dialogically, but it must be capable of pointing outside itself; it must somehow indicate another fragment with which it shares certain characteristics. Third, something profound must happen to the reader (or spectator) in the interval(s) between two or more fragments. In the gaps between fragments a structure must begin to appear, a structure that is never present in the text (or film) itself but that each discrete fragment must somehow signify.

Most readers reading Dos Passos lack such a theory of the interval; indeed, in most cases the lack has yet to be discovered. Critics approach the fragment-interval-fragment problem as if there were no problem – and in the sense that reading Dos Passos continues unproblematically, they are right. Foley, for example, quotes the following portion of Newsreel 68:

WALL STREET STUNNED

. . . .

MARKET SURE TO RECOVER FROM SLUMP

. . . .

Oh the right wing clothesmakers
And the Socialist fakers
They make by the workers . . .
Double Cross

. . . .

He was goin' downgrade makin' ninety miles an hour
When his whistle broke into a scream
He was found in the wreck with his hand on the throttle
An' was scalded to death with the steam

. . . .

RADICALS FIGHT WITH CHAIRS AT UNITY MEETING

. . . .

CARILLON PEALS IN SINGING TOWER

. . . .

on a tiny island nestling like a green jewel in the lake that mirrors the singing tower, the President today participated in the dedication of a bird sanctuary and its pealing carillon, fulfilling the dream of an immigrant boy

Foley comments that the "suppressed reports of financial disaster, the songs reflecting a resurgence of class struggle, the symbolic suicide plunge of Casey Jones, the false tranquility of the Bok carillon – these and other ironic elements reveal the varying attitudes of different social forces responding to the crisis" (1980, 450–1). Oddly, she does not bother to identify precisely what ironies are present nor how they are to be read. Should we assume that the resurgence of class struggle is an illusion symbolized by Casey Jones's journey ("suicide" may be too strong) or that his "suicide plunge" (representing individuals like Charley Anderson? Wall Street? the United States?) may be countered by a resurgent struggle? Should we assume that "MARKET SURE TO RECOVER FROM SLUMP" is totally ironic (or just a little?), given that the market was recovering by the time Dos Passos completed *The Big Money*? Should we assume that "fulfilling the dream of an immigrant boy" is wholly ironic, given this Newsreel's proximity to the reported deaths of Sacco and Vanzetti, or does "CARILLON PEALS IN SINGING TOWER" represent an optimism that cannot be undone by lying presidents and the pessimism of the ensuing Camera Eye (51)? Presumably, since Foley argues that Dos Passos's view of history is essentially pessimistic and not Marxist at all, she would see his irony working to subvert the optimism of a Socialist resurgence. Casey Jones (an engineer, after all, not a capitalist boss) would thus signify the failure of both Socialist and capitalist dreams of recovery, leaving us with Vag as the classically apolitical, alienated, isolate American wanderer. (A further irony from Foley's perspective might be the fact that a future unfolding along Marxist lines would necessarily prove Dos Passos's pessimism wrong.)

Melvin Landsberg provides an exactly analogous situation from a wholly different perspective. For Landsberg, the Newsreel sections are "excellent satire." Usually, he continues, "Dos Passos permits society, with its perverse values and practices, to condemn itself" (1972, 190). Among the discrete fragments Landsberg chooses from the entire trilogy to illustrate his point is one that Foley also quotes along with a footnote (mentioning Landsberg as her source) to the effect that this event, a fight in 1934 between Communists and Socialists, was central to Dos Passos's dissatisfaction with the Communist Party: "RADICALS FIGHT WITH CHAIRS AT UNITY MEETING." Foley associates this fragment with Dos Passos's vision of "historical doom" (451). Because Landsberg offers no context or interpretation, however, we have no way of establishing whether he perceives the same irony as Foley later will. This should be a moot point if Landsberg is correct in asserting that Dos Passos's satire should be self-evident. But because Landsberg does not espouse a Marxist position, as Foley does, we may at least guess that the disenchantment Dos Passos evinces here may be, for Landsberg, a temporary one, preparatory to entering new political territory. Furthermore, is Dos Passos satirizing "society" for allowing such maniacal behavior within it or merely satirizing the radicals who (ironically) think they are preserving society? If one focuses on Landsberg's description of the 1934 fight, the latter interpretation seems most likely. On the other hand, if we follow Landsberg's argument that this fight crucially affected Dos Passos's shift to a Jeffersonian democratic politics, might not the fragment possess a double irony, whereby society at large, now looked on more kindly by a more conservative Dos Passos, might indeed be satirized as weakly permitting this kind of nonsense? Or might this be a satire on the newspaper reporting that so trenchantly (and gleefully?) exposes the radicals' problems? Or might this not be satire at all, but instead a call for understanding the kind of social pressures that led to the "historical doom," to borrow Foley's phrase, of the Communist Party in the 1930s? In any case, the fragment does not permit society "to condemn itself"; it must be made to yield up significances that constantly change as other contexts are brought to bear. As critics adduce different interpretive contexts, irony might appear in Dos Passos's text for most readers yet be a different irony in each case.

These critics' omissions of context are perplexing only at first sight. Indeed, my point is not that Landsberg and Foley should provide contexts but that, even without specific contexts, most critics will assent to the premises underlying their readings. The irony of "CARILLON PEALS IN SINGING TOWER" may not be so transparent to all readers as it is to Foley, but most are prepared to activate some kind of ironic reading (most critical readings of the Newsreels do emphasize their ironic content). This is true in part because of the nonironic readings we are able to exclude, among the most important of which is to read the Newsreels as presenting the voices of mass culture in an unequivocal and neutral or even favorable way. We begin reading the Newsreels with the knowledge, or at least the supposition, that these grouped voices cannot be apprehended at face value; they are untrustworthy because of their nonliterary origins. These suppositions are underwritten by a literary–nonliterary distinction that is in many cases untenable; yet they are also resilient enough to make the blank intervals of Dos Passos's text seem perfectly comprehensible. Let us speculate for a moment on reading a single fragment: "large quantities of Virginia tobacco to be imported to England especially for the use of the British troops on the continent" (Newsreel 15). Chosen at random and offered to a reader unacquainted with Dos Passos's text, a fragment like this gives rise to any number of potential readings. With a certain kind of contextual knowledge about geography that most readers possess, the places mentioned here and the nature of certain economic arrangements transacted between them would begin to make sense. It might be much more difficult to place this transaction as occurring during the First World War. A different form of knowledge about language might lead many readers to identify the fragment as belonging in style to a newspaper idiom. In each case, the lack of a limiting context puts in doubt the recuperability of specifiable and stable meanings. We might get anything from interpretation-as-description ("it's about Virginia selling tobacco to England") to the wildly imaginative ("it's taken from a science fiction novel set in the future when tobacco is used in prebattle rites"). Once we allow contextual evidence from the rest of the Newsreel and novel, however, we liberate other readings that exclude the totally inappropriate while leading to still other adventures in reading. Now appraised of an actual historical era, we are able to use headlines like "WANT BIG WAR OR NONE" and "GENERAL WAR NEAR," together with other references to the war and more oblique references to state slaughter ("It is a terrible thing for the state to commit murder"; "disappearance of Major reveals long series of assassinations"), in order to read other meanings into that first fragment – meanings that are there only by virtue of these new contexts.

We might now, for instance, propose a link between this item's acknowledgment of an economic transaction and the larger economic complicities between the United States and Great Britain embodied in the Morgan Loans, which by 1917 totalled "one billion, ninehundred million dollars" (617) and to preserve which Dos Passos believed the United States entered the war. The accompanying biography of Andrew Carnegie, "Prince of Peace," which points to Carnegie's pursuit of peace "except in time of war," certainly buttresses a reading of complicitous war- and peace-time economies. Or we might identify an irony in the fact that while Virginia is exporting tobacco to British troops, Great Britain is preparing to import American troops as well as part of its war effort. The preceding Camera Eye (21), moreover, depicts in great detail a severe drought in the "exhausted land" of Northern Virginia, where the "land between the rivers was flat drained of all strength by tobacco in the early Walter Raleigh Captain John Smith Pocahontas days." Whereas the newspaper item uses abstract names ("the continent"), the Camera Eye identifies specific locales; whereas the item describes groups ("British troops"), the Camera Eye describes specific, idiosyncratic individuals. Beaten, broken individuals like Bowie Franklin with his "long scrawny neck an' his ruptured walk" and Miss Emily, who "took a drop herself now and then but she always put a good face on things lookin' over the picket fence," inhabit this exhausted land of Virginia. With Camera Eye (21) in mind, we are in a position to explore the hidden ideological effects of that newspaper report more closely. In its detached, objective fashion the report not only obscures the real people who inhabit Virginia but other possible foreboding analogies such as that between the "swamps dry and cracked crisscross like alligator hide" of Northern Virginia and the trench warfare of the continent. Furthermore, the newspaper item misses a crucial point that Dos Passos allows us to read back into this association of Virginia and Europe, which is that the "exhausted land" was in the first place a product of European exploitation from the "early Walter Raleigh Captain John Smith" days. This sale of tobacco to England puts us in mind of a whole series of exploitative transactions: people ruined, lands wasted, empires built and fought over, and all knowledge of those transactions fading away in the objective tone of the newspaper fragment. The newspaper's information masks, in other words, all that is really crucial to understand the true relationship of power among tobacco, the Old and New Worlds, and economic systems.

This reading proceeds, however, from several assumptions it would be well to make clear. The point about the relationship between the sale of tobacco and the Morgan Loans, for instance, depends in part on reading back from "The House of Morgan" biography in *1919,* where we learn that by "1917 the Allies had borrowed one billion, ninehundred million dollars through the House of Morgan: we went overseas for democracy and the flag." Dos Passos means (surely) that we went overseas for the Morgan Loans, but the point is that this reading also depends on one's ability to discover ironic meanings. We might buttress this ironic reading by activating Dos Passos's specific statements about the Morgan Loans in other articles; this would not prevent a few individuals with the trajectory of Dos Passos's career firmly in mind from seeing a hint of a forthcoming conservative backlash appearing unconsciously and nonironically at this moment. If we admit opinions expressed outside the text as evidence, we might even subordinate Dos Passos's own directly stated opinions about the Morgan Loans to Landsberg's considered opinion that Dos Passos was always fundamentally split as a "Harvard-educated middle class radical" (188). And Blanche Gelfant reads the desperate searches of Dos Passos's protagonists for identity as a function of the writer's "unwilling attraction to success and material rewards"

([1961] 1971, 181). In light of this, can we be sure that a deep-seated and perhaps unconscious pattern of resistance to the radical reading of American culture I proposed above does not exist? If we stay within the text and organize fragments into patterns of irony, we depend upon one irony to explain another; if we step outside the text, we confront still other disagreements about how to read Dos Passos's apparently straightforward pronouncements.

Far from permitting society to unravel its own perversities, Dos Passos, in the absence of authoritative statements, forces the reader to enter the text to negotiate spaces that persist in staying open. Another way of putting this is to say that the structure of readers' interpretive strategies – at least of those readers in the academy – will force them to view those spaces as needing negotiation. Effectively, we shall see, the two versions are doubled aspects of the same discursive practices. Of the individual discrete fragment almost nothing can be said; or, what is worse, too much can be said. At the same time, the spaces between juxtaposed fragments, which most critics reading Dos Passos assume are filled nonproblematically with a structure of settled convictions emerging from the dozens of possible contexts each fragment arrests and organizes, show a surprising resistance to closure. As an example, to take the most contentious point I made above, there is no stable evidence that the newspaper "masks" in any complicitous sense a "true relationship of power." We certainly cannot tell whether the original writer intended to force underground certain significances that appear in my reading or whether the fragment in question may have been taken from a longer article that did expose some of the conditions to which Dos Passos refers in Camera Eye (21). In one sense, these caveats are pointless, for the first casualty of this act of displacing fragments from their original context is intentionality. More precisely, we might argue, that act of displacement and ensuing recontextualization dismisses superficial intentions (to report, for instance, the shipping of tobacco to England) and invites the true (that is, the covert) meanings of the media to appear. Hence the true "intent" of the Virginia tobacco fragment, arising out of some realm of the political unconscious, might indeed be construed as keeping underground certain liaisons between the economies of England and the United States.

The difficulty with finally accepting this reading again has to do with reading the interval. The very structure of montage – whether juxtaposed fragments or the longer structural elements of narrative and Newsreels – must ultimately deprive us of the secure readings most critics propose about *U.S.A.*, and particularly about its ironies. Clearly, in a work as complex as this, any fragment of text must have dozens of possible contexts – those fragments that surround it, those at a distance that display some kind of similarity, as well as overarching contexts like Dos Passos's political beliefs. Each individual narrative technique (Newsreel, Camera Eye), moreover, furnishes a context for the others. Hence my reading above was able to use material from Camera Eye (21) to supplement Newsreel 15; in another situation, material from a Newsreel or biography might

be carried over to illuminate a Camera Eye. But this process of finding contexts – really, of limiting contexts – can only reach a stable position whereby we
are sure we have found the correct interpretation if some fragments in the total
field are found to possess a self-identical meaning that cannot then be traduced,
transformed, subverted, or supplemented. At such moments we would be able to
identify absolute perspectives and stand in the presence (the Derridean terminology is unavoidable) of Dos Passos's meaning. To find those moments in the
text, some critics have privileged one narrative technique – one universalizing
perspective – over the others. David Vanderwerken does so, arguing that the
Camera Eye sections are meant to provide "explicit authorial statement, an
unambiguous attitude toward his materials" and a "context in which to judge
the behavior portrayed in the narratives" (1977, 207). But for Barbara Foley, the
case is just the opposite: The Camera Eye sections represent Dos Passos's failure
to find a privileged perspective that would draw together subjective awareness
and the public historical domain (465). A statement like "all right we are two
nations" (Camera Eye [50]), coming as it does right at the end of the trilogy,
must represent for Vanderwerken a final truth to which all readings might
eventually be referred for legitimation. For Foley, the statement can only represent a troubled and pessimistic conclusion that other meanings in the trilogy
actually work against.

Likewise, to look at this problem from yet another perspective, it makes all
the difference in the world whether we agree with Shloss – that the trilogy
demonstrates a "larger coherence" (in which case all kinds of unified meanings might be discovered working together in a grand pattern) – or with
Marz – that the trilogy is fundamentally and irredeemably shattered. In the
latter case the noise of Newsreel 15 would certainly overwhelm the intricate
connections and resistances Shloss would figure in, and we would be tempted
to search instead for points of disruption, incompletion, and interpretive
anomalies. The source for Shloss's willingness to entertain coherence in
U.S.A. is Dziga Vertov, who suggests that the first stage in constructing a
montage is to choose materials that would crystallize the "assigned theme"
into the "plan of the theme" (1984, 89). Yet critics disagree violently on
what Dos Passos's "chosen theme" really is, whether they speak in formal
terms (coherence? incoherence?) or political terms (Marxist? progressive?
anarchist? or a mixture of this and more?). Even if we do not follow the
poststructuralist thought of Derrida, Fish, and company to its logical conclusion, Dos Passos's own shifting ideologies should prevent us from being
certain that perceived ironies are, first of all, correct and, second, equally
apparent to every reader. Because neither the individual fragment nor the
overall plan (the "chosen theme") offers a permanent basis for interpretation,
critics are left to mediate an unstable field of meanings that arises interstitial-
ly during the transit from one fragment to the next. No one fragment
constellates the entire field, though most critics are able to make fragments

cohere in a pattern that only begins to seem deficient when other radically different accounts are furnished. Dos Passos's montage, it begins to seem, invites us to perform the very same operations of recontextualization on *U.S.A.* that the Newsreels perform on the field of mass culture. Each process depends on a methodology of selection, rearrangement, and sedimentation within a structure whose premises are left up to the reader to discover and actualize.

And there is one final problem. If we bracket off what we think we know about Dos Passos, the media, adducing contexts and reading fragments, we find that individual fragments begin to develop poetic lives of their own. So one more irony of reading "CARILLON PEALS IN SINGING TOWER" is that while Foley sees only illusory hope, the headline itself has a decidedly poetic ring; it sounds worthy of W. B. Yeats. It would be hard to constrain the headline's aesthetic beauty within the voices of doom Foley generates from this Newsreel, yet harder still to read the fragment as part of a general theory about the aesthetic virtues of the media. Similarly, a fragment from Newsreel I, "Society Girls Shocked: Danced with Detectives," has an oddly Old English feel to its double alliteration, though it is unlikely that most readers pause to appreciate that fact. And if they do, it might only be to contemplate the irony of an echo of Old English saga appearing in this trivial tale of society girls being shocked to find they have danced with detectives. Yet this hint of the mock-epic (which I find congenial) is not wholly supported by the text, which turns out to be much richer than that; the headline does not insist, for instance, that the society girls are shocked *at* dancing with detectives; another person dancing might have caused this shock. Or they may have danced with detectives after receiving the shock. A whole series of micronarratives are possible here. It might be argued that the headline only achieves this complexity after being removed from its initial context by Dos Passos, its potential meanings liberated by the act of artistic selection. My point, though, is that no one has (yet) thought to explore the possibility that Dos Passos is setting out to identify the richness and potential complexity not just of the popular mind but of the newspaper idiom. Such a reading would be particularly apt if we grant an overlapping of Dos Passos's and the media's imaginative domains. To attribute the complexity of this fragment solely to Dos Passos's strategy of appropriation turns out to be a multifaceted critical maneuver. Indeed, if Dos Passos can be said to liberate a multitude of meanings by virtue of his act of appropriation, critical acts of reading tend to limit them all over again by reading the Newsreel fragments as merely trivial, historical markers, or ironic indices to the mass mind. By excluding, for example, the possibility of a new poetics of newspaper culture as one possible reading of the Newsreels, critics call into play certain premises about the relative values of mass culture and Dos Passos's work. It is a maneuver easily made, all the more so for being made invisibly.

III

Meaning overburdens the text of *U.S.A.* To the extent that Dos Passos refuses to cordon off the imaginative work of the trilogy's PR men, a space is opened that no wholly ironic reading of, say, Moorehouse's "literature from a factory" can expunge. The meaning of Moorehouse's "literature" will always be more than *non*literature even though the play of significances it liberates will paradoxically persuade us that there is a kind of literature that "literature from a factory" is not. Similarly, the fragment "large quantities of Virginia tobacco to be imported to England" points in the direction of many interpretive strategies. It could lead us to an analysis of the objectivity characteristic of the newspaper idiom; it could lead us to condemn that objectivity as a sign of false consciousness; but it could also lead us to perceive certain profound similarities between Dos Passos's documentary fiction and the precise, objective "degree zero" of style we find in the fragment. Again, "CARILLON PEALS IN SINGING TOWER" possesses a range of potential meanings and barely perceptible connotations that cannot just be parlayed into an ironic reading like "the knell of doom for America," though this may certainly be one powerful reading. As Hearst and Moorehouse experience unexpected resistance to grasping the power they desire, so do the Newsreel fragments, in their vibrant and freewheeling constellations of names, facts, and situations, resist and transcend the limiting contexts most critics put forward. Although it seems self-evident that the richness of the Newsreels must be attributed to Dos Passos's work of authoring, such a reading does not pay sufficient attention to the intransigence and ineluctable density of these conjoined scraps of material. While Dos Passos's tactics may have the effect of liberating undisclosed meanings from some political unconscious, they also effectively place under the microscope the oddities, the *bizarreries,* the everyday carnival of American life in the media, that has grown mundane only under the weight of repetition. In this sense, Dos Passos's work of selection, estrangement, and patterning may simply, or may also, bear witness to the aura embodied within these headlines and news items.

Dos Passos's tactics of accommodation disprove the commonly held notion that the Newsreels are an out-and-out attack on the mass media. Dos Passos's own work of estranging media material from its original contexts allows that material, at times, to push forward its own voice in all its rawness and raggedness and to proclaim an energy that is not fashioned wholly through Dos Passos's reworking. To read *U.S.A.* as truly polyphonous, to take Dos Passos at his word when he says that in his trilogy "everything should go in" (quoted in Landsberg, 189), is, however, a double-edged maneuver. On the one hand, true polyphony promises a true egalitarianism along the lines of Shloss's reading of the politics of Vertov's film techniques, in which individual shots are arranged serially and cumulatively without any attempt to subordinate some elements to others. All of the shots, in fact, participate in the fleshing out of the "chosen theme." On the other hand, according to most critics Dos Passos's chosen theme is not celebration but critique, which he achieves by way of an ironic rather than a cumulative juxtaposition of fragments. This is to say that Dos Passos does not assign each voice (of the media, Moorehouse, Uncle Tim, Jack Reed, Thorstein Veblen, and so on) an equal or neutral value; some are subordinate to others. We can distinguish literature from "literature from a factory," Moorehouse from true imaginative writers, and a fragmentary document about "CARILLON PEALS IN SINGING TOWER" from Dos Passos's own innovative style of documentary fragmentation in the Newsreels. And we do this because we correctly identify shaping and controlling patterns of, say, the irony that allows Dos Passos and his readers to harness the potentially explosive and anarchic medley of American voices. But on several occasions in this chapter, going on the evidence of critics who all recognize irony but all describe different, not to say mutually incompatible, ironies, I have argued for a radical instability in the trilogy's ironic meanings. On this basis, we unleash again the notion of an unrestrained polyphony of voices and defer once again the certainty we need to distinguish Dos Passos from the inventions of the PR people. Indeed, if I correctly read the difficulty of reading irony in *U.S.A.,* it must be possible for someone (a reader, say, not educated within the academy) to read the range of writing in *U.S.A.* – from the rapid-fire, spectacularly unspectacular prose of the narrative sections, to the incorporated media material in the Newsreels, to the enigmatic fragments in biographies and Camera Eyes – and fail utterly to perceive how Dos Passos writes off mass culture.

But such a reader would lack the kind of guiding strategies that allow critics to infer, from the buying up of Uncle Tim's outstanding paper and various other attempts to silence radical newspapers, that the media in general manipulate and misguide the American public. (This interpretation, to repeat, cannot be certified absolutely until we can finally dismiss the worrying implications of Gelfant's article – that Dos Passos harbored contradictory psychological and political impulses – or until we can find a precise methodology to distinguish Dos Passos's critique of mass culture from a desire to register and celebrate American speech.) Most of all, it would be to lack the specific context of a professional community together with all the supporting apparatuses university departments of literary study provide. To read the trilogy poststructurally, as I have at various points in this chapter, is quite different from reading it (however speculatively) through the eyes of a naive reader outside the academy, even though both poststructuralist and naive reader may deny the legitimacy of literary meanings somehow arising out of bits and pieces of newsprint. Actually the positions are quite different. The latter fails to see the possibility or does not recognize the value of, say, reading "literature from a factory" as a statement Dos Passos means us to perceive as ironic. The former of course recognizes the interpretive framework that allows "literature from a factory" to be apprehended by certain groups as "*non*literature from a factory," but chooses to emphasize a surplus of meaning that has the effect of illuminating the once-invisible premises of that framework and disrupting them. The crucial point of difference is that a poststructuralist analysis carries with it its own institutional baggage – a hagiography of critics, notably Derrida, a jargon-ridden discourse, and a small audience of professional critics and philosophers – all of which tends to inscribe its knowledge of sliding and insupportable boundaries solidly back into the framework of the academic institution. The truly unsurprising aspect of poststructuralist analysis is how far it consolidates the boundaries of the institutionalized discourses that it pretends to disturb. Theoretically, poststructuralist theory presents a powerful argument for always deferring a stable grasp of points of difference; practically speaking, it is engaged in practices that perpetuate the organizing principle that allows writers of and about literature to fence off a special terrain of discourse.

Turning back to my own analysis of Dos Passos, it should be clear that though I have argued for a more problematic reading of his strategy of incorporating media voices in all their raw immediacy, I have not been able to – and could not now – collapse his work back into some undifferentiated cacophony of American speech. Far from denying the presence of distinctive features on which critical discourse could gain purchase, one (covert) function of my reading has been to show that Dos Passos is an engrossing and complex writer whose engagement with mass culture becomes an issue for critical debate only because that engagement is not complete. My own rhetoric of engagement, appropriation, and estrangement presupposes a level of self-reflexive awareness on Dos Passos's part; moreover, it presupposes a professional audience that attributes authority to critical work in part because its discourse matches none other in the sociocultural realm outside the academy. Critics perform criticism successfully because the general public does not; if the general public did, the act of criticism would no longer be professionally viable. In this sense, this chapter began cordoning off a realm in which to indulge critical practices from the moment I first engaged Dos Passos's text, even though I have also argued that the need to cordon off such a realm arose in, and is always immersed in, an age of mass culture. For the same reasons, the academyless naive reader I postulated above could not gain a voice within the academy even though his or her reading might prove more radical (in the sense of different, unusual, extreme) than anything the academy could offer – to the extent that it removed *any* privileged basis for apprehending literature and did so in a noncritical discourse. That reading would merely fail to correlate with any premise, postulate, or style that critics could perceive as authoritative, and would thus be dismissed. The reason that this naive reader could not in turn authoritatively dismiss the critic's reading is because the latter's is more persuasive. The critic's reading correlates with premises grounded in the real power structure of the critical profession, which is in turn affiliated with the powerful institution of the university.

This theoretical position holds several consequences for reading *U.S.A.* First, the more fully we enter the polyphony of the novels, and the more we attempt to register the meshing voice traces from all areas of American society, the more difficult it is to establish parameters and guidelines within which a literary text might emerge as distinct from its incorporated voices. Yet to study critical readings of *U.S.A.* is to become convinced that such guidelines do in reality exist; for though each critical position I have elaborated has jarred with the next, none has disputed the basic structural paradigm that preserves an authoritative literary space over and against a realm of mass culture. Thus, both Shloss and Marz assign the Newsreels a place in a "social order in radical disarray" (Shloss, 157) even though Shloss's vision of the work moves toward symphony whereas Marz's moves toward cacophony. And though Foley and Landsberg probably disagree about what irony they observe in the Newsreels, both are unwittingly right to leave their readings silent. Critical practice presupposes a matrix of values, principles, and canonical choices that in general obviates the need to keep legitimating one's chosen study; of these principles, the ability to distinguish (authentic) literature from (inauthentic) mass culture is the most profound and wide-ranging. Any specifiable frame, such as the line of demarcation between Camera Eye and Newsreel sections, holds the potential to activate structuring principles that are already and always present in the critic's mind. Along with Landsberg and Foley, we see some kind of irony, in part because we do not even know we expect to see it. To all intents and purposes, it is as though the interstices of Dos Passos's text did carry specific instructions to the reader about how to constellate fragments and make them richly significant.

Indeed, Dos Passos carries out the task of distinguishing his text from the mass cultural domain all the more successfully because of the lack of specific instructions. We are able to read Flack's letter without seeing its text and we scorn Delia's definition of literature without knowing precisely what literature is; in the same way, Dos Passos can assume a general proclivity toward writing off mass culture. In these circumstances critical participation need not be created so much as shaped. A hint like "this power over the dreams/of the adolescents of the world/grows and poisons like a cancer" (1116) provides a stable enough foundation for reading the Newsreels critically, though we may be hard put to it in individual Newsreel fragments to distinguish mass dream from mass cancer. It would not be difficult to imagine contexts in which a piece of writing like "General Miles with his gaudy uniform and spirited charger was the center for all eyes" in Newsreel 1 could be construed as effective – if we were willing, for instance, like many critics with Dreiser, to subordinate style to substance, or if we simply liked the way its ordinary tone sets up the shocking events that ensue. Nonetheless, once we register the passage as a piece of journalese, we find our interpretive options limited. A cliché like "center for all eyes" reads only like a cliché. We find, also, that it is unnecessary to position the passage alongside other items in order to articulate these meanings. This is only the third item in Newsreel 1, and thus occurs before any reader could have done much by way of recognizing irony, but the relevant context ("journalese") predates and preconditions our reading. It is in the space between the passage and our informing context that a derogatory opinion of the passage is shaped. To modify an earlier point, the spaces between discrete fragments in Dos Passos's text read as though they carry specific instructions because the fragments invoke an invisible pressure to marginalize that which bears the sign of the mass media. We require intervals in order to fabricate a coherent and extensive theory about Dos Passos's accommodation of mass culture; but we come to the fragment about General Miles with an ingrained ability to make educated guesses (the phrase is a rich one) about its meaning and cultural value. We recognize and "talk up" the coherence of *U.S.A.* only after the work has silently tested the coherence of our own reading strategies. What this means is that the trilogy does not force certain meanings to appear; it allows certain preconditions in readers' assumptions to guide the interpretive act in ways that possess the force and authority we might otherwise attribute to direct authorial statement.

Oddly, Dos Passos's refusal to offer final and authoritative statements in *U.S.A.* works to make critical readings of it all the more certain and secure. A fragment like the one about General Miles swamps the interpretive frameworks critics typically bring to it: A dozen contexts could be adduced and a dozen images linked to other areas of the novel, none of which are limited by Dos Passos's imperatives. But the lack of categorical statements on Dos Passos's part, far from leading to a palsy of the interpretive will, can only lend support to each hypothesized reading, which in the absence of affirmed or contradictory authorial positions finds legitimating evidence everywhere. This seems to lead back by another route to the never-ending proliferation of critical positions postulated in section II of this chapter. But interpretive anarchy would only be a true danger if there were an infinity of critical positions within the profession. In fact they are limited. Each position, moreover, is marked by criteria of selection and judgment that serve to distinguish those texts worthy of study from those that are less or unworthy, a principle that is not fortuitous or arbitrary but a key legitimating function of professional work. In the profession of literary studies, the most constant protocol – even though strategies of implementation may constantly change – is that which defines a powerful but culturally marginal realm of mass culture over and against a realm of literature. In this sense, the problem of readers reading Dos Passos turns out not to be a problem at all, for any reader within the institution of critical studies may approach the text of *U.S.A.* and compose a reading that will be persuasive not because it accurately assesses Dos Passos's intentions about a particular fragment, or about all the fragments, but because it activates constitutive principles of critical study. To read the passage about General Miles as a criticism of him or militarism in general is a tribute not to Dos Passos's powers of selection but to the particular competencies of the critical community, which apprehends and stabilizes certain kinds of language as culturally marginal. This stabilizing is not only always possible but, even in the face of theories that appear to destabilize our ability to make distinctions and have them hold in place, always being done.

The makeup of the critical profession invites a very different reading of *U.S.A.* and of its often contradictory interpretations. While each critical study of the trilogy seems to have fallen short of eliciting or recognizing the complexity of Dos Passos's accommodation of mass culture, each has performed the crucial task of embedding creative text and critical text within a professional arena where the limits of a particular accommodation can be established. In the sense that the very act of discussion within literary studies presupposes at least a residue of cultural value, even the most violent attack on Dos Passos must quickly add to the already-sedimented layers of critical discourse about the novel and testify anew to its prominence in the canon. The existence of a body of criticism, as much as its composition, establishes an author's value to the canon; and the practice of criticism legitimates the object of discussion. All critics affirm this level of discourse: Professionals cannot opt out of the business of validating their discourse and object of study without losing their professional status. All the critics I have touched on here begin with the premise that *U.S.A.* is worthy of study and that therefore Dos Passos has carried out certain maneuvers on material incorporated from mass culture that defuse, clarify, or limit its effect. It is within this general context of unspoken agreement that critics go on to register interesting but relatively minor differences of opinion about Dos Passos's work. The existence of these theories suggests one more important conclusion, which is that we can no more get back to a true, original, and pure text of *U.S.A.* than create a truly original interpretation of the novel. The pressure of so many institutionalized readings of the trilogy (as multifaceted as they are) has fashioned a context that we cannot shake off and that has indelibly marked our ability to read the novel. *U.S.A.* really does write off mass culture. The critics affirm this, even though their routes to that affirmation differ considerably. Only the truly alternative reading produced by someone unable to make (professionally) in-formed judgments or even educated guesses could "misread" fragments of journalism *as more valuable than Dos Passos's accommodation of them.* Within the profession, such a reading could only come about through a kind of collective amnesia.

One way of approaching this question of the shaping power of professional discourse, in fact, is through the issue of collective memories – an issue of which Dos Passos is well aware in *U.S.A.* The trilogy concludes in Camera Eyes (49) and (50) with a double recollection of the deaths of Sacco and Vanzetti and of the "old words" their deaths summon back. These scenes, written nearly ten years after the original events, return us to Dos Passos's thoughts about memory and writing soon after the anarchists' deaths. In his article "Sacco and Vanzetti" Dos Passos castigated the tendency of the media to exist solely in the present. One of the most extraordinary things about industrial society, Dos Passos argued, is "its idiot lack of memory. Tabloids and movies take the place of mental processes, and revolts, crimes, despairs pass off in a dribble of vague words and rubber stamp phrases without leaving a scratch on the mind of the driven instalment-paying, subway-packing mass" (quoted in Pizer 1988, 99). One way of reading the Newsreels is to see them as exercises in countermemory: They establish a process whereby fragments are removed from their original time frames and made, in one sense, ahistorical. It is true that a few fragments refer to major historical events and thus perform a convenient function of roughly locating narrative events in history. More often, the references are too minor to be easily placed; and, more often still, a fragment like "CRIMINAL IN PAJAMAS SAWS BARS; SCALES WALLS; FLEES" (Newsreel 40) possesses a general relevance to the era that might be interpreted in many ways. Whichever interpretation we use will tacitly ignore the original memory, buried somewhere in the media, of the criminal's name and the circumstances of the jailbreak. The removal of the headline from its context does not point us in the direction of old newspaper files but inward, to the remainder of the text, and perhaps liminally to a general era (the 1920s). The fragment appears anonymously, stripped of a context that would provide precise biographical and historical data, and stripped too of the trace memories of that particular article in the minds of millions of Americans.

These memories disappear as inconsequential, to be replaced with different forms of trace memories. Each fragment, first of all, carries the "memory" of its disarticulation. The perversely enigmatic nature of so many of these fragments, beginning and ending in midsentence, slurred together or held apart by ellipses, gaps, and other typographical oddities, might be said to embody the environment of their genesis in the media. Their vagueness assures us that they lack a context; their disembodied nature bespeaks the lack of a coherent body politic; the multiple echoes they set up with other such fragments convince us that there are secret structures of power, some unconscious, some manipulative, that these fragments tap into, mask and, with the proper key, reveal. And the fact that items of news so often float freely in time suggests that their relationship to underlying structures of history may have been in the first place superficial. A similar situation occurs in the narrative sections, where, as several critics have pointed out, the characters exist in a striking presentness; they experience the nausea of life without recollection and without reflection. The discrete happenings of their lives are weakly aligned with the future, in the sense that ambition shapes so many of their decisions, yet the determinedly rapid-fire, scattershot quality of Dos Passos's prose condemns all characters to a collective amnesia. A passage at random:

> When they went in the restaurant the headwaiter looked at them sharply and put them at a table in the corner of a little inside room. Joe ordered a big meal and some beer, but Janey didn't like beer, so he had to drink hers too. After Janey had told him all the news about the family and how she liked her job and expected a raise Christmas and was so happy living with

the Tingleys who were so lovely to her, there didn't seem to be much to say. Joe had bought tickets to the Hippodrome, but they had plenty of time before that started. (286)

This wartime reunion of brother and sister forgoes all the intimacies one might expect from long acquaintance. Joe does not remember, or think to ask, whether or not Janey likes beer; they have nothing much to say to each other. Lacking a shared past, the couple also make all past occurrences present. Janey tells Joe about her job, but only within a syntactic construction that tells us from the first word ("After") that her whole monologue is a process of leading up to an important and culminating present moment – which concerns in this case an emptying of speech. Likewise, the fact of Joe's buying tickets for the Hippodrome becomes a casually reported occurrence, pertinent only, it seems, for its role in setting up the waste of time in which nothing much is said. In general, the past appears in the text as a kind of afterthought to provide the barest minimum justification for present particularities. In the case of Janey, who likes to live "in the midst of headlines," a clear correlation exists between her ability to live always *after* her recollections and the truncated, amnesiac world of the Newsreels.

But Newsreels and narratives testify not only to a represented world of forgetfulness but to strategies of estrangement and reordering. In the Newsreels, typographical distortions recall a labor of cutting and arranging, a labor that must have been gone through to arrive at fragments dispossessed of their original contexts. "Horsewhipping Hastens Wedding," claims one fragment of headline in Newsreel 48, and we recognize, by virtue of our failure to complete the shadowy story this headline subtends, a disarticulation that could not be part of the original story, though it might be perceived as intensifying a true narrative about American culture that the original context could only mask. Less obviously, Dos Passos effects the estrangement of Janey and Joe (and other characters) by way of strategic subordinations of past occurrences to present time. This ensures that the reader plays a double role: caught up in the obsessive presentness of discourse but also forced to recollect the events of a character's life in a way that the characters never manage. Dos Passos's strategy of interwoven stories makes the role of the reader's memory particularly obvious. The thread of the narrative must be picked up after an interval of many pages, and, in the case of Charley Anderson, after the entire volume of *1919*. In both sections the text demands, in place of the media's "idiot lack of memory," special techniques of remembering. In the case of the narrative sections, we supply memories to amnesiac characters, first in order to reflect on continuities the characters do not perceive and second, to become aware that they do not. Our act of remembering makes memory an interpretive crux in evaluating the characters.

In the case of the Newsreel montage, we use at least three conjoined skills, the first of which is to understand that Dos Passos's act of fragmentation obviates the need to recuperate original contexts; a precondition to that understanding is our certainty that the original context could not add anything meaningful to our often baffled apprehension of the fragments. We could not otherwise read the Newsreels at all without access to old newspaper files or without several reference guides on hand; to the extent that we do not, those contexts have already been dismissed as beside the point (whatever it is) of Dos Passos's exercise. This places us in a complex reading situation. We recognize that the dislocation of items from their contexts might prove a successful way of representing the media's "idiot lack of memory"; yet, insofar as we know that the point is not to turn to the back files of newspapers, we ourselves exercise a strategy of forgetfulness. Any reader who does not consult the back files has already demonstrated a reading competence deriving from an accommodatory relationship between literature and mass culture. In this case, that competence is to "forget" that which could have no relevance and "remember" how to read a montage of fragments that appear to lack specific contexts. Actually there are many contexts, among which the most important is the collective memory awakened by Dos Passos's montage. This memory, a dense underpinning of cultural values, strategies for reading and, above all, abilities for recognizing differences, identifies certain kinds of expertise and competence characterized most completely by professional communities of readers.

Importantly, this memory is quite unlike that invoked by Vertov and Eisenstein, even though Dos Passos's innovations in montage remind us of their film aesthetics. Vertov's work presupposes a common mind, an accumulation of discrete units; his montage does not reveal that mind so much as always assume it. His "most basic formula" is to *"see and show the world in the name of the worldwide proletarian revolution"* (Vertov, 40); seeing and showing seem almost identical, as if a simple seeing, free of idiosyncratic selection of detail, must figure forth the revolution. Likewise, a revolutionary (and simple) showing must by virtue of its genesis be accessible to anyone embraced by revolutionary communism. His moviemaking is a celebration of the work that does not have to be done on the part of his audience to participate in the film experience. His audience must recognize themselves in the montage and, because the movie mimetically represents their experience, be able to translate readily the meaning of the intervals. Emerging out of the shape and structure of a communal body politic, Vertov's filmmaking cannot help but be significant to its audience; interval theory enacts communal practice. For Dos Passos, strikingly similar techniques lead to very different consequences, and the reason lies not so much in the nature of Dos Passos's audience in the 1930s as in the discursive premises and practices available to him.

IV

Throughout the 1920s and 1930s, Dos Passos pushed forward a thorough and provocative investigation into questions of style, audience, and powerful writing. Most interestingly, he inquired deeply into the role of the professional writer in ways that illuminate and extend the preceding discussion as well as revising current opinions about his political and cultural vision. All these issues converge for Dos Passos in the problem of how to gain and then hold cultural authority – a problem frequently couched in terms of how to demarcate a powerful, "masculine" and "real" realm of literature as opposed to the Belles Lettres practiced by bourgeois culture.[7] In "Toward a Revolutionary Theatre" ([1927] 1988b), he argues that the "day of the frail artistic enterprise, keeping alive through its own exquisiteness, has passed. A play or a book or a picture has got to have bulk, toughness and violence to survive in the dense clanging traffic of twentieth century life" (101). And this toughness extends to the author. In 1932, for instance, he described the manipulation of emotions at the 1932 Republican Convention in Chicago by means of the "mechanics of communication": A "man in his shirtsleeves handling a battery of spots can give the effect of a great wave of mass emotion in a convention hall. The possibilities of control of the mass are terrifying." In the next sentence, Dos Passos's final, rhetorical question, "Who's going to be man enough to stand at the switchboard?" (1932, 179), transforms the actual operators he has been watching into a symbolic figure who can presumably stand at the switchboard of American society itself. This may be either a lament (will anyone ever prove man enough?) or a prophecy (perhaps the writer will accomplish the task). In either case, the man is distinguished from the mass of men whom he controls and organizes by means of whatever tough, manly virtues are enough for the dense, clanging world of the twentieth century.

We saw in Chapter 1 that critics have routinely equated this desire on the part of American writers to "really do something" with the writing profession that seemed to afford an appropriate opportunity: journalism. And there are grounds for extending that argument to the work of Dos Passos in *U.S.A.*, for Dos Passos himself claimed that the novels developed out of a series of reportages (see Landsberg, 200). And however we read his representation of the mass media, the fact remains that the only pure writers depicted in the trilogy's biography sections are Randolph Bourne and the reporter Jack Reed. In "Playboy," Reed is denominated, perhaps straightforwardly, as "the best American writer of his time." Shaped, virtually against his playboy leanings, by "workingmen husky guys he liked out of luck out of work," by theories of socialist revolution, by the fact that as a Westerner "words meant what they said," Reed seems to epitomize a truth-in-writing that resurfaces as the "old words" at the end of *The Big Money,* and that confounds a changing world dominated by secret police and intelligence services. Or is it that the changing world confounds Jack Reed? Although Dos Passos wrote in 1928 that the "only excuse for a novelist" was as a "sort of second-class historian of the age he lives in" (1988e, 115), this biography of Reed, written a couple of years later, belies that doubt about a novelist's role and belies, too, the confidence that words mean what they say. In the Soviet Union, Reed wrote "till he dropped"; but his commitment does not make self-evident the meaning of this story of a Westerner caught up in the East. "Reed was a Westerner words meant what they said," Dos Passos repeats in the coda to "Playboy," and juxtaposes that with "He threw everything he had and himself into Smolny, dictatorship of the proletariat." Smolny, we have just learned, glows "whitehot like a bessemer,/no sleep in Smolny,/Smolny the giant rollingmill running twentyfour hours a day rolling out men nations hopes milleniums impulses fears." What does Smolny signify? Powerful harbinger of a Communist future in which Reed's playboy tendencies and Harvard education are smelted down in the machine of society? Or the kind of totalitarian machine Dos Passos thought he glimpsed during his visit to the Soviet Union in 1928, where Reed's working till he dropped is only appropriate to a life-threatening construct in which his writing talents are not thrown but thrown away? Or both awe and doubt at once? In any case, Reed seems an anachronism to a world where "everything has to be relabeled and catchwords lose their meaning from week to week" (1988g, 148), what with the "mighty rollingmills" of Moorehouse and his PR business, Smolny and its "giant rollingmill," and secret documents and "spies everywhere." History itself no longer offers an overt, coherent, settled shape for even a first-class historian to register. "Reed wrote" is Dos Passos's final flat epitaph on Reed's writing. It suggests a writing without issue, a writing swallowed up by Smolny, even a kind of pure writing uncompromised by the mighty word-mills of America and the Soviet Union and *hence* without issue. Reed wrote, but the true story is embedded in treacherous fragments like "no sleep in Smolny," connoting everything from the sleepless energy of a revolutionary body politic to a hell-like insomnia, a fragment that is thoroughly compromised, comprehended anew, and resignified by each different reading context.

Dos Passos tries to clarify his position with regard to powerful writing in his introductory remarks to the 1932 reprinting of *Three Soldiers* (1921). This wide-ranging essay, concerned with everything from modernism to professionalism to writing strategies, is Dos Passos's most interesting exploration of the questions facing us here. At first sight, little in Dos Passos's comments would seem out of place in an essay by Henry James: the expanded market for professional writers and a correlative pressure to devalue one's writing; the trivial nature of most writing floated on the market; and the commodification of novel writing, which Dos Passos, echoing Frank Norris, likens to "feeding the machine, like a girl in a sausage factory shoveling hunks of meat into the hopper." "Professional deformation" – Dos Passos's term for the constricting forces of commodification experienced in the "trade of novelist" – is partly to blame for the demise of the hope and energy of 1919 when "Picasso was to rebuild the eye" and "whenever you went to the movies you saw Charlie Chaplin." Dos Passos moves easily between commodification and an obsessive fear of an effeminate culture. "Somehow," he writes of the deluge of print, "just as machinemade shoes aren't as good as handmade shoes, the enormous quantity produced has resulted in diminished power in books. We're not men enough to run the machines we've made." The writer, furthermore, must decide

> exactly what he's cramming all these words into print for; the girlish-romantic gush about selfexpression that still fills the minds of newspaper critics and publishers' logrollers, emphatically won't do anymore. Making a living by selling daydreams, sensations, packages of mental itchingpowders, is all right, but I think few men feel it's much of a life for a healthy adult. (147)

Dos Passos's rhetoric reminds us strongly of the sense of cultural malaise afflicting writer after writer of the late nineteenth century. But everywhere in this piece Dos Passos records a strategic inversion whereby the trade of writing is consigned (by a girl) to the hopper of girlishromantic gush, while "straight" writing, the business of a healthy adult (man), is produced by one who would dominate the "machine of production." "Working with speech straight is vigorous absorbing devastating hopeless work," all the more hopeless for being produced by someone who can never transcend the machine he hopes to dominate, but it is "work that no man need be ashamed of." The rhetorical shift achieved here erases the image of the hard-drinking, hard-fighting, man-of-the-world journalist who seemed to typify all that was wrong with the literary life, and place in its stead the image of an effeminate daydream seller whose goal is only therapeutic (to please consumers who "need to buy a pinch of intellectual catnip now and then"). Dos Passos preserves, within the arena of professional deformations, a distinction between the "daydream artist" and the straight writer; it is only surprising that the "devastating hopeless" task of writing straight guarantees the writer a manly authority.[8]

What is still more surprising – because it tangibly increases the vulnerability of his position – is that the model author Dos Passos chooses to represent the differences between these cultural positions is James Joyce. Dos Passos of course admitted Joyce's influence on his work, but the point is that in this context he seems a strange choice; one might consider a writer in the Hemingway mold a more suitable protagonist. And from the beginning Dos Passos is forced to defend his choice, first dismissing as unimportant the criterion that "Joyce produces for the highbrow and the other [the daydream artist] for the lowbrow trade," and then imagining a probable attack on his position: "You answer that Joyce is esoteric, only read by a few literary snobs, a luxury product like limited editions, without influence on the mass of ordinary newspaper readers." Dos Passos goes on to answer his supposed critics: "give him time," he writes, for the "power of writing is more likely to be exercised vertically through a century than horizontally over a year's sales." The "influence of his powerful work," furthermore, has "already spread, diluted through other writers, into many a printed page of which the author never heard of *Ulysses.*" But those answers are provocatively incomplete. Joyce's work is powerful, but Dos Passos does not discuss the sources or nature of that power. To dominate the machine of production is in part to outlast it, but Dos Passos does not explain how that long-term influence might spread anonymously from page to printed page; Joyce's work is esoteric, but Dos Passos does not reveal how its influence might translate into styles suitable for "the mass of ordinary newspaper readers" (or how that mass might be made suitable for Joyce). Dos Passos argues for the hegemony of Joyce's writing while refusing to specify the conditions under which this admittedly esoteric writing might direct and shape the formations of American culture. Taking "The Pit and the Pendulum" as a model might help us appreciate how Joyce's influence could spread through invisible networks and relays of speech; nonetheless, we should note that the fundamental condition for this influence – the unassailable fact of Joyce's "powerful work" – goes un-argued. We can infer a good deal about "writing straight" from the nature of Joyce's seminal work, but nothing in the piece, beyond Dos Passos's assertion, offers a rationale for Joyce's preeminence.

Like the intervals of Dos Passos's montage, what goes unsaid in this essay provides clues to the author's and our critical strategies. We can begin to articulate those silences by referring to *U.S.A.* and to Dos Passos's other essays of this period, in particular those that explore from different angles that key notion of professionalism. In the Introduction to *Three Soldiers,* professionalism signifies little more than the novelist's trade. In the earlier "Whom Can We Appeal To?" ([1930] 1988f), however, the professional comes in for more elaborate treat-ment. Restoring civilized values to America, Dos Passos writes, must fall to other groups than those reading a magazine like the *New Masses* – an acknowledgment that is perhaps unintended. Dos Passos argues that the readers of *New Masses* are already convinced about the need for revolutionary change and hence any appeal to them must be a "waste"; his covert assumption is that another appeal to the same readers must prove futile by virtue of appeals having been made so many times before to so little overall effect. True power, Dos Passos claims, belongs to the professional strata of the middle class: "there is a layer: engineers, scientists, independent manual craftsmen, writers, artists, actors, technicians of one sort or another, who insofar as they are good at their jobs are a necessary part of any industrial society." This, Dos Passos continues,

> is the weekly-magazinereading [*sic*] class that people appeal to when they talk about public opinion. Education and our professional deformation has made most of us too cowardly and too preoccupied with making a living and living respectably and raising children to want to make events, but

through our technical training and our fair average of leisure we are the
handlers of ideas. Ideas can't make events but they can color them. . . . It's
the job of people of all the professions in the radical fringe of the middle
class to try to influence this middle class . . . so that at least some of its
weight shall be thrown on the side of what I've been calling civilization.
(132–3)

Dos Passos here is very close to the Gramscian notion of hegemony, in which
organic intellectuals (the "radical fringe") are to guide the thought, opinions,
beliefs, and values of their class, though Dos Passos seems to arrive at this position
by way of the power he attributes to manipulators of consciousness like J. W.
Moorehouse. In his letter "Wanted: An Ivy Lee for Liberals" (1930), which
broaches the same theme of recruiting professionals for the preservation of
civilization, Dos Passos fantasizes about employing one of the "super-public-
relations counsels" for subversive ends; and as he imagines the steps this mythical
PR manipulator might take, Dos Passos charts out the territory he would like
others to follow.

Dos Passos is even closer to the position of Thorstein Veblen who, as Dos
Passos put it in "The Bitter Drink," his biography of the economist, "still had a
hope that the engineers, the technicians, the nonprofiteers whose hands were on
the switchboard might take up the fight where the workingclass had failed." In
agreeing with Veblen that technicians should be "at the switchboard," Dos
Passos counts on two major factors. First, Dos Passos argues, because professionals
are not directly involved in the regulation of capital, they play a relatively neutral
role in the class war; second, because they play a vital and irreplaceable role in
the functioning of a complex, technological society, they are perfectly placed to
direct the fashioning of ideas and opinion in that war. Professionals then are to
be both in and out of the game; they are in possession of a symbolic capital that
should not be confused with finance capitalism and thus somehow suited to
direct a society that is organized and dominated by the formations of capital.
There seems a grave split in Dos Passos's theory of social change insofar as the
very neutrality that makes professionals so useful a counter in the class war would
have to be sacrificed in order to grasp an active role in leadership. But oddly, the
example of the Soviet Union that Dos Passos provides to encourage the
radicalizing of the professional classes suggests that the status and position of
professionals did *not* significantly change. The loss of professional neutrality
would pose no problem for Gramsci, whose theory of hegemony is rooted in
Marxist doctrine and for whom neutrality (even if it were possible) would have
no virtue in itself. But Dos Passos's drift in "Whom Can We Appeal To?" is to
"convince the technicians and white collar workers that . . . they can at least
afford to be neutral." The question Dos Passos begs is not so much how the
middle class's organic intellectuals are to radicalize it – though he is silent about
this issue too – but which form of radicalism they are to oppose to dominant

social and economic formations. Readers of "Whom Can We Appeal To?" printed in *New Masses,* would presumably draw their own conclusions about the constitution of that "radical fringe." But "Wanted: An Ivy Lee for Liberals," published in the more moderate *New Republic,* eschews the potentially aggressive role laid down for the radical middle-class intellectual in favor of a pessimistic and even confused conclusion. "Rereading this statement [from "Whom Can We Appeal To"]," Dos Passos writes, "I find it pretty unsatisfactory." The trouble is, he continues, that "the whole structure of the political ideas of the people who are neither members of the Communist party nor pro-capitalists is built of rotten timber and must, I think, be replaced by something more in accord with the historical facts. Until that is formulated, any appeal to 'humanity,' 'civilization,' 'mercy,' must necessarily be on pretty shaky foundations." That "something" in accord with historical facts has not yet, it seems, been formulated; and though Dos Passos's depiction of the complicity between the owning class and professionals has absorbed Marxist rhetoric as well as perspective, there is little sense in either essay or letter that Marxist doctrine and its followers are powerful enough to effect the preservation of civilized values.

This sense that Dos Passos views the potential neutrality of the professional classes as a stabilizing counterweight – a force for preservation rather than for leadership – will surprise few critics. But the point is not that these essays, in their reticence about putting forward coherent political positions, foreshadow Dos Passos's mid-decade shift to a more conservative perspective, but that they each articulate a certain professional stance that ultimately connects us back to the question of why James Joyce appears to be such a useful model for Dos Passos. For he is not only concerned with stabilizing civilization but with ensuring the separateness of the professional realm. Which is to say that works like "Whom Can We Appeal To?" and "An Ivy Lee for Liberals" read two ways at once: as an appeal to professionals to assume a more directive role and as a covert appeal to maintain the autonomy of professional classes. Professionals cannot make events; at best they can "color them." By "education and training," in fact, they are "unfitted for political action." Far from condemning that unfitness, however, Dos Passos seems more concerned in "An Ivy Lee for Liberals" that professionals compromise their autonomy through an unwitting complicity with the owning classes. The "political education instilled by our colleges" has "taught them [those with technical training] to walk unconsciously in step with the owning class and to do any kind of servile dirty work required by the man who signs the checks." Instead, Dos Passos continues in the next sentence, one should "convince these people that it wouldn't hurt them to be neutral." And speaking of the other side of the political spectrum, Dos Passos argues that it "ought not to be so very difficult to convince them here [professionals in America] that their personal destinies are not being directly attacked by the Communists." Appropriately, Dos Passos concludes "An Ivy Lee for Liberals" with a series of hesitations and silences, as though recognizing at last the multiple and often contradictory significances of professional neutrality.

In the Introduction to *Three Soldiers,* Dos Passos equates professionalism with trading in commodities; but his essays suggest professional functions much closer to those I outlined in my first chapter. They affirm a sense of technical workers as ideally autonomous, their power deriving from their ability to resist absorption by a mass society, whether we understand by mass society the present state of consumer capitalism or its potential replacement by communism. And, like all professional endeavors, they affirm a scientific perspective (couched throughout in terms of disengagement and an inquiring objectivity) as the underpinning of their claims to social status and truth. These claims for objectivity should not be seen as merely a subterfuge for justifying Dos Passos's inability to enter the class war on the side of the Communists – a plea by a middle-class liberal for the right to remain neutral. Although he does not detail the new society that might emerge from the rise of the professional classes, there is little essential difference between his vision and the role professionals (and many commentators on professionalism) have actually claimed for the nature of their work within a capitalist society. Indeed, the professional classes could not have been useful to Dos Passos in the first place if the peculiarity of their social position and its actual power had not been manifest. In this sense, his statement in "Whom Can We Appeal To?" that professionals "should be made to realize that they have power and that by intelligent organization they could make themselves respected" merely asks the radical readers of *New Masses* to encourage the formation of communities that have been consolidating their power for decades by the time he writes. And Dos Passos acknowledges his affiliations to professionalism not only in his choice of professionals to effect massive social change (as the group above all others to appeal to) but in the particular configurations of professional power and responsibility he chooses to represent. When in the later essay "The Writer as Technician" ([1935] 1988h) Dos Passos argues that the main problem for the technician in a capitalist or socialist economy is "to secure enough freedom from interference from the managers of the society in which he lives to be able to do his work," he is only articulating the unspoken meanings of earlier essays. He is also articulating a primary criterion of professional work that has its roots far back in the nineteenth century.

All of this has profound implications for Dos Passos's fiction and essay writing alike. By the time of "The Writer as Technician," he recognizes more fully that his affiliation to an ethos of professionalism brings with it particular discursive features. He writes, for instance, that

> the professional writer discovers some aspect of the world and invents out of the speech of his time some particularly apt and original way of putting it down on paper. If the product is compelling, and important enough, it molds and influences ways of thinking to the point of changing and

rebuilding the language, which is the mind of the group. The process is not very different from that of a scientific discovery and invention. The importance of a writer, as of a scientist, depends upon his ability to influence subsequent thought. In his relation to society a professional writer is a technician just as much as an electrical engineer is. (169)

Although the next paragraph distinguishes between the work of the "isolated technician" and the "collective type of writing" produced by "advertising offices, moving picture studios, political propaganda agencies" and newspapers, this passage suggests that both forms of writing accrue authority by way of structurally parallel tactics. That is, a political propagandist as much as a creative writer may "influence subsequent thought" by putting into play writing strategies that demand certain specialized skills. Both are technicians, depending on institutionalized communities to bestow on them the authority their speaking requires, however differently their words are then allocated places in the realm of culture.

Comparing a writer's work to the function of scientist and engineer combined begins to identify some of the features that the process of influencing the mind of a society – which the Introduction to *Three Soldiers* left vague – must possess. Incidentally, it helps to explain why the collective and isolated work of writing "technicians" might be produced to such different cultural effect. Once again, Dos Passos refuses to specify the details of the process – it is "not very different from that of a scientific discovery." But the next sentence, instead of explaining how a scientific discovery is transmitted to the public, retraces old ground by remarking that the importance of creative work is predicated on the extent of the writer's or scientist's influence. Again, Dos Passos's argument circumvents the very information it promises to deliver. But if a writer's power is built on the same structural principles as those pertaining to the scientist and engineer, certain consequences should follow. Professional autonomy (or the appearance of it) arises out of the consent of a number of different communities: the immediate community of competence to which the individual is bound by legal, contractual, and epistemological ties; and, in still more complex fashion, the economic and class structures of society at large, which recognize the authority and functionality of the various professions. It is this dense, tightly regulated web of economic, legal, and consensual relations – the kind of enveloping structure that grants power to the lawyers and judges who engineer the deaths of Sacco and Vanzetti – that must be present in order to disseminate the influence of a writer like Joyce from page to page.

In "Washington and Chicago, II: Spotlights and Microphones" (1932), Dos Passos composes a parable of professional power that illuminates this relational structure and dramatizes many of the points he argues in other essays of this period. Sitting behind the spotlights at the 1932 Republican Convention, Dos Passos remarks on the "powers of the technicians who tune the loudspeakers and handle the lights." Those powers concern, in part, the expert production of dramatic and emotional scenes during the convention, all the more expert because produced silently and invisibly. Thus it appears that the spotlights have "invented a little comic figure on a platform"; they "dextrously produce a little beaked figure in black." The man at the switchboard (by the name of Joe) remains offstage throughout the performance, like Dos Passos himself, sitting behind the batteries of lights and looking down on the "circus" below. Oddly, the technician's power is revealed as power only at the point it goes awry; thus, problems in the microphones reveal elements of the party platforms that should, according to the script, have been muted. The "booing and backtalk of the galleries," for instance, is transmitted to the radio audience, and the unwelcome prohibition plank comes across loudly to the hall. These spontaneous power surges serve a double function for Dos Passos, demonstrating on the one hand that from behind the spotlights a form of power is being exercised, and on the other that the power wielded by these technicians could be used differently for subversive and salutary ends. But there is a script, and the technicians, far from inventing these moments of theater, are themselves invented by the still more anonymous scriptwriters. Although the spots invent little figures on stage, the spots too "spring to attention" at the singing of *America;* and at one unscripted moment, when ex-Senator France appears on stage, Dos Passos comments that the audience "didn't get a chance to see what the spotlights would have done if they'd had to extemporize, because the offending marionette was immediately dragged off by the stagehands and the show continued according to the script."

Once more, the essay invites multiple readings. Although Dos Passos focuses on the way the "whole technique and machinery of politics has been changed by the mechanics of communication," his inquiry penetrates beyond the mechanical manipulation of emotions on the convention floor to those experts who have skilfully charted the course of the convention. The scriptwriter rather than the lighting engineer is Dos Passos's most cunning – and imitable – opponent; but all share access to the same forms of power. His final question "Who's going to be man enough to stand at the switchboard?" links together the lighting technician, the unknown scriptor of the entire convention, and Dos Passos himself, who brings these secret relations to light. Dos Passos, in a sense, plays all roles: illuminator, writer, and rewriter of the secret scripts prepared for this event. But though his image of the man at the switchboard emphasizes the role of the writer as an isolated technician – perhaps man enough to be (in Dos Passos's words) the "Great Engineer" that the president himself attempts and fails to be – that image runs counter to the way Dos Passos depicts professional power in the essay. That power is inherently relational. The "guy at the phone" yells to Joe at the switchboard; both answer to the political propagandists whose show this is; and all owe their prestige and status, in a sense, to what the "circus" on the convention floor represents in terms of economic, political, and ideological power. It is hard to imagine how the technicians could exercise their power along the lines of the anarchic, spontaneous power surges that nearly disrupt the convention. To do so would transform them into Dadaist saboteurs, and thus not, by the terms of their own professional charters, professionals at all.

It is this point, that professional writers at the switchboard of society require communities able and willing to support them and grant them social authority, that Dos Passos keeps approaching and then eliding in his discussions of professionalism. That gap between inventing original writing out of the speech of one's time and then having that writing mold and influence the mind and language of a generation is never closed by Dos Passos. But that gap is closed, historically and practically, by the professional study of literature in the university; what is more, its closing is everywhere countenanced and predicted by the way in which Dos Passos describes professional work in his essays. In the Introduction to *Three Soldiers,* Dos Passos set himself the problem of defending Joyce, who is "without influence on the mass of ordinary newspaper readers" and only appeals to a "few literary snobs." But, as the subtext of Dos Passos's arguments has suggested all along, professional power relies on the kind of special, competent communities that allow those with technical training, scientific knowhow, and special forms of writing to accrue power in the first place. In the case of writing, cultural authority depends on the persuasiveness of a few literary snobs (or, let us say, professional critics) rather than the mass of newspaper readers. This point is one that Dos Passos, again almost in spite of himself, comes close to acknowledging in several essays. In "They Want Ritzy Art," his essay on the New Playwrights Theatre (the radical theater that he helped organize and run), Dos Passos writes that it aimed specifically at "things that matter to a large and largely workers' audience." The "main difficulty in getting such an organization under way," however, is that the "whole drift of American cultural life is against it. That tendency is that experiments in thought and presentation are for a few high-brows and that the general public that attends prizefights and baseball games will take only the most smooth-worn routine in the theatre." It may be, he concludes, that though worthwhile "the task is an impossible one." Historically, the task of reading and legitimating a work like Dos Passos's own play for the theater, *Airways, Inc.,* has been carried out by professionals who are (mostly) in accord with Dos Passos that the mass of readers prefer smooth-worn routines, and whose function – like Dos Passos's in his fiction – is to make "smooth-worn" and "routine" signify in ways that preserve the cultural legitimacy of terms like "original," and "fresh." In Dos Passos's transposition of an audience composed of workers (which has never been achieved) to a general public, which can be observed any day of the week and whose mass tastes can only be scorned, we recognize the alignment of Dos Passos's cultural outlook with that promoted within the academy.

This secret complicity between Dos Passos's work and the professional groups of readers who have most often engaged his work can be discerned most readily in his 1928 *New York Times* essay about e.e. cummings's play *Him* (1988c), an essay that, in its cogent defense of modernist technique, offers a new and intriguing perspective on the reception of experimental writing. Along with modernist painting and Freud, Dos Passos begins, has grown up a "style of writing that might be called oblique in the sense that it attempts to generate feelings and ideas rather than put them immediately up to the understanding." Modernism in writing often uses "shorthand or the Morse code" in order to sabotage the conventional, linear plot lines inherited from the nineteenth century. This is the technique of *Him,* which Dos Passos argues in terms of a familiar analogy is the "method of a scientist rather than of a storyteller." Though *Him* might strike the reader as stylistically different from Dos Passos's work, an underlying commitment to detachment and objectivity, held in common with all professional enterprises, characterizes the work of both writers. Dos Passos makes no attempt in this essay to distinguish between a working-class audience and the general public; instead, he specifies the failings of educated and professional readers. This results in an important shift of emphasis. "They Want Ritzy Art" contemplates the possibility of an experimental theater aimed at a working class audience, in full knowledge that experimental writing implies its converse – a few highbrow, specialized readers.[9] In "They Want Ritzy Art," Dos Passos avoids the problem by condensing it into a few equivocal sentences. The *Times* article takes this subterfuge a step further by attacking the very audience it quietly assumes to be not its adversary but its real ally.

Education, to begin with, is depicted as closing down the possibilities of narrative expression; thus the statement that the "majority of educated people have been taught to believe that the only way of expression in words is the narrative exposition style" suggests that they have been taught wrongly. But Dos Passos saves his vitriol for those educated readers whose duty is also to write. The result of reading *Him,* Dos Passos writes in a sentence whose syntax is as confused as its logic, is that

> particularly among professional writers, critics and the like who feel they know it all and that any use of words other than according to their own habits that they learned in high school is a personal insult to them, start snorting and blustering around and saying, "Rubbish, nonsense." And the talk about not being able to understand new methods in music, painting, writing, comes, it seems to me, from trying to judge them by standards other than their own. (110–11)

It would be easy to read this essay as a standard exercise whereby avant-garde writers define their modernity against the staid, outmoded bourgeois critic. But this would be to mistake the whole point of the essay, which is not to dismiss the value of professional critics but to increase it. The essay is to provide new ways of perceiving and understanding to "professional writers, critics and the like who feel they know it all," and thus help them to know better. Indeed, his analysis of cummings's *Him* actually shows him performing the critical role more effectively than the critics themselves, arguing, despite his deliberately homely metaphors of peeling artichokes and onions, for greater complexity and for a range of reference that includes Freud, painting, and science as well as nineteenth-century poetry. This attack on false cultivation and learning could only be read, in the case of Dos Passos, as a thoroughgoing dismissal of educated readers if we suppose that the legitimating function of this audience could be taken up by the working class – a supposition that "They Want Ritzy Art" appears to subvert. The essay on *Him,* in fact, makes no pretense of supplanting a professional audience in favor of another (say, the working class) either more teachable or more in tune with experimental writing. This "preachment," to use a term Dos Passos favored, is designed to inform, educate, and thus bolster the cultural value of professional readers and writers. Far from denying their right to speak, Dos Passos wishes to translate their snorting and blustering around into an appropriate, effective, and powerful idiom.

The essay, in other words, covertly acknowledges the fact that experimental writing in the twentieth century has been the preserve of communities of expert readers whose criteria for literary writing are virtually indistinguishable from Dos Passos's: the value of oblique, complex, innovatory art, and a strategy of identifying and cordoning-off both routine work and the general public to which it appeals. The point is not that Dos Passos consciously wishes to join ranks with the middle-class readers he seems to scorn, nor even that an unconscious conservative bent appears under the radical rhetoric. Rather, Dos Passos's work everywhere implies a complicity between modernist writer and professional reader, the one producing work that presupposes an elite readership, the other intent on consolidating professional authority by way of a complex, multileveled engagement with the texts best able to support it. *U.S.A.* has woven into its very fabric an implied legitimating readership that is very different from the group of hoboes, boilermakers, and social workers who gather in Camera Eye (50) to hear the old words renewed by Sacco and Vanzetti's deaths. While Camera Eye (50) ends with "we stand defeated America," this can hardly be said of the specialized critical audience (a "we" distinct in important ways from the "we" of the entire American population) that has made this moment one of the most intensively studied in the novel.

A necessary consequence of the task of cultural legitimation falling to the academy is that the United States has no unified audience possessing homogeneous reading skills. Whereas Eisenstein, Vertov, and many writers in the *New Masses* could at least hypothesize the existence of a unified audience within which each individual would be capable of activating montage in the same way, the actual composition of readerships in the West suggests quite the opposite. Montage structure in the West has been propagated by avant-garde movements and then legitimated, not by the quickly dying movements themselves or by succeeding movements, but by the long-term memory of the academy. The reason that critics are correct about *U.S.A.* – even when they seem to disagree –

is because of the conditions of reception prevailing in the West. The historical conditions surrounding the production of *U.S.A.* could only lead to its reception as valuable work within the profession of literary studies, which separates out "collective" work from that of "isolated technicians" and guarantees a different cultural placement for the latter's. We as critics could not read *U.S.A.*, appreciate the meanings of its intervals, and provisionally agree on them without a shared, enabling discourse already being in place that shapes the way we think about the text and apprehend each other's interpretations. In his essays of the late 1920s and early 1930s, Dos Passos acknowledges the nature of that audience and its discourse despite his outright hostility to what he saw as effeminate literary snobs. Given the cultural and historical makeup of his era, his efforts to become the man at the switchboard of American society could have no other issue.

6

Miss Lonelyhearts

Nathanael West's Comic-Strip Novel

⸻

*[Miss Lonelyhearts] was smiling an innocent, amused smile,
the smile of an anarchist sitting in the movies with a bomb
in his pocket.*

Miss Lonelyhearts

In *Miss Lonelyhearts* ([1933] 1962a), Nathanael West's book about a world more grimly "newspaperized" than Henry James's could ever be, Miss Lonelyhearts tries out for a role whose performance could only be thought anachronistic in the twentieth century: the man of letters. More precisely, perhaps, Miss Lonelyhearts tries to avoid the contemporary life of letters – these "inarticulate expressions of genuine suffering" (32) – to which he is sentenced by the protocols of mass publishing. Like the movie version of the Battle of Waterloo in *The Day of the Locust,* the term "man of letters" evokes a strange iteration of past splendors when, as John Gross describes in *The Rise and Fall of the Man of Letters* (1969), gentlemen amateurs pursued the genteel vocation of belles lettres. Those splendors are nominally recalled in Miss Lonelyhearts's pursuits, but appear only as bathetic imitation. A latter-day Dr. Johnson, a Grub Street hack without literary pretensions, Miss Lonelyhearts gives us a vertiginous sense of that honored and archaic-sounding title made new under ignominious circumstances: the writer whose only letters are those received from other people, and whose only written productions serve to promote a rampant commercialism to which Truth and Beauty mean larger circulations. Not that Miss Lonelyhearts adequately performs the role of the professional writer. Having once recommended suicide to his readers as an appropriate escape – a strategy guaranteed, as Shrike points out, to reduce the paper's circulation – Miss Lonelyhearts increasingly fails to recommend anything at all as his antagonism toward his task grows. The man of letters gives way here to the hack without words whose descent into inarticulacy the novel chronicles.

Miss Lonelyhearts's literary filiations are potentially immense. A nineteenth-century *flâneur* out of Charles Baudelaire, wandering and observing the nightmare streets of the city, Miss Lonelyhearts walks into a very unpoetic wasteland of meaning where "No repeated group of words would fit [the] rhythm" (11) of the streetcars and shouts of hucksters. In the speakeasy underworld of the city, occasionally reminiscent of Bohemian Paris or the fertile coffeehouse culture of eighteenth-century London, and certainly evocative of the reading and discussion groups Nathanael West attended in the 1920s (Martin 1970, 110–11), Miss Lonelyhearts and his friends gather to talk about art and literature. At one point Miss Lonelyhearts finds his friends complaining, in terms that Henry James and Nathaniel Hawthorne would have understood, about "the number of female writers" (13). But this profoundly disillusioning conversation (these female writers "all needed . . . a good rape," proclaims one of them) suggests their loss of belief in "literature . . . and in personal expression as an absolute end" (14) inculcated at college. These men proceed from the same premises as the young John Dos Passos, whom Dos Passos in *U.S.A.* remembers as living within the Harvard bell jar of a weak late-nineteenth-century aestheticism, and whose belief in Beauty clashed with a brute, alien reality. The "pressure outside sustained the vacuum within," Dos Passos wrote in Camera Eye (25), identifying a stultifying equilibrium that Harvard, grown "cold with culture," could not upset. For both West and Dos Passos, new pressures demanded the invention of new writing strategies, to be forged out of a vacuous culture of aestheticism, a new modernist idiom, and out of the limited expressive possibilities of mass culture. Miss Lonelyhearts himself reminds us of the difficulty of those aspirations. He is a pseudonymous man of letters, journalist, androgynous everyman, writer and reader, yet none of these, for he does not write, can barely read the letters, spurns the void of journalism yet discovers no other more satisfying cultural arena.

As we have seen, current theories of the literary response to mass journalism frequently hold this environment of alien technologies and languages responsible for some of the most powerful impulses of Progressive Era American literature. Journalism, promising "culture into action" and access to a world of hard facts and realities conventionally hidden in genteel literature, seemed to offer to the literary writer new perceptions, languages, and tactics. But in *Miss Lonelyhearts,* the journalists play a very different role than their Progressive forebears. Old buzzwords like accuracy, facts, truth are subjected to the imperatives of a new marketplace in which Miss Lonelyhearts's columns conceal the desperate letters he receives and newspaper articles eschew muckracking to examine an America of "goat and adding machine" rituals (7). With images that have become more familiar to the twentieth century than the muckrakers' enlightenment values of social transformation, journalism is associated with violence, deformity, and trash. Returning to the city from the country, for instance, Miss Lonelyhearts sees "a ragged woman with an enormous goiter pick a love story magazine out of a garbage can" (39); in the little park he sees a newspaper that "struggled in the air like a kite with a broken spine" (5). And in a grim extension of the myth of the hard-boiled reporter, newspapers become signs of aggression throughout. Mrs. Doyle, for instance, "rolled a newspaper into a club and struck her husband on the mouth with it" (234). And, as if to return the favor, Peter Doyle conceals in a newspaper the gun with which he plans to kill Miss Lonelyhearts. Like Clyde Griffiths, Miss Lonelyhearts is also completed by the newspaper, which brings the Doyles to him as readers of his column, and then masks the gun that (we assume) kills him.

West's brilliant satire of the newspaper business uncovers, as we shall see, much that later historians of mass culture have come to identify as the profound shortcomings of our media-saturated society. In particular, the novel implies a cultural dynamic whereby the expressive possibilities of the mass media are augmented by appropriating the vocabulary and images of high culture; in many ways, Shrike and Miss Lonelyhearts outperform Dos Passos's PR wizards and surpass George Flack's borrowing from a rhetoric of fine perception. Unlike any of the characters we have seen so far, Shrike and Miss Lonelyhearts recognize their complicity with an appropriative mass culture; they play a dual role of participants in and readers of the newspaper world they both support and revile. Oddly, so does Nathanael West. As thoroughly as Dreiser's *An American Tragedy, Miss Lonelyhearts* evokes a world in which literary principles are colonized by mass forms of expression; what is more, West himself established the relationship. Whereas in James, Dreiser, and Dos Passos we look to a rhetorical accommodation of the expressive conventions of mass culture, in *Miss Lonelyhearts* the nature of that accommodation is transformed by West's own announced intentions for the novel. It was to be a "novel in the form of a comic strip," as though the only formal principles suitable for describing a pervasive mass culture were to be drawn from its own discursive premises rather than from a literary world elsewhere. West negotiates in complex ways between satirizing a powerful mass culture and acknowledging an allegiance to its possibilities for formal innovation.

West's position thus sounds like the one I have already outlined for Dreiser and Dos Passos; what distinguishes *Miss Lonelyhearts* is that West does not merely accommodate techniques from mass culture but self-consciously refers to and deflates those accommodatory maneuvers. West's anarchic attempt to introduce a bomb into the movies (as the epigraph to this chapter suggests) is certainly no more remarkable than the antagonism he shows toward literary traditions, for over and over again he invokes an outmoded literary culture whose traditional forms, strategies, principles, and meanings no longer have cultural validity. In this sense, West is quite different from the likes of James, Dreiser, and Dos Passos, who depend on *not* defining a cogent theory of literariness in order to activate in the reader preexisting cultural and literary significations. West invokes and brings great pressure to bear on the category of the "literary" itself, and in so doing runs the risk of subverting the premises that should confer meaning on his work – not only in what he says about literature but in the formal and linguistic strategies he employs to create "literature."[1] *Miss Lonelyhearts* brings to a focus the complex modernist strategies I have tried to describe throughout this study – and also puts them in question. At what point does the novel push so far in the direction of a formal and linguistic iteration of mass cultural expression that West's critique of mass culture can and should be turned against his own work? Indeed, is it possible that *Miss Lonelyhearts* functions like a sophisticated creation from the culture industry – replete with eye-catching violence, banal allusions, caricatured situations and characters – not because it is a satire but because it is colonized by the comic-strip culture it only appears to condemn? West's writing locates and transforms the energies of modernism even as it looks forward to a postmodernism that stretches the accommodation of mass culture to its extreme.

Paradoxically, his subversion of literary meanings is contingent on the presence of institutionalized meanings that were unavailable to, say, Henry James. By the late 1920s, when West was composing *The Dream Life of Balso Snell* and *Miss Lonelyhearts,* a very different set of cultural circumstances was brought to bear on the possibilities of literary expression. In this new age of college-trained readers, manifestos, little magazines, and transient but productive bohemias, literary culture was growing self-reflexively aware of its modernism. An art of allusion and juxtaposition developed by the likes of Eliot and Pound, whereby a word or phrase might evoke the entire life of a past cultural tradition for the competent reader, did more than create new formal strategies. It lay the foundation for a systematic organization of literary periods and genres, established a canon and hagiography of culture heroes, and crystallized concepts of literariness. *Balso Snell* is West's classic statement of and about a newly institutionalized literary culture, and the artist, as West writes (quoting from Chekov), "must always be occupied with undermining institutions" (1957, 30). Drawing on his immense erudition, West created in *Balso* a pastiche of literary names, book titles, styles, conventions, quotations, and mannerisms, all of which imply the existence of established reputations, quotable masterpieces, and customary literary poses sedimented into self-perpetuating canonicity. Even that bible of modernism, Joyce's *Ulysses,* is invoked and hollowed out by Balso Snell's "Moooompitcher yaaaah. Oh I never hoped to know the passion, the sensuality hidden within you – yes, yes. Drag me down into the mire, drag. Yes!" (61). The insane John Gilson, whose journal Balso Snell reads, worked in a library surrounded by "a hundred billion words one after another according to ten thousand mad schemes," each book smelling like the "breaths of their [dead] authors" (17). Gilson thus becomes a type that West rewrites in the characters of Balso Snell, Miss Lonelyhearts, and Shrike: the worker in words who constantly gestures toward literary precursors in full knowledge that they are institutionalized, outmoded, and dead. This problem of heritage works its way even more potently into the later work of West, whose novel in the form of a comic strip registers affiliations to the comic-strip culture he otherwise derides, and who derides the literary culture that is generally seen as the sole enclave of powerful writing.

I

In the new dispensation of a "newspaperized" world, Miss Lonelyhearts, whose classic "New England puritan" (3) looks mark him as heir to America's literary as well as religious traditions, finds himself at a cultural crossroads where the signs "literature" and "mass culture" once again come into play. Prodded by the sight of the woman picking a magazine out of a garbage can, Miss Lonelyhearts brings a familiar indictment against mass culture: "Men have always fought their misery with dreams. Although dreams were once powerful, they have been made puerile by the movies, radio and newspapers. Among many betrayals, this one is the worst" (39). Though voiced by Miss Lonelyhearts, this statement seems an adequate interpretive key to the novel; the implications of this betrayal, however, are complex. The "business of dreams" (22) functions not only by making dreams into commodities but by making its producers aware of the structure of the belief on whose occlusion its stability depends. As Foucault and Pierre Macherey have argued, the ideological equilibrium of bourgeois society rests on accepting as natural and universal what is in fact socially constructed and controlled by specific formations of power. The sense of betrayal exhibited by Shrike and Miss Lonelyhearts signifies not only their forced recognition of a new cultural puerility but also the loss of naturalness it occasions. Mass culture inveighs against the inherent weightlessness and disposability of its own productions, exposing constantly its alliance with commodity form and the marketplace. It displays, in Berthold Brecht's terms, its in-built *verfremdung*-effect. Nathanael West departs from the model of Dreiser's Clyde Griffiths in having certain characters (Tod Hackett in *The Day of the Locust* included) become aware of this effect. In this respect, Miss Lonelyhearts's diagnosis of his own spiritual and psychological ills is a masterpiece of self- and cultural-awareness:

> Perhaps I can make you understand. Let's start from the beginning. A man is hired to give advice to the readers of a newspaper. The job is a circulation stunt and the whole staff considers it a joke. He welcomes the job, for it might lead to a gossip column, and anyway he's tired of being a leg man. He too considers the job a joke, but after several months at it, the joke begins to escape him. He sees that the majority of the letters are profoundly humble pleas for moral and spiritual advice, that they are inarticulate expressions of genuine suffering. He also discovers that his correspondents take him seriously. For the first time in his life, he is forced to examine the values by which he lives. This examination shows him that he is the victim of the joke and not its perpetrator. (32)

By presenting himself to Betty as "he," the butt of the cruel joke of this newspaperized world – but not really accountable, not really to be identified with the real Miss Lonelyhearts – he manages to disassociate himself from the premises of the joke in which he is so clearly implicated. The joke may have serious consequences for characters who need real solutions to intransigent problems (even more so because his readers persist in mistaking his parodic columns for wisdom), but it remains a poor one nevertheless, capable of being riddled, parodied, and subverted.

Miss Lonelyhearts' position as a respected player in a disreputable "*newspaper game*" (35) places him within a series of neat double binds. Presented with a huge audience of readers, Miss Lonelyhearts finds himself lapsing constantly into incoherency; fully aware of his ethical responsibility to them, Miss Lonelyhearts ends up facing, spiritually and rhetorically, the void that Henry James claimed lay within media saturation. In *The Reverberator* James engaged that void by eliding Flack's text, whose noisy but vacant publicity encountered its appropriate destiny in textual silence. West, using a tactic he will exploit more fully in *The Day of the Locust,* prints fragments of newspaper copy in such a way that its fade into obscurity becomes increasingly predictable. Thus Miss Lonelyhearts's first leader is "impossible to continue" (1). Shrike's rewriting breaks off with an ellipsis (4) as does Miss Lonelyhearts's later column about Christ (39). Another abortive attempt to write ends with "Life is . . ." (26). Miss Lonelyhearts's imagined headlines appear and fade with the regularity and monotony of Dos Passos's Newsreels: "Mother slays five with ax, slays seven, slays nine. . . . Babe slams two, slams three. . . ." (25). Collagelike, these scraps of newsprint hang in the space of the text as though in mute testimony to their reproducibility. Newspaper "copy" lives up to its name, for if on the one hand it is riddled with ellipses and hesitations, on the other it calls for the rewriting of what has already been written. Miss Lonelyhearts is still trying to write his first leader (beginning "Life *is* worth while") when the words of his later column trail away with "Life is . . ."

Iteration is the predominant rhetorical and psychological mode of West's mass culture. Miss Lonelyhearts "could not go on finding the same joke funny thirty times a day for months on end," especially as these letters are "all of them alike" (1). In response, his columns are all alike in their rhetoric and in their repeated failure to conclude. Constant iteration is made to replace the equilibrium of unquestioned structures of belief, papering over an inevitable slippage of confidence even as the iterative mode draws attention to its artifice. Conversely, it is because the artifice is so obvious that characters must vigilantly try to renew the validity of the functional paradigms, as Miss Lonelyhearts himself suggests at the El Gaucho restaurant after hearing Mary Shrike talk about her father the "portrait painter, a man of genius": "Parents are also part of the business of dreams. My father was a Russian prince, my father was a Piute Indian chief, my father was an Australian sheep baron, my father lost all his money in Wall Street, my father was a portrait painter. People like Mary were unable to do without such tales" (23). "Man of genius" follows "portrait painter" as mechanically as Miss Lonelyhearts iterates Mary's story as one of his examples, all told to the mechanical rhythm of "my father was." Like Clyde Griffiths and many of the characters of *U.S.A.*, Mary Shrike suggests a consciousness structured by the formal repetitions of mass culture. According to Miss Lonelyhearts, Mary Shrike "always talked in headlines" (20). Her speech is anonymous, communal, and forever pointing beyond itself, like the headline, to larger discursive structures of which it is an extension and indicator.

By way of demonstrating the hegemony of the mass media, all speech in the novel tends toward characteristic linguistic strategies of the media. Like Dreiser, West constantly demonstrates his mastery of the cliché, which invests the speech of his characters so thoroughly that many of them have no linguistic life beyond the repertoire of formulaic expressions produced by mass culture. Mrs. Doyle begins her confession to Miss Lonelyhearts: "It's a long, long story, and that's why I couldn't write it in a letter. I got into trouble when the Doyles lived above us on Center Street. I used to be kind to him [her husband] and go to the movies with him because he was a cripple, although I was one of the most popular girls on the block" (29). Her "long, long story" (already her third repetition of that phrase) recalls the narrator's description of her husband as "one of those composite photographs used by screen magazines in guessing contests" (45). Her story too is a composite of conventional phrases like "I got into trouble" and "I was one of the most popular girls on the block." In one of her few moments of insight, Mrs. Doyle admits that her problem may be "too much movies" (30). Likewise, when Miss Lonelyhearts attempts to heal the rift between Mrs. Doyle and her husband, his speech betrays its textual origins and he finds that he has "merely written a column for his paper" (49). Shrike plays a similar role, producing a clipping of an article in a speakeasy, producing Miss Lonelyhearts's letters at the party and, as we shall see in more detail, producing in his lengthiest and most eloquent speech at Miss Lonelyhearts's sickbed a brilliant parody-through-repetition of the culture industry.

West first conceived of *Miss Lonelyhearts* after reading letters written to "Susan Chester," pseudonym for a reporter at the *Brooklyn Eagle,* at least one of which is reprinted in fragmentary form in West's text (Martin 1970, 109–10). The comparison to Dreiser's partial reprinting of newspaper reports and the Grace Brown letters suggests a coincidence of strategy if not of intent. It would not do, however, to confuse West's vision of an iterative mass culture with that of Dos Passos's or of Dreiser's (whose "muddle class" realism West derided [Martin 1970, 69]). In *An American Tragedy,* the processes by which a mass culture inhabits consciousness were invisible to the characters themselves. The Lycurgus Griffiths were capable of understanding the social uses and consequences of a journalistic mediation of reality, but no one understood the clue to such repetitive tragedies clearly inscribed in the newspaper's own report of the "ACCIDENTAL DOUBLE TRAGEDY" at Pass Lake. Similarly, Dos Passos's role "at the switchboard" of American technologies of power placed him in the familiar modernist position of cultural mediator, selecting, arranging, and reprinting the fragmentary evidence of a wholesale shift in culture and consciousness in such a way as to allow recurring patterns to surface. That operation of uncovering the coded or mystified languages of mass culture in Dos Passos's Newsreel sections, however, demanded a competence accorded to few historical personages (such as Thorstein Veblen), and no characters. In *Miss Lonelyhearts,* Mary Shrike, Mr. and Mrs. Doyle, and perhaps Betty, share with George Flack, Clyde Griffiths, Charley Anderson, Janey, and most of Dos Passos's biographical studies, a lapsed awareness about the extent to which the culture industry shapes and governs the self. The power of mass culture over its consumers, these characters imply, lies in its ability to fabricate models of selfhood for them that flesh out, actualize, and complete a sense of the real. At the same time, that completion is only possible by a diminishment of the self to a point where the inadequacies of the models cannot be observed.

The problem with Shrike and Miss Lonelyhearts – though it marks the point at which West diverges from the other authors I discuss – is that their allegiance to mass culture is overburdened and compromised by their acute penetration of its paradigmatic narratives, gestures, images, and languages. Although Miss Lonelyhearts fails to dissociate himself physically from the newspaper game, it is nevertheless true that the fantasy of dissociation in the novel remains a powerful one, enabling Shrike and Miss Lonelyhearts to live out, rhetorically and in fantasy, the escape that forever eludes them (until death). In "Miss Lonelyhearts on a Field Trip," for instance, Miss Lonelyhearts's inability to finish his column leads him to an "imagined desert where Desperate, Broken-hearted and the others were still building his name" out of "faded photographs, soiled fans, time-tables, playing cards, broken toys, imitation jewelry" (26). Miss Lonelyhearts imagines himself in this parody of a religious ritual as another Tiresias, focusing another wasteland composed, like T. S. Eliot's, of detritus ("empty bottles, sandwich papers,/Silk handkerchiefs, cardboard boxes, cigarette ends/Or other testimony of summer nights"). Though his imagined retreat from the unbearable letters leads him back to the idiom of brokenness and fragmentation he sought to escape, the point is that even this inadequately realized fantasy promotes an awareness of what is to be escaped. By composing his audience and the disordered remains of culture into a kind of collage, Miss Lonelyhearts reserves for himself at least the bare possibility of enacting the role of observer, selector, and arranger already made powerful by modernists such as Eliot, Picasso, Pound, Braque, Dos Passos, and many others.

In *Miss Lonelyhearts,* fantasies of escape make the characters' adjustment to the newspaper game less and less possible. The kind of adaptations available to Shrike and Miss Lonelyhearts forbid the unself-consciousness necessary for them to accept (as the other characters do) that game as unquestionably and unmitigatedly real. Yet their failure to envisage true cultural alternatives means that they constantly marginalize the discourse to which they remain dialogically committed. To Betty, in "Miss Lonelyhearts and the Party Dress," Miss Lonelyhearts proclaims, "I've quit the Miss Lonelyhearts job," yet in the final chapter we find him submitting "drafts of his column to God" and misinterpreting Doyle's shout as yet another desperate letter from "Desperate, Harold S. Catholic-mother, Broken-hearted, Broad-shoulders, Sick-of-it-all, Disillusioned-with-tubercular-husband." And Miss Lonelyhearts's lugubrious sermon to the Doyles, when he realizes that he has "merely written a column for his paper," suggests the same sense of rhetorical displacement. Aware that he has "substituted the rhetoric of Shrike for that of Miss Lonelyhearts," he is unable to speak in his own voice, yet equally unable to ignore the meaning of that substitution. A curious schizophrenia emerges at the moment when Miss Lonelyhearts attempts to deliver a "message" (48) to the Doyles, as to all of his desperate readers; his perception of the inauthenticity of his public voice implies the presence of an authentic self capable of discriminating one from the other. In this limited sense, he performs the role occupied by the Jamesian narrator in *The Reverberator*, defining a consciousness potentially distinguishable from those voices inhabiting the public domain. Yet his potential for discrimination does not allow him to disengage whatever authentic kernel of self remains.

Still more obviously, Shrike's set-piece speech to Miss Lonelyhearts on his sickbed constitutes a series of manic narratives that uncover – and yet in a sense empower – the discursive structures that function as the precondition for his speech. Shrike's topic is escape; his mode is parodic juxtaposition:

> Let us now consider the South Seas . . . You live in a thatch hut with the daughter of the king, a slim young maiden . . . In the evening, on the blue lagoon, under the silvery moon, to your love you croon in the soft sylabelew and vocabelew of her langorour tongorour. [*sic*] Your body is golden brown like hers, and tourists have need of the indignant finger of the missionary to point you out. They envy you your breech clout and carefree laugh and little brown bride and fingers instead of forks. But you don't return their envy, and when a beautiful society girl comes to your hut in the night, seeking to learn the secret of your happiness, you send her back to her yacht. (33)

Shrike touches on key images of romantic fantasies of escape from industrialized society: the Fayaway-type maiden, the vision of an organic, nonmechanized way of life epitomized most fully by the South Sea islands. The image of the "beautiful society girl," far from intruding into this fantasy, seems quite at home – as many movies attest. In the voice of a Mary Shrike (or Faye Greener in *The Day of the Locust*) these images would identify the character as a conduit for an anonymous, public discourse. Shrike organizes the narrative into parody, and parody implies control. An existing style is reproduced in exaggerated fashion and in such a way that this appropriation of its distinctive features results in a new perspective and comprehension. Shrike's extravagant word play begins to defamiliarize what would otherwise remain hackneyed and significant only in the fact of its reproducibility. In particular, the bizarre onomatopeia of the sentence beginning "In the evening, on the blue lagoon" highlights the influence of popular songs; rather pointedly, the triple assonance of "oo" culminates in "croon." In the same passage, references to the daughter of the king in whose eyes is an "ancient wisdom," whose "breasts are golden speckled pears, her belly a melon," recall the Song of Songs. Juxtaposed musical languages suggest Shrike's command over diverse idioms. "Her belly a melon" and "to your love you croon" yoke together the traditional and the contemporary, thus introducing a point of difference essential for exposing this narrative of South Seas escapism as a cultural fabrication. Shrike's witty pastiche of the "soft sylabelew and vocabelew" of contemporary music and mass narratives demonstrates his comprehension of their vocabulary, thus marking his resistance to a characteristic conflation of such narratives with reality.

Yet the parody is an uneasy one, and not just because Shrike's "soft sylabelew and vocabelew" thereby affirms how ingrained the words and rhythms of popular culture must be in him. Insofar as parody always places the parodied and the parodier in a mutual relationship, Shrike feels that he participates in the exhaustion of media productions. As his own commentary suggests: "The South Seas are played out and there's little use in imitating Gauguin" (33). Shrike, aware of his language as a series of "played out" verbal gestures, points to their exhaustion and simultaneously affirms his dependence on them. Emptied of meaning by iteration, this narrative of the South Seas can only be played out yet again by Shrike in a by-now pointless display of the narrative's pointlessness. All of Shrike's major speeches foster this mode of self-consuming parody, whereby parodic style dubiously "plays out" its own clever, self-possessed, subversion-through–iteration of prior stylistic features. Parody can exert control if it eclipses the object of parody and thus affirms a larger and more authoritative perspective – one that the original perspective cannot or will not know about itself. But there is a sense here in which the object of parody proves stronger than the parodier, for the "played out" forms and narratives of mass culture preempt the kind of rhetorical play Shrike creates. Can Shrike's elaboration of this South Seas narrative be said to be satirical when the movie industry outperforms Shrike with its own insistent and deadening elaborations? Can "langorour tongorour" be said to defamiliarize the style of popular lyrics when lyrics of the 1920s practiced similar (or worse) contortions? It remains an open (though important) question – despite Shrike's perception of his dilemma – whether his word play subverts conventional modes or whether the productions of mass culture anticipate and outperform, in terms of mediocrity, repetition, and exaggeration, any parodic strategy Shrike might adduce. We shall shortly consider the possibility that West's own satiric maneuvers function differently from Shrike's; it is worth stating in anticipation, nevertheless, that West's avowed purpose to create a "novel in the form of a comic strip" will pose similar questions about an accommodatory intent being eroded by the manner and style of the appropriation.

Shrike and Miss Lonelyhearts maintain a distinctly problematic relationship to the "played out" fictions that have nevertheless come to occupy the core of their culture and into which they invest their own verbal play. What makes that relationship even more complex in *Miss Lonelyhearts* is their attention to the correlative category of literature. One consequence of Miss Lonelyhearts and Shrike's probing of their professional limitations is that, unlike the characters of *The Reverberator, U.S.A.,* or *An American Tragedy,* they invoke and articulate a discourse about high culture. The novel's speakeasy culture supports a number of affiliations to literary scenes past and present. Miss Farkis "works in a bookstore and writes on the side" (6); one of Miss Lonelyhearts's friend's rape stories concerns a "gal" who "went literary," writing like an aesthete "about how much Beauty hurt her" (14); another such story describes a female writer evidently joining the school of Hemingway when "this hard-boiled stuff first came in" (14). And Shrike in all of his speeches demonstrates a great familiarity with a wide range of Western cultural monuments. The problem is that Shrike parodies literary principles and conventions with as much facility (and incidentally posing as many interpretive problems) as he did the played-out South Seas. The two following passages illustrate this point:

> You fornicate under pictures by Matisse and Picasso, you drink from Renaissance glassware, and often you spend an evening beside the fireplace with Proust and an apple. . . . Alas, after much good fun, the day comes when you realize that soon you must die. You keep a stiff upper lip and decide to give a last party. . . . The guests are dressed in black, the waiters are coons, the table is a coffin carved for you by Eric Gill. You serve caviar and blackberries and licorice candy and coffee without cream. (34)

> The gospel according to Shrike. Let me tell you about his [Miss Lonely-hearts's] life. . . . First, in the dawn of childhood, radiant with pure innocence, like a rain-washed star, he wends his weary way to the University of Hard Knocks. . . . And then, the man, the man Miss Lonelyhearts – struggling valiantly to realize a high ideal, his course shaped by a proud aim. But . . . the world heaps obstacle after obstacle in his path; deems he the goal at hand, a voice of thunder bids him "Halt!" . . . And so he climbs, rung by weary rung, and so he urges himself on, breathless with hallowed fire. (54)

The first passage occurs immediately after Shrike dismisses the South Seas. It recalls a scene from Joris-Karl Huysmans's *A Rebours* (1884), a novel well known to late-nineteenth-century aesthetes, which describes a feast similarly decked in black (itself a parody of the funeral feast, for Des Esseintes is mourning the late decease of his virility). Shrike's tactic of allusion is quintessentially modernist; in the best tradition of Eliot, Pound, and Joyce, the allusion is undocumented, thus calling upon Miss Lonelyhearts's (and our) competence to make the connection and then make it signify. In the second passage, which occurs at Shrike's party, he creates a magnificently absurd pastiche of centuries of quest literature. His "gospel" is a manic tour of secular and religious quests, from the religious ("hallowed fire") to Medieval epic ("deems he," "wends his weary way") to the sentimental ("like a rain-washed star"). Even T. S. Eliot, creator of one of the more influential of modern grail quests, speaks through "a voice of thunder." Once again we are called upon to make connections and make them signify.

But what do they signify? It can scarcely be said that Shrike parodies Huysmans's scene, for Des Esseintes's feast, like the narratives of mass culture Shrike invokes, already pushes good taste to its limits; it would not be extraordinary for Des Esseintes's table to be a coffin. At the same time, Shrike is not holding up Des Esseintes's feast as exemplary; Miss Lonelyhearts, as he says, is not "stupid enough to manage" such an escape. In similar fashion, Shrike's quest speech is less a parody of quest literature than a mocking of the mock-heroic. Whereas Alexander Pope might have evoked a heroic-sounding rhetoric to deflate the pretensions of the decidedly unheroic so that language itself would come to be arraigned against the forces of dullness, Shrike manages to make a potentially heroic-sounding rhetoric encounter its own limitations. The rhetorical flourish of "deems he the goal at hand" does nothing more than gesture toward a once-powerful discourse. We might argue that Shrike, unable to make a perfectly legitimate literary mode function, is thereby hoist with his own petard: the would-be satirist self-subverted. To do so, however, would be to blame Shrike for a state of affairs that holds throughout the novel, which is that the names, strategies, and productions associated with high culture are often evoked but nowhere powerful. Like South Seas escapism, traditional high culture – including such immediate precursors as Matisse, Picasso, Eliot – appears to Shrike "played out" in its double sense of "enacted" and "exhausted." It is doubtless true that Shrike, in his readiness to refuse institutionalized names and values, shares much with the Dada movement West admired. Following the lead of Dadaists like Tristan Tzara and André Breton, West had demolished in *Balso Snell* all kinds of institutionalized literary practices and values, and Shrike might be seen as a latter-day Dadaist cutting with anarchic energy the ties to literary tradition that conventional readers would expect. Indeed, one scene in *Balso Snell* portrays an audience of the "discriminating few," "smart, sophisticated, sensitive yet hardboiled, art-loving frequenters of the little theatres" (30), only to cover these art lovers with a deluge of excrement. Without ever having undergone Henry James's humiliation on the London stage, and without the experience of James's long writing career, West in his first published work was more than ready to *bafouer* the bourgeoisie – and worse.

The contexts of Shrike's speeches, however, make an important difference. For the narrator of *Balso Snell* to parody Joyce's Work in Progress ("Moooom-pitcher yaaaah!") suggests an in-joke perpetrated on another inhabitant lost in the funhouse of literature. The joke questions the value of Joyce's strategy, backhandedly compliments his skill, indicates West's right to enter into dialogue with Joyce's text, and perhaps suggests his search among inherited styles for an idiom of his own. By invoking in *Miss Lonelyhearts* the "other" of mass culture, however, West creates an oppositional dynamic repressed in *Balso Snell*. Literature is no longer the terrain of free play where a wandering narrative voice discovers and dissolves its literary inheritance, but a commodity within a new eclectic cultural organization whose primary mode is appropriative. Shrike's parodies appear in a new light when we see that they conform to the media's thoroughgoing appropriation of a rhetoric of high culture. Should we read his parodies as a bitter intellectual's brilliant parody of newspaperspeak or as a newspaperman's poor parody of high culture?

We have already seen the appropriation of high cultural modes operating in *The Reverberator* and the *U.S.A.* trilogy, but in these novels the theft is mystified, as it were, by the incapacity of the perpetrators to comprehend their actions. It is Miss Lonelyhearts's and Shrike's prerogative (and despair) to be fully aware of the nature and terms of that appropriation, as the first chapter demonstrates. Miss Lonelyhearts's column for the New York *Post-Dispatch,* the deadline for which is "less than a quarter of an hour away" when the novel opens, is begun by Miss Lonelyhearts and completed by Shrike. (Here are no moments of inspired creation, no works of genius produced in solitude.) Miss Lonelyhearts composes this leader: "Life *is* worth while, for it is full of dreams and peace, gentleness and ecstasy, and faith that burns like a clear white flame on a grim dark altar." His crass rewriting of Walter Pater ("To burn always with this hard, gemlike flame, to maintain this ecstasy, is success in life") is soon picked up by Shrike who, in his attempt to offer "something new," rewrites both Pater and Miss Lonelyhearts: "*Art Is A Way Out . . . Art Is One Of Life's Richest Offerings.*" Shrike and Miss Lonelyhearts constantly rewrite cultural traditions for a new context, bringing once-authoritative texts (the Bible, Pater's *The Renaissance,* probably Matthew Arnold's *Culture and Anarchy*) uselessly to bear on the inarticulate misery embodied in the letters. But rather than embedding the letters within a context of belles lettres, the kind of values Shrike associates with art – escape, creation, appreciation, richness of experience – are defused and rendered inoperative by the work of selection and fragmentation required by the newspaper game.

Shrike is an anomalous figure whose discourse seems constructed from several sources: the Dada-like anarchist smashing literary shibboleths, the newspaperman unable to rescue (or not caring to rescue) traditional cultural values from the abyss, and the modernist author rearranging a cultural heritage within a new matrix. It is characteristic of Shrike's parodic style that it obscures the object of parody; its true anarchy arises from the fact that we cannot tell where his clichés end and the reversal of clichés begins. Shrike's replacement for Miss Lonelyhearts's unwritten leader, for instance, presents real interpretive problems: "When the old paths are choked with the débris of failure, look for newer and fresher paths. Art is just such a path" (4). Is Shrike parodying newspaper rhetoric, or parodying Miss Lonelyhearts's personal style, or genuinely writing the leader for Miss Lonelyhearts, or performing all at once? Actually, all of these questions converge under the rubric of the newspaper game. Because writing seriously for the newspaper is to produce the kind of writing that in a literary context would prove stale and formulaic, and because literary protocols value originality, defamiliarization, and difference, Shrike's leader stands self-condemned – unless we envisage a new context that provides for the accommodation and subversion of the formulaic. Such is clearly the case with Eliot's "O O O O that Shakespeherian rag" in *The Waste Land,* for instance, which I discussed in Chapter 1. Here bad writing transmutes into the profound once we bring to bear a traditional and proper evaluation of Shakespeare's name and work. With Shrike's leader, more options are open: Either we interpret it as genuine, publishable newspaper rhetoric (in which case we cringe at Shrike's ineptitude), or as a parodic approximation thereof, in which case we still cringe but now in full realization of Shrike's clever maneuver, which has reproduced the form and language of the newspaper while covertly gesturing toward formal and linguistic principles without which the formulaic could not be measured and found wanting. In loose terms, we might designate the first position as that of reporter, the second as that of modernist writer, wherein the reportorial suddenly changes significance under the pressure of its recontextualization as literature. Finally, we might suppose that Shrike is fully aware of his clichés and of what is truly original, but wants only to set in motion an endless series of parodies whereby clichés suitable for the newspaper are subverted by what is original (say, Huysmans's bizarre feast) and what is original is subverted by the appropriative mode of mass culture. This we might assimilate to Dada – or even to contemporary poststructuralism.

In one sense, the above discussion of Shrike's motives scarcely matters. The competence of most readers of West's text nowadays will allow them to identify "When the old paths are choked with the debris of failure, look for newer and fresher paths" as the old choked path of mass journalism; the shaping of the literary institution in the twentieth century will virtually enforce such a reading. By demanding that we use our competence in ways made familiar by other modernist texts, West's text thus preserves a distinction between mass-produced language and that language, defined by its difference, we call the literary. Nevertheless, it makes a difference how we read Shrike's discourse about art. Does West in fact articulate a coherent theory of art within his narrative through the voice of Shrike? Or does Shrike merely draw attention to the literary principles he then goes on to revoke, so that in the novel icons of high culture are placed alongside scraps of newsprint like some Dada collage in which tradition, modernity, and modernism are swept away together, leaving intact only anarchic principles of pure action, mere energy? The questions matter because for the first time we have characters capable of comprehending the value (or traditional value) of literary culture and who inscribe those values into their writing and speech. Whereas the reader of *The Reverberator* was required to invoke prior literary standards in order to perceive the limitations of Flack and the Dossons, Shrike and Miss Lonelyhearts embody principles that the reader must work with or against or through. The dilemma we face as readers of *Miss Lonelyhearts* is not merely that Shrike (in particular) savages the literary and artistic figures we might expect West to emulate, and attacks them in such a way that we cannot easily use it as a sign of Shrike's limitations, but that canonical figures of high culture are made into common currency. Given West's own statement that the novel was to be "in the form of a comic strip," we have to inquire next to what extent his novel is subject to the same compromises and limitations.

II

West's remarks about his comic-strip novel, sketched in *Contempo* magazine in his usual sparse style, run as follows:

> As subtitle: "A novel in the form of a comic strip." The chapters to be squares in which many things happen through one action. The speeches contained in the conventional balloons. I abandoned this idea, but retained some of the comic strip technique: Each chapter instead of going forward in time, also goes backward, forward, up and down in space like a picture. Violent images are used to illustrate commonplace events. Violent acts are left almost bald. (1933, 1)

Several critics have argued for the relevance of West's comments to *Miss Lonelyhearts.* Randall Reid (1967) and Joan Zlotnick describe West's extensive interest in comic strips and some of the possible sources for his technical innovations, from "Bringing up Father" to William Hogarth's satiric picture sequences to Max Ernst's collage novels. Zlotnick also notes his use of caricature, compressed dialogue, and "pictorial pantomime" (1971, 237–9). Each chapter contains few characters; scenes rotate swiftly; there are no subplots. Most obviously, perhaps, though West introduces the subject almost casually in his *Contempo* article, slapstick violence performs a double role as narrative content and stylistic convention. Thus, in slapstick fashion, unknown assailants twice attack Miss Lonelyhearts: "Somebody hit Miss Lonelyhearts from behind with a chair" (18); "He stepped away from the bar and accidentally collided with a man holding a glass of beer. When he turned to beg the man's pardon, he received a punch in the mouth" (15). Even the last scene, in which Miss Lonelyhearts actually chases the fleeing Peter Doyle before this would-be avenger accidentally pulls the trigger, has overtones of grotesque comedy. On the one hand, the baldness of violent acts in both comic strips and *Miss Lonelyhearts* evokes a culture in which violence is so gratuitous and endemic as to be barely noticeable. On the other, comic-strip descriptions of violence possess their own grim choreography. Pow!

Zap! and pictured stars signify within an elaborate and stylized language of violence which, because of its artificiality, distances us from a full and immediate apprehension of physical pain, only to allow the subsequent reinscription of violence in countless other productions of mass culture. When, after being punched in the mouth, Miss Lonelyhearts finds himself "playing with a loose tooth" (15), his gesture is as stylized and painless a representation of pain as the stars or vortices that denote unconsciousness in the comics. And like any comic strip representation of violence, this convention will be played out again in various stages of Miss Lonelyhearts's numb withdrawal, especially during the final scene, which describes Miss Lonelyhearts's injury with the detachment of the comic-strip idiom: "Miss Lonelyhearts fell, dragging the cripple with him. They both rolled part of the way down the stairs."

Although West (not surprisingly) abandoned the idea of speech in conventional balloons and could not recapture the static two-dimensionality of a picture, he more than compensates by making *Miss Lonelyhearts,* to an inordinate extent, into a novel of frozen gestures and set-piece speeches. Shrike, who cultivates the deadpan after the fashion of "moving-picture comedians" (6), makes a point of speeches that have little dramatic function. Shrike's first major speech doubles as a seduction-speech (7–8), but his sermon at the sickbed is never answered, and no one is shown listening to his final quest speech. The religious terms in which the monologues are invariably couched ("sermon" [8], "prayer" [1,9], "gospel" [54]) suggest how completely they conform to static oratory rather than to the dramatic situation at hand. Mary Shrike and Mrs. Doyle, both of whom relate stories apropos of nothing (23, 29–30) as though the gesture of speaking were enough, are his doubles in this. Speaking from behind such a mask of anonymity, Shrike has conventionally been viewed as a partially realized character, even a caricature styled after the comic strip (Zlotnick, 237). Nor does the loose sequence of vignettes compose much of a plot. *Miss Lonelyhearts* is a novel of ellipsis and fracture, in which linear plot development is generally sacrificed for self-contained actions (such as Miss Lonelyhearts's encounter with the "clean old man") taking place within the "squares" of the chapters. At the same time, the frames of the chapters thwart the development of actions, cutting short speeches (4, 54), ending chapters with the voice of Shrike, Betty (13), and Broad Shoulders (43) rather than Miss Lonelyhearts, and transforming potentially pivotal events, such as Miss Lonelyhearts and Betty's trip to the country, into inconsequential episodes. Like Roy Lichtenstein's paintings of comic-book images, in which bodies, faces, and objects are dominated by the frame into which they frequently disappear, and in which words (in conventional balloons) gesture toward a narrative completeness they never possess, West's *Miss Lonelyhearts* reproduces comic-strip form as a series of static actions and speeches within limiting frames.

In America, West claimed, "violence is idiomatic" (1932, 132) and if in comic strips "Violent acts are left almost bald," this alone may suggest their fitness to embody a maniacally violent American culture. Comic strips perform a double function by invoking social attributes (an America of "Violent acts") as well as a commensurate expressive strategy ("Violent images are used"). Yet the comic strip's propensity toward violence whose utility for the contemporary writer appeared plain in the *Contempo* article, is transformed in *Miss Lonelyhearts* into stark parody. For comic-strip violence of the order appearing in daily newspapers and in Sunday color supplements, is repetitious and banal. To Gilbert Seldes, whose *The 7 Lively Arts* (1924) was the first extended attempt to render homage to the arts of mass entertainment in America, the "slam ending," in which the strip concludes with a blow dealt by one character to another, was also inartistic and conventionalized to the point of cliché (222–6). But violence is also endemic to the world of Krazy Kat, whose creator, George Herriman, was according to Seldes one of the two great artists of the age – the other being Charlie Chaplin. As those names suggest, comic-strip and comic film-strip violence tends to promote a comic violence in which the victim generally manages to turn the tables, reestablish individualism, and even affirm a more complete social coherence. Chaplin and Krazy Kat survive all calamities to appear in yet another film, yet another comic (film) strip. Miss Lonelyhearts, in contrast, suffers the "bald" violence directed against the comic victim without undergoing a Chaplinesque transformation from victim to victor, and without the aid of an Offisa Pup, Krazy Kat's protector. *Miss Lonelyhearts* portrays comic routines of violence that are no longer funny and affirmative because no longer governed by our faith in the reappearance of the protagonist. We might say that West caricatures the sentimentalized detachment and affirmativeness of cartoon violence, appropriating it only to reject its premises of a comic conclusion.

However, distinguishing different registers of violence proves a difficult task in a novel like *Miss Lonelyhearts,* which seems to have borrowed wholesale from the repertoire of movie and comic-strip "slam endings," blows, and gratuitous repetition (as when Miss Lonelyhearts strikes Mrs. Doyle repeatedly to escape her clutches [50]). Nor is it certain that the comic-strip abruptness of the novel's conclusion signifies Miss Lonelyhearts's death. That interpretation depends on our ability to reconstruct a series of equivocal actions into satisfying contingencies. Mr. Doyle "pulled his hand out," which caused the gun to explode, which caused this consequence: "and Miss Lonelyhearts fell." Clearly, "and" can support at least two hypotheses: First, that the explosion of the gun, placed in intimate conjunction with his falling, suggests that the gun blast kills or injures him. Second, that his falling is unrelated to the gun (or caused by surprise) and that therefore Miss Lonelyhearts will rise like Krazy Kat from his latest "beaning" to suffer still more comic violence.[2] We can thus imagine the ending as being oddly affirmative. The point is that we interpret the ending to conform to expectations already engaged by our reading of the text and by our general literary competence; the ending, conversely, affirms or consolidates that reading. We may read the ending as appropriate to the novel's entropic vision of decaying relationships and rhetorical fragmentation (Shrike's last speech about Miss Lonely-hearts's life ends with an ellipsis). Or we may read the ending as appropriate to and *appropriated by* a comic-strip culture whose primary mode is a perverse mixture of sentimentality and violence and which thus transforms the novel into a lightweight caricature, dependent on fake emotion and banal allusion for its effect.

At the same time, West's comic-strip concept suggests a radical clearing and refiguring of literary ground. Not only are traditional nineteenth-century forms of the novel inappropriate to a rapid-paced, "comic-stripped" world, but modernism itself looks to be rewritten in a new and startling idiom. In West's reading of the comic strip, "many things happen through one action" and the images, instead of just going "forward in time" as in written narrative, also go "backward, forward, up and down in space" – statements that evoke the manifestos of literary modernism. West promotes his own brand of Imagism; each chapter was to act like Ezra Pound's Image (or like T. S. Eliot's objective correlative) to focus past and present, emotion and intellect, within one "complex." As Pound put it in "A Few Don'ts by an Imagiste" (1913):

> An "Image" is that which presents an intellectual and emotional complex in an instant of time. . . . It is the presentation of such a "complex" instantaneously which gives that sense of sudden liberation; that sense of freedom from time limits and space limits; that sense of sudden growth, which we experience in the presence of the greatest works of art. (121)

Short as it is, West's *Contempo* article proves itself to be one of the more provocative little-known literary manifestos of the twentieth century. Because narrative progression in a comic strip is wedded to a two-dimensional picture that requires us also to read its spatial organization, the comic-strip image, like Pound's Image, frees the writer from conventional space-time coordinates. In particular, the comic strip bypasses the linearity of prose. Presenting its information almost instantaneously, one frame of the comic strip assumes the gestural compression and tautness (what West called "Violent images") of the Chinese characters that so fascinated Pound. Many things "happen through one action," just as the ideogram for dawn – a sun rising above the horizon – conveys a noun by way of narrative, and narrative by way of pictorial equivalents (Kenner 1971, 103). But this is not to say that West merely rewrites Pound and Eliot. Pound was fond of talking about an artistic *risorgimento* to be born out of Victorianism and the rubble of postwar Europe, but in its laconic way West's own little manifesto proves just as revolutionary, just as much a violent act against inherited literary culture (which by now included the work of the early modernists). There is a certain irony, for one thing, in West's accommodating the work of expatriate Americans within such a quintessentially American expressive form as the comic strip. Quietly, West enters the debate between writers like William Carlos Williams and Pound about the virtues of writing in the American grain and suggests the ease with which Pound's brand of modernism can be formulated out of local materials. These local materials, however, despite their apparent utility to the writer interested in "making it new," seem to inspire an interest in popular culture and commodity form hostile to the cultural principles of modernism. Indebted as West might be to modernist ideology, his re-presentation of that ideology within the context of the culture industry could scarcely be countenanced by writers such as Pound and Eliot, whose *Cantos* and *The Waste Land* were not to be confused with any popular "Shakespeherian rag."

Are we then to read Miss Lonelyhearts as a modernist work in the imagist idiom that we experience (in Pound's words) as one of the greatest works of art? Or as a homespun retort to Eliot and Pound that ends by iterating its cultural context only too well? Or can we separate the text's historical complicity with a comic-stripped culture from its formal innovations and thus show West holding to a theory of cultural betrayal even as he aspires to the culturally appropriate technique of the comic strip that betrayal has somehow produced? West's description of his novel in the *Contempo* article does seem to recognize only formal debts. The novel was to be "in the form" of a comic strip and was to retain, after the abandonment of his initial plans, a token "comic strip technique." Form, West implies, is marginal to whatever essentially constitutes his novel. Indeed, in the syntax of West's proposed subtitle, "A novel" preceded its modifier "in the form of a comic strip," as if form could only supplement a work that remained a priori a novel. To propose "A novel in the form of a comic strip" is after all to preserve a concept of the novelistic – that which pertains to a novel as opposed to anything else. Yet formal innovations are precisely what West emphasizes in the *Contempo* article as making the novel relevant and new; they are surely responsible for whatever cultural status it attains. But if they are responsible, why are the formal possibilities of the comic strip not subject to the thorough critique of mass culture the novel invests in its grotesque images, its characters who talk in headlines, and in Miss Lonelyhearts's categorical statements about the betrayals of contemporary mass media? In either case, it is hard to see how West divorces form from the ideological and cultural meanings of the novel.

What is certain is that most critics identifying the scandal of West's comic-strip novel have proceeded to deflate, rationalize, or in some other way account for its borrowings lest it should be regarded as no different than the comic-strip world it invokes. Hence interpretations of West's attack on mass culture frequently omit his formal appropriations or emphasize the resistances deployed by the appropriative mode or demote comic-strip texts to the position of *con*text. Zlotnick, for instance, begins by noting the "irony" that in a "novel which by implication attacks the comic strip, West used the techniques of the strip" (238), and ends by affirming West's attack on comic-strip culture. As she remarks, "the medium is not the message." Zlotnick's interpretive strategy, confronted by West's formal accommodation of a cultural realm that the novel specifically resists, first marginalizes that accommodation as "irony" and "paradox" (239) before disclaiming the problem as a misreading of the transferrable power of the comic-strip medium, even though the presence of that medium has lent its weight to the initial formulation of the paradox.[3] At the other extreme – though not quite in contrast – Jonathan Raban argues that West's medium is wholly the message. West's novels display a "menagerie of rhetorics" that, far from function-ally representing a splintered world, are "pathetically incomplete" (1971, 376). Both critics effectively evade the problematic nature of West's text even as they point toward its nature. What begins as paradox for Zlotnick is transformed into a traditional opposition by occluding the power of medium, while what might have been a routine opposition for Raban (a mutilated novel confronting a splintered world) suggests a capitulation to a threatening world of pulp media. Both critics gain closure by reinstating a traditional opposition between litera-ture and mass culture; it is only that in the latter case that West has appeared on the wrong side of the cultural divide. But if a "novel in the form of a comic strip" can be read as a prescription for innovative writing (which it certainly appears to be), *Miss Lonelyhearts* constantly invites being construed as a comic-strip novel whose innovatory power is borrowed from whatever images, actions, and expressive forms the comic strip produces. The novel invites us to pursue, rather than bracket off, the scandal of its cultural status by appraising how intimately comic-strip culture has infiltrated and constituted it.

As a final attempt to define the problematic cultural status of *Miss Lonely-hearts,* let us explore the question of allusiveness as a potential index to why and how we perceive the novel as novelistic, its modernity as modernist, and its concern with letters as literary. Allusive fragments have always figured as a key modernist strategy. "*La Prince d'Aquitaine à la tour abolie* / These fragments I have shored against my ruins," writes Eliot in *The Waste Land,* smuggling in under cover of ruin his principles of composition: "I *have* shored," thus an action completed and irredeemable; "I have shored against my ruins," thus an action accomplished by "I" that is mysteriously distinct from the ruins being shored; "*these* fragments," hence a determinate solution to an incomprehensible prob-lem. Eliot achieves a victory over form by making functional the possibilities of formlessness, just as the Prince d'Aquitaine in the ruined tower remains a prince, and of Aquitaine: these meanings and this form still promise recuperable sig-nifications. But the jumble of references and allusions to elite culture in *Miss Lonelyhearts* – Eliot, Beethoven, Bach, Brahms, Titian, Shakespeare, Aquinas, and more – seems to assure a random, anarchic, even mindless principle of selection. Speaking of Brahms, Beethoven, and Bach, Shrike asks "Do you think there is anything in the fact that their names all begin with B?" (34). We might well ask instead what kind of authority attaches to their names in a novel where Miss Lonelyhearts's "imagined desert" includes "Desperate, Broken-hearted" as letter writers, "Miss Lonelyhearts" and "Shrike" as writers, and a shadowy cast of (in Shrike's phrase) "stinking intellectuals" (6). We have already noted the absence of articulated literary precepts in works by James, Dos Passos, and Dreiser. What is remarkable about *Miss Lonelyhearts* is the extent to which modernist techniques of allusion, juxtaposition, the iconography of cultural monuments, and the accommodation of newspaper and movie discourse, all lie on the surface of the text, where they are "played out" in conscious recognition of their cultural inconsequence.

But if we assume that West's technique of allusion does function within a modernist idiom – so that, for instance, the phrase "*Art Is A Way Out*" signifies a possibility of cultural redemption beyond the reach of an omnivorous mass media – another problem arises. For why should we privilege West's technique when self-referential allusiveness can be found everywhere in other forms of mass expression? Children's shows, TV sitcoms, movies, cartoons, and comic strips often make play with the inherited conventions and inherent properties of their media. Similarly, it is not unusual for TV shows and movies to allude to or excerpt from the repertoire of images, gestures, situations, and characters peculiar to that medium. Steven Spielberg's *Indiana Jones* movies, for instance, are composed in tribute to, and from a desire to outdo, dozens of action-chase-adventure movies now lost to popular culture. His movies are a film connoisseur's delight, affording filmgoers the same kind of opportunities to rediscover resonant actions from B-production movies as readers probably experience in plumbing *The Waste Land*'s allusions to infrequently read authors like Middleton, Goldsmith, and Kyd. It might be argued, in fact, that an *Indiana Jones* film arises out of institutional processes similar to those that shaped *The Waste Land* and, because it allows the naming of relevant works, comparisons, and evaluations critical to canon formation, leads to similar ends. The allusiveness of Spielberg's work evokes a film culture in which a modernist technique of quotation and its correlative process of canon formation have already become functional. Moreover, the work of a director like Spielberg (and he is not alone in this) suggests that the literary canon has also entered the cultural arena of the mass media. References to the Ark of the Covenant and the Holy Grail, however diluted or explained within the movie by dialogue, call into play a minimal literary competence on the part of most moviegoers. Such allusions, we may feel, degrade oral legend and original writings, flattening out the subtlety and profundity of a T. S. Eliot to cynical manipulation while transforming Eliot's critique of contemporary culture into a tool for selling tickets. Nevertheless, the appeal of an *Indiana Jones* movie to categories of high culture is an objective fact of the experience of watching; its formal strategies, parasitical upon the technical achievements of modernism, cannot be discounted as easily as its profundity or significance as cultural monument. The allusive techniques of any category of mass culture, like modernist writings, always open up for display the features specific to one discourse and thus tend to legitimate that discourse as special and distinctive. An *Indiana Jones* movie, cartoons that allude to other cartoons or to the nature of their artistic fashioning, the TV show "Moonlighting" – all these cultural artifacts refer to the conditions of their making in such a way as to construct a discursive field and define an appropriate audience. And they do so by making accessible techniques that hitherto have been preserved by – and the preserve of – the few.

How then, if at all, does West's use of allusion differ from the technical achievements of mass culture? How do the formal properties of West's text signify differently (and more) than the productions of mass culture? Should we read West's strategies as symptomatic of his culture or as effecting a transformation of accommodation into critique? Or can we even tell the difference?[4] In one sense, as I have pointed out in other chapters, these questions have already been answered insofar as *Miss Lonelyhearts's* canonicity precedes and virtually disarms the problem of its literariness; only its curious self-subversion makes the attempt to consider this problem anything more than academic. But that self-subversion, paradoxically, also suggests why it does not answer to the comic-stripped culture of which it is nonetheless historically and ideologically part. In *Miss Lonelyhearts,* it is not self-referentiality but the particular kind of attention the novel confers on self-referentiality that betrays its historical relatedness to the kind of literary strategies embedded in the texts of high modernism – that, indeed, makes it more distinctive than its modernist models. West radically destabilizes inherited discourses. Any text, author, and style, whether literary or nonliterary, is potentially available to the characters and narrative voice to be recontextualized and revealed as one more mode to be utilized and consumed. And because West activates a range of allusions across the cultural spectrum, his text tends to disrupt any single cultural context we adduce. It is our condition of not knowing how to take West's literary game playing that points to *Miss Lonelyhearts's* difference from superficially similar self-referential maneuvers in mass culture.

Critics, then, have been both wrong and right to turn *Miss Lonelyhearts's* allusiveness to their advantage by reading it as though it were *The Waste Land,* susceptible to the kind of detailed, subtle, learned exegeses that critics favor. References to odysseys, religious allusions, images of sexual dysfunction, have all been used and still can be used to support a view of the novel as weighty, important, and original – everything that is distinct from the banal, repetitious, violent world of mass culture. But it is West's prerogative to imprison the heritage of high culture within a novel dominated by inarticulate letters and Shrike's predatory raids on literary monuments, and thus to question both the value of that heritage and the premises of writing novels in a comic-strip era. This in itself may suggest an avant-garde posture whereby received notions of the literary are rewritten as bourgeois, outdated, reactionary, and so on, in order to liberate the truly new. But West, still more subversively, pushes the avant-garde as far as it will go – that is, until it meets and begins to blend with the forms, materials, and authority of mass culture. Along with a few other artists in the twentieth century – the Dada artists, Andy Warhol, Roy Lichtenstein – West has the capacity to draw together the boundaries of art (or the literary) and mass culture in such a way that the boundaries begin to collapse, thus revealing the ideological expectations and presuppositions associated with the production of art in the twentieth century. It is because of the text's bewildering or even indeterminate cultural affiliations that one may call *Miss Lonelyhearts* a brilliant satire (as I did) as easily as one may call it "pathetically incomplete" (as Raban does).

Transformations of narrative voice reveal the whole of Western culture as *Miss Lonelyhearts's* text; in turn, *Miss Lonelyhearts* might be seen as the quintessential text, dialogically conceived and executed, of twentieth-century culture. The novel's fragmented, partial, rapid-fire world bespeaks its historical moment at the cultural crossroads of the twentieth century; its signposts point back toward modernism and Dada and forward to kitsch, camp, pop art, and postmodernism. It is writing at the point where controlled parody (of mass culture) hovers on the edge of unconscious self-parody. It is writing at the point where Shrike's speeches, the letters, and newspaper columns cannot adequately be evaluated as good satire (that is, bad writing that we recontextualize as West's genius) or as bad satire composed in a throwaway comic-strip style. The text's exposure of its own operations blurs into the self-parodic processes of mass culture. On the other side, West's critique of the cultural and psychological failures of mass culture is curiously hamstrung by his appropriation of what might appear a discredited mode of expression (the comic strip) in order to discredit his own literary heritage. The novel seems to countenance an apparently never-ending process of recontextualization by means of which it defeats each attempt to define a stable literary context, but equally defeats each attempt to write off the novel – or privilege it – in terms of its relationship to mass culture. Yet it is precisely this self-consuming doubt about its own cultural status that makes the novel seem so valuable. The novel's problematic indifference to cultural difference only makes it seem more tantalizingly powerful and still more replete with esoteric potential than it was before – and thus still more relevant to a struggle for hegemony repeated across the terrain of modernist culture.

7

Making the Usual Kind of Sense

Hollywood, West, and the Critics in
The Day of the Locust

He tried to get out of going to the pictures with them, but couldn't. . . .
The Day of the Locust

Toward the end of *The Day of the Locust,* Homer Simpson's impotent sexual jealousy regarding Faye Greener, the would-be screen goddess, forces him into mental breakdown. The incident is scarcely a key one: like most scenes in the novel, it is episodic in structure and merely confirms what is already known about Faye and Homer. Yet Homer's inarticulacy conveys a striking sense of the fragmented stories, languages and texts prevalent in West's Hollywood.

> He [Tod Hackett] sat down and tried to make sense out of what Homer had told him. A great deal of it was gibberish. . . . He hit on a key that helped when he realized that a lot of it wasn't jumbled so much as timeless. The words went behind each other instead of after. What he had taken for long strings were really one thick word and not a sentence. . . . Using this key, he was able to arrange a part of what he had heard so that it made the usual kind of sense. ([1939] 1962b, 168)

Oddly, for a man whose only song is the "Star Spangled Banner" (102) and who puts a "great deal of faith in sayings" like "Good riddance to bad rubbish" (168), Homer's language reminds us more of a fragmented, multilayered modernist text. The symbolic density of Homer's "one thick word" displaces linear or narrative progression, while conventional time sequences collapse into an impression of timelessness. His gibberish becomes a kind of objective correlative for his Hollywood travails. Cast in the role of reader, Tod searches for a "key" to make the "usual kind" of narrative sense out of Homer's compressed and jumbled thoughts. And the restructured text that Tod achieves is at once enlightening and useless; its key whose function is to make the "usual kind of sense," may yet be the wrong one. "After Tod had hurt him by saying that nasty thing about Faye," Tod's replayed version of Homer's one thick word goes, "Homer ran around to the back of the house and let himself in through the kitchen, then went to peek into the parlor" (168). Tod continues for three pages, offering a supremely concise summary of the events of one night, yet making "nonsense" of the actual chaos of Homer's emotions.

Tod's predicament is our own, for *Locust* invites us to make the "usual kind of sense" of it, yet as often defeats and baffles us with its elisions, its rapid shifts of action and narrative voice, and with its refusal to develop a coherent plot. This scene is an example: a flashback that emerges out of a kind of narrative limbo. For though we know that Tod is making sense of Homer's chaotic speech, it is hard to make sense out of Tod's presentation of it. "After Tod had hurt him by saying that nasty thing about Faye" sounds like free indirect discourse, but we know that Tod is arranging "a part of what he had heard." But though Tod arranges, his own voice is mysteriously absent as he relates Homer's tale without comment, even though a statement like "[h]e wasn't angry with Tod, just surprised and upset because Tod was a nice boy" invites just that. Tod, moreover, seems to have miraculous recall of Homer's speech patterns. It is as if Tod temporarily suspends his personality, abruptly becoming an omniscient narrator who could legitimately present every nuance of Homer's language. But now there is another problem, for an omniscient narrator after the wild party would have to present this whole scene in the pluperfect: that is, "after Tod had hurt him by saying that nasty thing about Faye, Homer *had run* around to the back of the house." As it stands, Tod's version sounds like the kind of free indirect discourse we should have been reading during the party. Quite apart from that, Tod is presented to us as a hater of the "fat red barn" school of realist painting and the creator of the surreal "The Burning of Los Angeles" – scarcely the character, one would think, to construct conventional meanings. As much as this scene fills in gaps and presents the illusion of coherence, the more we study its relationship to Tod's and Homer's character and to the narrative the more it seems disorienting and, in Kingsley Widmer's nice phrase, "odd-angled" (1982, 69). It is, as Norman Podhoretz remarks, a "difficult book to get one's bearings in" (1964, 72). Precisely because of its disorienting quality, *The Day of the Locust* is the ideal work to reexamine our bearings in that bewildering territory where text and professional critic meet mass culture.

I

Widmer's image and my own rhetoric of "flashback" and "replay" brings to mind one possible key to making sense of the novel: cinematic modes of narration. Biographically and narratively speaking, the connection is an obvious one: West lived and worked in Hollywood during the thirties and died there at the end of the decade. Interestingly, critics have most often seen the Hollywood connection in West's work as a liability and condemned its plotless, fragmented structure. If West's technique is cinematic, Hollywood itself offers no usable models, and his immersion in Hollywood seems complete enough, in the eyes of the critics, to preclude the possibility of his modeling his work on the Soviet filmmakers – as Dos Passos does to critical acclaim. West's debt to Hollywood seems obvious enough that fragmentation fails to *signify* in his work. James Light states both sides of the problem neatly. He claims that *The Day of the Locust* "owes more to West's writing of screenplays than to any other source. In writing for the screen West learned the cinematic advantages of writing short scenes or 'shots'" (1961, 175). But he concludes his chapter on the novel with this criticism: "the middle of *The Day* seems at times to be rambling without effective direction" (177). West, as director, seems to have abdicated his role as *auteur*. Edmund Wilson, too, in his review of the novel on its publication, sees a similar problem but attempts to define it in a larger context. "I think that the book itself suffers a little from the lack of a center in the community with which it deals," but adds this qualification: "I am not sure that it is really possible to do anything substantial with Hollywood except by making it, as John Dos Passos did in *The Big Money*, a part of a larger picture which has its center in a larger world" (1950, 54–5).[1]

Wilson's images fruitfully remind us of Theodore Dreiser's case against Paramount, in which he had complained "they can't picture me as writing something I never in the world would have written." Dreiser's odd conflation of media, we found, was an attempt to wrest from Paramount the aesthetic high ground. If the film company was going to "picturize" Dreiser's writing, the author was going to rewrite the picture as text. Wilson also rhetorically appropriates Hollywood. Hollywood is a collection of picture-making enterprises that can be repictured on a grander scale – as if Hollywood film art suddenly finds itself looking into another camera eye (this time belonging to a Dos Passos or even a Sergei Eisenstein) as the subject of someone else's documentary. Or perhaps Wilson has in mind the "larger picture" of a painter – a figure of speech that is just as appropriate to *The Day of the Locust,* which ends with Tod Hackett imaginatively packing his Hollywood experience into the frame of his canvas, and which brims with the names of great painters rather than of great movie makers. However we read Wilson's trope, the fact remains that he, like Dreiser, demands a "larger picture" in which, by framing, contextualizing, and centering the centerless noncommunity of Hollywood, the message of the film industry may finally be read and understood. According to Wilson's review, that message is, first, one of centerlessness and, second, one of emptiness. Finding a "center" for Hollywood signifies, on Wilson's larger canvas, marginalizing the whole institution; its meaning surfaces at the moment its lack of meaning is revealed.

Wilson has, in other words, made the usual kind of sense of Hollywood: He follows the by-now familiar pattern of invoking mass culture in order to write it off, and he does so by invoking a center, a larger picture, and a larger world whose exact dimensions are never stated. Is this larger picture to be found in socialist thought, in the tradition of Western high art, or in the wider geographical entity of the United States that Dos Passos captured so successfully in the

U.S.A. trilogy, and that might allow us to see through Hollywood's pretensions to being the cultural capital of America? It scarcely matters; we need only recognize the difficulty of doing something substantial with Hollywood, Wilson suggests, to perceive its actual insubstantiality. Likewise, we need only recognize Hollywood's centerlessness to posit the existence somewhere of stable frames of reference that allow centers and margins to form, together with reliable means of finding them. Just as the writers I have studied accommodate expressive forms out of mass culture in order to bring the "other" to light (that is, literature, however inchoate these authors' formal definitions of literary work might be), Wilson consigns Hollywood to the margins of culture. Wilson's critique of *Locust* – and it is backed up by many other critics – implies that West's narrative tactics are simply not equal to the task of rewriting and thus writing off the expressive forms of Hollywood. *The Day of the Locust,* the critics suggest, reproduces rather than accommodates the narrative strategies of Hollywood film art, and in so doing loses sight of the narrative framing that constitutes its cultural prerogative. These critics imply in their general insistence on West's secondary canonical status that *Locust* reproduces Hollywood film art too well. The novel marginalizes itself, they imply, losing its bearings among the fragments, gaps, and inanities of the film culture it concerns.

We should note from the beginning, however, that West is well aware of the difficulties of making sense of Hollywood film – something that becomes evident in the remarkably varied way he dramatizes the narrative endings of Hollywood. During a visit to his friend, Claude Estee, for instance, Tod begins watching a pornographic film which is abruptly interrupted when the projector goes haywire. The film suddenly "whizzed through the apparatus until it had all run out" (75), causing a temporary cessation and a "mock riot." Unlike Tod's unfolding of Homer's "one thick word" into straightforward prose, the projector collapses familiar patterns of narrative organization into visual gibberish. In this particular case we are tempted to cry "Fake!" "Cheat!" "The old teaser routine!" along with the disgruntled spectators, for at this point West's narration of the plot of "Le Predicament de Marie," which had begun with lurid detail, simply ends. Tod goes "back to see the rest of the film" (26), but we remain unsatisfied with this tantalizing story fragment that removes the acts of sex toward which the pornographic film inevitably moves. Our predicament is very different from Marie's who, confined within a farce's rich plot, must dispose of a number of bodies in hiding places around her room. We must account instead for gaps in the text that frustrate any expectation of a traditional, linear plot; in this case, the unfinished "Le Predicament de Marie" remains embedded within a visit (Tod's to Claude Estee) that seems equally anecdotal and inconclusive. Indeed, if West recreates in *Locust* the multiple "shots" of a movie script, the frequent abrupt scenes, elisions, and narrative leaps of the novel nevertheless fracture the tight plotting and predictable climaxes of the typical movie.

Faye Greener, whose every word and action illustrates the truth of her admission that "acting was her life" (105), displays characteristics similar to the "apparatus" whose film had "run out." Her "odd mannerisms and artificial voice" (94) puzzle Homer at first; and Tod categorically states that she was an "actress who had learned from bad models in a bad school" (104). But, in one of West's finest strokes of irony, she is also the primary storyteller of the novel: "[She] told him [Tod] that she often spent the whole day making up stories" (104). Her first example of a story calculated to make her fortune in Hollywood begins "[a] young girl is cruising on her father's yacht in the South Seas," and ends when "a big snake grabs her. She struggles but the snake is too strong for her and it looks like curtains. But the sailor, who has been watching her from behind some bushes, leaps to her rescue." Faye's story reminds us of the South Sea idyll related by Shrike in *Miss Lonelyhearts* as part of a litany of potential escapes from the wasteland of modern culture. But where Shrike deliberately parodies the clichéd language of popular fiction, Faye, with phrases like "it looks like curtains," becomes the medium through which "played out" fictions are replayed – and, what is more, replayed by the "hundreds and hundreds" (106). Her "pack" of grotesque fictions suggests a plenitude that masks a deeper exhaustion, a more complete absence of individual creativity.

But perhaps more interesting than the number of Faye's stories is her failure to complete them. Tod "asked her how she thought the picture should end, but she seemed to have lost interest" (106). By delegating responsibility for finishing the picture to Tod ("Tod was to go on from there"; "You can work it out easy enough"), Faye fails at the critical moment to author her fiction. Her failure is illuminating, for her stories are in a sense already complete. The stories that Faye lays claim to as uniquely her own are merely repetitions of preexisting models culled from the movies and other media.[2] It is not surprising that Faye has "hundreds and hundreds" more stories; she becomes an apt vehicle for the proliferation of stories created by the medium of film. Faye is the "medium" though which popular fictions express themselves; she is the projector for a library of films. But despite their common origin in the libraries of formula fiction, there are differences between Faye's stories and "Le Predicament de Marie." For while the latter story ends with frustration for the reader, we guess in advance – even half fear – the predictable completion of Faye's tale. When she imagines an ending, at Tod's prompting, it satisfies our (worst) expectations: "Well, he marries her, of course, and they're rescued. First they're rescued and then they're married, I mean. Maybe he turns out to be a rich boy who is being a sailor just for the adventure of it, or something like that" (106). Faye's miscue ("First they're rescued and then they're married, I mean") speaks volumes, suggesting not only her indifference but the easy interchangeability of the elements of her tales. The throwaway phrases "of course" and "something like that" imply an infinite number of potential endings, but each is as inevitable and apt (or unsatisfactory) as any other. Her conclusion frustrates because it fails to confound or intrigue.

West's analysis of filmic representation reaches its climax in the long scene describing Tod's ramble through the Hollywood film sets. The description of Hollywood's retelling of the Battle of Waterloo in particular, in which the collapse of the fake Mont St. Jean mockingly echoes Napoleon's actual calamity, becomes a set piece of dramatic upstaging on West's part. Hollywood's representation of the Battle of Waterloo requires the subjunctive: The armies battle "as if" they were at Waterloo. West's genius is to use the indicative: "At the far end of the field, he [Tod] could see an enormous hump around which the English and their allies were gathered. It was Mont St. Jean" (133); or "Things looked tough for the British and their allies. . . . The desperate and intrepid Prince was in an especially bad spot." Mimicking an uncritical camera eye, the indicative voice seeks to persuade the viewer that an edifice of scaffolding and canvas "was" Mont St. Jean and that an actor "is" a "desperate and intrepid Prince." The very certainty of "was" suggests the camera's capacity for mimesis and carries an authoritative ring, as if re-presentation had given way to pure, unmediated presentation. At these moments, the narrative voice strives to present a camera-eye's view. But the same voice abruptly unmasks its own game playing: "The French killed General Picton with a ball through the head and he returned to his dressing room." The conjunction "and" yokes together two grammatically similar clauses that possess incompatible referents, and thus set up a series of jarring impossibilities: General Picton could not return to a dressing room and dead men cannot in any case return. Similarly, the "colors of the Lunenberg battalion . . . were captured by a famous child star in the uniform of a Parisian drummer boy" and the "Scotch Grays were destroyed and went to change into another uniform." Historical names do not link with historical referents, but rather point up the warping that characterizes Hollywood's attempt to recapture the past.

Tod Hackett, conversant with the events of the historical battle and designer of some of the actors' costumes, begins to restore a historical dimension. As Mont St. Jean collapses under the weight of the charging cuirassiers, Tod realizes that this was "the classic mistake . . . the same one Napoleon had made." Yet Tod quickly corrects this statement, which for a moment sounds like that persuasive camera-eye perspective, conflating past and present into "the same one": "Then it had been wrong for a different reason. The Emperor had ordered the cuirassiers to charge Mont St. Jean not knowing that a deep ditch was hidden at its foot to trap his heavy cavalry. The result had been disaster for the French; the beginning of the end." At last the pluperfect is restored. Realizing that the Emperor "had ordered" the cuirassiers to charge rights our perspective, allowing us to introduce the comparative element previously denied by the Hollywood camera eye. As Hollywood's production disintegrates on the slopes of Mont St. Jean, moreover, the narrator steps forward as privileged observer to complete our knowledge of the events. Hearing "lath and scantling snap as though they were brittle bones," and listening to the "sound of ripping canvas," we find ourselves backstage on the set, privy to the shattering of the fragile props that support the Hollywood illusion. The narrator also displays knowledge of the future – "The man in the checked cap was sent to the dog house by Mr. Grotenstein just as Napoleon was sent to St. Helena." And "just as" makes explicit the connection between historical fact and representation that the Hollywood camera, in its determined attempt to cancel the notion of likeness by way of an overwhelming verisimilitude, refuses to make. As the film version of "Waterloo" implodes along with Mont St. Jean, the narrator confirms our suspicions that Hollywood verisimilitude lies – not because it fails to record reality accurately enough, but because its success in representation obscures the kind of discriminations that the text alone is able to perform.

West's textual games aim at uncovering the fact of Hollywood representation. His initial narrative strategy mimics the camera's, for as Mr. Grotenstein's cameras are unable to differentiate medium from content, so does West's generic "and" humorously refuse to discriminate between actors and historical characters. But the more the narrative voice weaves in and out of the camera-eye perspective, reproducing it, juxtaposing it with other analytic perspectives before stepping out of Tod's field of vision entirely to report on future events, the more we see the effect of camera work. In a scene like the shooting of Waterloo, West goes far toward supplying the "larger picture" whose lack Wilson lamented. Tod even observes this scene standing on a hill above the set, so that though the man in the checked cap "had failed to see that [Mont St. Jean] was still being worked on," Tod sees the disaster unfolding and is able to formulate the analogy to Napoleon's "classic mistake." Tod plays the part of the privileged observer, epitomizing the "roving, panoramic technique" James Light ascribes to *The Day of the Locust* (1965, 175). The narrator, who at times sees more than Tod and at other times appears indistinguishable from Tod's voice, helps out; the scene succeeds in lampooning the directors of Hollywood while framing, comprehending, and disparaging that illusive camera eye. By the end of this scene, the indicative voice has recaptured its authority: "The man in the checked cap was making a fatal error"; "The man in the checked cap was sent to the dog house." Grammatically identical to "[t]hings looked tough for the British," these sentences belong to an omniscient narrative voice that is simply to be believed. The "larger picture" thus does not depend upon grammatical competence but a competence in reading contextually. One voice, inspired by the camera eye, views Mont St. Jean and the historical Mont St. Jean as identical; another, concerned with the edifice's behind-the-scenes construction, observes that the "paint was not yet dry and all the struts were not in place" and thus emphasizes mediation, likeness, and reproducibility.

Still another of Tod's "readings" of the Hollywood lots allows us to extend this train of thought. Just before encountering Waterloo, Tod witnesses what appears to be the final resting place of Hollywood dreams:

In the center of the field was a gigantic pile of sets, flats and props. While he watched, a ten-ton truck added another load to it. This was the final dumping ground. He thought of Janvier's "Sargasso Sea." Just as that imaginary body of water was a history of civilization in the form of a marine junkyard, the studio lot was one in the form of a dream dump. A Sargasso of the imagination! And the dump grew continually, for there wasn't a dream afloat somewhere which wouldn't sooner or later turn up on it, having first been made photographic by plaster, canvas, lath and paint. Many boats sink and never reach the Sargasso, but no dream ever entirely disappears. Somewhere it troubles some unfortunate person and some day, when that person has been sufficiently troubled, it will be reproduced on the lot. (132)

Evident here is West's fascination with accumulations of cultural artifacts. The studio lot reminds us of the Dali-esque "Chamber of American Horrors" in *A Cool Million,* which features "a Venus de Milo with a clock in her abdomen, a copy of Powers's 'Greek Slave' with elastic bandages on all her joints, a Hercules wearing a small, compact truss" (1957, 239). In both cases West creates a controlled space in which multiple juxtapositions quickly unravel the fabric of "realism" and "normalcy." In turning dreams into "plaster, canvas, lath and paint," the lot parodies traditional artistic techniques of mimesis. Unable to ignore the comic compression of these scenes, the reader perceives more readily the exhaustion of their structures. The lot paradoxically confirms the exhaustion, the paucity of invention, of a proliferating film industry. And eclecticism suggests only a bankrupt culture. The collision of traditionally prized works of art with elastic bandages and trusses in the "Chamber of Horrors" distorts and cheapens the original work. Dissolving traditional unities in sets portraying cultures from around the world, Hollywood epitomizes and insistently parodies the allegedly archetypal American experience of the cultural melting pot.

"Reproduced" is a key term, suggesting both Hollywood's fertility of invention in bringing dreams to "life" and its ultimate sterility, for these reproductions are not only dumped – they are also in the first place "made photographic." Photography perfects the mimetic function of art, allowing exact and reproducible copies of reality. And reproducibility allows Hollywood to mass produce commodities at an ever-increasing rate. Thriving on machine-perfect duplication, Hollywood confirms the duplicity at its heart. Whether we look to the "plaster, canvas, lath and paint" of the sets, or Hollywood's houses, also constructed of "plaster, lath and paper" (61), the film capital presents only multiplying facades. Thus the reproducibility of Hollywood art appears again in Homer's house, which features two rooms that are "exactly alike in every detail. Even the pictures were duplicates" (81). We have already seen in our discussion of Dreiser's *An American Tragedy* and the court case to which it led that reproducibility is culturally suspect – the best example, ironically enough, being the claim of Paramount's attorney that Dreiser had cold-bloodedly plagiarized newspaper reports. That accusation feeds off the lack of respect accorded mass-produced artifacts since the beginning of the industrial era and bears out the truth of Walter Benjamin's assessment that the new arts of mechanical reproduction, by destroying the singularity of the work of art, undermine the work's "aura" – that quality of authentic being imputed to singular, unique cultural productions. But reproducibility also redeems the breakdowns of Hollywood film art as productions like "Le Predicament de Marie," "Waterloo," and Faye's movie scripts are ultimately restored. Tod goes back to see the film once the projector has been repaired, Waterloo will be "fought over again the next day" (134), and Faye's stories will continue to flow with or without the optional endings. In Hollywood, single events become infinitely replayable and refilmable. Since any event or story can be refilmed and resold, none is unique or ever completed. Incompletion, therefore, perpetuates Hollywood art; its singular and enduring quality is that it is virtual. Hollywood ruptures the sequence of historical time. It dismantles the architectural, artistic, and religious characteristics of different cultures and then reassembles them in plaster and lath. Hence Waterloo, and hence the grotesque scenery of the film lots, where "a bamboo stockade, an adobe fort, the wooden horse of Troy" and "a corner of a Mayan temple" all coexist in various states of decay (131).

West reassembles Hollywood in similar fashion. The novel's narrative forms a catalogue of discordant impressions through which Tod's voice itself fades in and out, sometimes being absent for long stretches of the novel. The conjunction of Tod's panoramic perspective and the omniscient narrative voice, so effective during the battle of Waterloo, fluctuates wildly. As we have seen, his later attempt to make sense of Homer's gibberish raises all sorts of problems for anyone concerned with gaining a trustworthy and objective portrait of Homer. From the banality of Faye's stories to the trenchant satire of the "Waterloo" production, from Tod's making the usual kind of sense to his final wild screams, the narrative of *Locust* continually warps and changes. The novel, so the critique (and my defense) goes, is incomplete, ragged, episodic, collapsing like Mont St. Jean under the charge of so many different narrative voices, bit parts, and unfinished narrative lines. Critics who condemn the provisional, fluid, and sometimes awkward shifts of perspective in the novel, it might be argued, miss its logic of imitative form. As Hollywood film, collapses, and dumps – as films whizz through projectors too fast for the eye to follow – West's narrative follows suit. In a scene like the battle of Waterloo, where juxtapositions of different perspectives entail sorting and organizing different frames of reference, his technique works beautifully. The scene represents Hollywood's tactics of reproduction in such a way as to suspend their logic; imitative form playfully yet successfully embroiders on Hollywood design. And this argument also allows us to reinterpret the problem of Tod's reading of Homer's "one thick word." By invoking the conventional linearity of realist prose, Tod surrenders the dazzling rhetorical charge of the Waterloo scene. He espouses the logic of another world and another time; he fails to comprehend fully the lessons of the Hollywood aesthetic.

II

The preceding argument suggests that the novel does conform to a model of accommodation and that West's splintered narrative "writes in" Hollywood modes of representation only to write them off in the "larger picture" the novel activates. The very fact that West reproduces so intimately the cultural features he seems to satirize, however, suggests that this argument will scarcely settle the question for those critics who claim that the novel founders on the fallacy of imitative form – that Hollywood incoherence leads to West's narrative and cultural incoherence. Many of these questions about West's unsettling narrative hinge on the way one reads Tod Hackett and his cultural office as part-time narrator, painter, observer of, critic of – and participant in – the new Grub Street of Hollywood. What and who does Tod represent? In what senses does Tod fulfil the role of culture representative? In what senses has that role become a successful counterpart to Miss Lonelyhearts's failed performance as "man of letters"? To what extent, indeed, can we see him as the most significant character of this study – a latter-day portrait of the artist who, in his opposition to Hollywood culture, finally marks out the site of authentic art? The question has obsessed critics of *The Day of the Locust,* in part because Tod's seemingly bona fide artistic credentials collide with a number of (highly visible) psychological flaws. His rape fantasies make him a particularly unsympathetic observer, while his work as a designer for Hollywood productions raises questions about his devotion to pure art. In the end, Lavonne Mueller writes, Tod "'sells out'" (1973, 226). Like those critics who ascribe a compromising cinematic verity to the narrative voice, Mueller goes on to argue that, as Tod is being crushed in the final mob scene, he "forgets his art and with cinema-like magic creates his own kind of vengeance. While lapsing into a reverie about his canvas, he enacts his escape by imagining himself in the role of a show–biz director in his own creation." Walter Wells goes further by stripping Tod of all his artistic potential. Tod's art does not only lack content, it lacks even existence: "Tod's yet-to-be-painted picture somehow 'prove[s] he had talent.' All that Tod ever does complete of his prophetic painting is a series of preliminary 'cartoons'" (1973, 62).

But West does not allow such an easy conjuring-away of Tod's art. Wells's subtle emendation of "proved" he had talent to "prove[s]" masks the original sense of "And 'The Burning of Los Angeles,' a picture he was soon to paint, definitely proved he had talent" (60). A similar intervention by an omniscient narrator tells us later that "In 'The Burning of Los Angeles' Faye is the naked girl in the left foreground being chased by the group of men and women who have separated from the main body of the mob" (108). In both cases, the narrator offers proof positive that the projected painting will indeed be completed and that Tod is to become an artist of some talent. The real point at issue, however, is not the fate of Tod's painting but the determinacy of a cultural and artistic context that would evoke stable coordinates for a term like "talent." That is to say, we cannot judge from the text whether the revelation of his "talent" is predicated upon natural genius or upon the vagaries of a marketplace that, at another time, might bestow status on the productions of a Claude Estee or Mr. Grotenstein. Both possibilities – value as a function of genius and value as a function of economic investment – are potentiated within *Locust*. Tod's thoughts about which artistic principles are relevant to Hollywood culture do, however, provide a workable aesthetic framework, even though they cannot prove the worth of his own work. We learn, in the first chapter, that

> he was determined to learn much more. They [those coming to California to die] were the people he must paint. He would never again do a fat red barn, old stone wall or sturdy Nantucket fisherman. From the moment he had seen them, he had known that, despite his race, training and heritage, neither Winslow Homer nor Thomas Ryder could be his masters and he turned to Goya and Daumier.
>
> He had learned this just in time. During his last year in art school, he had begun to think that he might give up painting completely. . . . he had realized that he was going the way of all his classmates, toward illustration or mere handsomeness. When the Hollywood job had come along, he had grabbed it despite the arguments of his friends who were certain that he was selling out and would never paint again. (60–1)

In a way, this passage is as chronologically bewildering as Homer's "one thick word." Reconstructed (to make the usual kind of sense), the passage suggests that, first, his frustration at art school leads to his grabbing the Hollywood job, which then made him determined to shape an aesthetic appropriate to the people who came there to die. Far from forcing him to "sell out," Hollywood offers inspiration and rich material to the aspiring artist bored with traditional means of representation. Opting for Hollywood thus has a satisfying logic to it – and so does the inverted chronology of the passage, which concludes with an expectation of failure we have already found to be false. Nonetheless, West's narrative pacing is oddly disorienting: Tod's acknowledgment of his true artistic subject precedes his arrival in Hollywood and discovery of his subject (in the fourth sentence), while the comment about his "training" refers to the art school experience that comprises the content of the next paragraph. Similarly, in that second paragraph, the indeterminacy of exactly when Tod learns his true subject in Hollywood ("just in time") switches back to his last year at art school, and then forward to the end of his last year there.

If this passage enacts the same kind of abrupt and disorienting narrative leaps we experience elsewhere in the text, its temporal disjunctions at least seem significant in terms of his pursuit of artistic standards. For Tod leapfrogs his recent (realist) heritage of Winslow Homer and Thomas Ryder in order to invoke the pertinency of other eras and cultures – pertinent, that is, to the confused or effaced chronologies of Hollywood filmmaking. Tod opts for an aesthetic of eclecticism and of odd temporal conjunctions – a *bricolage* of images that accommodates the peculiar landscapes of Hollywood. Hence:

> He had lately begun to think not only of Goya and Daumier but also of certain Italian artists of the seventeenth and eighteenth centuries, of Salvator Rosa, Francesco Guardi and Monsu Desiderio, the painters of Decay and Mystery. Looking down hill now, he could see compositions that might have actually been arranged from the Calabrian work of Rosa. There were partially demolished buildings and broken monuments, half hidden by great, tortured trees, whose exposed roots writhed dramatically in the arid ground, and by shrubs that carried, not flowers or berries, but armories of spikes, hooks and swords.
>
> For Guardi and Desiderio there were bridges which bridged nothing, sculpture in trees, palaces that seemed of marble until a whole stone portico began to flap in the light breeze. (131–2)

Tod's meditations at least suggest the presence of privileged contexts – the work of "old masters" made newly authoritative – that stabilizes the disorienting jumble of scenes from other times and cultures.[3] The work of the old masters "frames" landscapes that appear to have come apart, or to have been constructed awry: "there were bridges which bridged nothing." By bridging historical eras, their work allows Tod to form chaos into composition. Indeed, though landscapes overlap, priorities have been reshuffled; hence Rosa's work, rather than the camera or the eye of a Mr. Grotenstein, becomes seminal, a fixed point around which Hollywood landscapes cohere. (Once again, Tod's associations are made from a privileged perspective, for he is "[l]ooking down hill.") Tod's invocation of the artists' names demonstrates the lasting power of the old in contrast to the ephemeral productions of Hollywood (produced merely by "some unfortunate person" [132]). His new perspective effects a transfiguration of the old – an image that also seems appropriate to this passage whose rhetoric of "tortured trees," "arid ground," and "armories of spikes, hooks and swords" looks back to Christian symbolism (perhaps by way of *The Waste Land*).

In light of this, how are we to evaluate Tod's own opus, "The Burning of Los Angeles"? Whether or not we can judge its artistic value from the novel's descriptions of it, the painting evokes a host of traditional associations – in particular, that resistance to inauthentic culture imputed to genuine art, captured most bluntly in Shrike's ironic "*Art Is A Way Out.*" For while Tod imagines working on his painting in the mob outside Kahn's Persian Palace Theatre, his theme is one of escape: "he had worked on it continually to escape tormenting himself"; "to make his escape still more complete he stood on a chair and

worked at the flames in an upper corner of the canvas" (184–5). Tod's escape
into painting might signify little more than substitution – a projection of
half-repressed desires and fears onto canvas. The painting, which features Faye as
"the naked girl in the left foreground being chased by the group of men and
women who have separated from the mob" (108), can be seen as one more of
Tod's frequent sadistic fantasies. Nevertheless, if Hollywood and the mimetic
form of *Locust* evoke incompletion, Tod's ambitious attempt to make his escape
from pain "still more complete" as he works on his painting deserves serious
consideration. If his physical escape is finally stymied by the mob, and if his
apocalyptic imaginings are transformed into his sterile repetitions of the am-
bulance's siren howl, what he does bring to fruition implies an authenticity
lacking in most of the novel's sexual, social, and artistic relations. And we have the
narrator's word for it that the painting, at some point after this narrative has run
out, will witness to Tod's "talent."

For we might argue that "The Burning of Los Angeles" not only finishes the
novel but completes it. Scored with the traces of Tod's experiences and dilemmas,
the painting preserves the uniqueness of his collisions with Hollywood society. A
sprawling panorama, at once satiric and apocalyptic, at once ludicrous and
profound, the painting recapitulates a Hollywood that we and Tod have already
imagined. Tod pictures "a great united front of screwballs and screwboxes," using
the "innumerable sketches he had made of the people who come to California
to die"; and "[a]cross the top, parallel with the frame, he had drawn the burning
city, a great bonfire of architectural styles, ranging from Egyptian to Cape Cod
colonial" (184). The "bonfire of architectural styles" composes the painting's
horizon, just as it has structured our perception of Hollywood's houses and sets
in the novel. And this painting does indeed frame or "contain" chaos. What
strikes us about the painting is not so much its jumbling of Tod's Hollywood
experiences, but its sense of structure – an impression that Tod underscores by
employing the language of art criticism to describe his painting. Thus "[t]hrough
the center, winding from left to right, was a long hill street and down it, spilling
into the middle foreground, came the mob" (184). Tod's directions are precise,
locating us in our movement away from, and in relation to, the "center." The
very syntax of the sentence, taking a sinuous course from the center through the
participles "winding" and "spilling" to the mob, enacts the painting's organization, and harnesses at the same time the potentially disruptive effect of "spilling."
Painting and rhetoric together give structure to the chaos they describe.

Or nearly so. For once again the narrative voice "spills" out in a number of
seemingly arbitrary directions. The first long paragraph of description, for
instance, looks back to the narrative strategy of "Waterloo." The indicative voice
supplants the subjunctive, so that the mob who "sang and danced joyously in the
red light of the flames" takes on an ontological stability it could not (as yet)
possess. Here, the transfiguration of Tod's virtual imaginings into solid form is
prepared for by the narrator's comment that "the way to [the painting] in his

mind had become almost automatic": We see immediately that these transfigurations signal a kind of indirect discourse. But after describing the flight of Faye and others from the pursuing mob, the narrator recounts that "Tod himself picked up a small stone to throw before continuing his flight" (185). To be consistent, this sentence would have to read "Tod *was picking* up a small stone." But the depicted action (Tod picking up a stone) suddenly becomes part of a continuum (Tod picking up a stone and then fleeing). It is as if the static painting gives way, on impulse, to a movie. A projector, as it were, jerks into life as surely as one ground to a halt during the showing of "Le Predicament de Marie." And the next paragraph offers more of the same. Though we comprehend the relevance of the indicative voice for an imagined painting, how are we to read this next transformation?

> He had almost forgotten both his leg and his predicament, and to make his escape still more complete he stood on a chair and worked at the flames in an upper corner of the canvas, modeling the tongues of fire so that they licked even more avidly at a corinthian column that held up the palmleaf roof of a nutburger stand. (185)

Now a new Tod's-eye perspective emerges. The narrative clues that previously stabilized our understanding of the indicative voice as a representation of an imagined scene now vanish: not "he imagined that he was standing on a chair" but "he stood." Either Tod has silently stepped back to observe himself observing the painting or the indicative voice signals the completion of an action (his standing on the chair) that has no ontological status in the mob, on the canvas, or anywhere else. Perhaps we cannot even choose between them, and the chair, like the narrative voice, remains forever virtual. In any case, "he stood on a chair" simply makes the action sound more complete than it could or should be – and that carries over to the tongues of fire, which lick at the Corinthian columns as if the artist's modeling really is fanning their destructive powers.

Our glimpse of Tod's painting is thus beset with contradiction; but each contradictory reading can make us more secure about Tod's, the painting's, and the text's accommodatory powers. On the one hand, its composition raises the possibility of a comprehensive framing that would make Hollywood and its film art comprehensible. A stylized imitative form, eschewing "fat red barns" for the work of Goya, Daumier, and Janvier (and for that matter contemporary surrealists never named in the text), might allow the act of centering for which Wilson and other critics have yearned. A hierarchy of cultural productions might then be extracted from the text: the old masters, modern filmmakers, and Tod as the as-yet-incomplete completer, whose role is to fashion and then try out transhistorical artistic principles appropriate to Hollywood. On the other hand, the whole narrative edifice seems as flimsy as the nutburger stand whose roof is due to flash into flames. Early in the novel, Tod creates a little allegory of the builder who must "distribute his stresses and weights and . . . keep his corners plumb" rather than surrender to fancy. But "plaster and paper know no law" (61), according to the law of Hollywood building sites. West – that other employer and manipulator of paper – also seems to know no narrative law. An unpredictable discontinuity characterizes his narrative voices, which employ a transfigurative mode seemingly for its own sake. The old masters, in this reading, are not invoked as guarantors of eternal cultural stability, but as part of a never-ending free play of meaning whose slipping "center" lies in the persistence with which explanatory models and embracing frames of reference are disabled. Readers have created the most damning critique of the novel by attributing this slippage of meaning to the film art the novel ostensibly derides. By constructing his wandering, near-plotless plot in ways that seem more reminiscent of Hollywood script construction than modernist nonlinear narrative, West appears to transgress the very distinction that could grant authority to his attack on Hollywood culture. The problem with West's narrative arises, therefore, at the moment when his modes of representation are seen to center in a marginal or even empty cultural enterprise and hence to confuse accommodation (in which inherited forms are transformed) with reproduction (in which they are not). Like Miss Lonelyhearts, who speaks only to find that he has "merely written a column for his paper," West runs the risk, so these critics suggest, of writing Hollywood large rather than writing it off.

III

The preceding exegeses of the novel depend on certain presuppositions it would be wise to make clear. First, both critiques of the novel's fragmentariness and my defense of it rest upon the assumption of a hierarchized but heterogeneous culture. A "larger picture" defines what Hollywood pictures lack; culture defines mass culture in a mutual but exclusive relationship. Critics read West's tactics of accommodation as mere reproduction, whereas my analysis argues back from West's descriptions of Hollywood to the narrative organization of the text and seeks to show legitimate, definable, stable points of difference. Clearly, both readings presuppose a necessity for some kind of rhetorical and narrrative intervention on West's part; West's critics simply fail to see its traces. In a way, critics like Wilson and Light formulate the more radical reading of the novel. My own reading merely sets out on the basis of more complex premises to explain away their problematic. My reading, in other words, seeks to make the usual kind of sense, even though no one has previously thought to legitimate the novel in just these ways. My further argument that the nature of West's accommodations might be simply undecidable, is still less radical. Either we assume in post-structuralist fashion that all texts make undecidable the literature/mass culture split, in which case the issue hardly seems worth pursuing for long, or we assume (as I do) that there is something uniquely undecidable about West's novels – in which case questions of authenticity, hierarchy, and cultural authority return in full force.

My analyses of both *Miss Lonelyhearts* and *The Day of the Locust* are consequential for understanding modernism. What remains to be done is to correlate these readings with recent trends in thinking about postmodernism. If, as I have suggested, West's novels lie on the cusp of post/modernism, how do theories about postmodernism allow us to articulate the narrative features I have addressed? Equally germane, how do West's novels enable or disable postmodern theory? Precisely because *The Day of the Locust* engages the issue of cultural (de)centering so profoundly, the text serves as a convenient testing site for some of these newly forming critical strategies. The key element of postmodern discourse for our purposes is the pervasive argument that cultural boundaries are in the process of (or in danger of) collapse. As some of our most authoritative critical voices speak of (or against) pluralism, heteroglossia, and centerlessness, cultural unity – or, rather, a unified (high) culture defined in part by its opposition to various sub-, non-, or pseudo-cultures – seems increasingly dubious. Enough attacks have been made on the monolithic cultural patriarchy of literary studies that the kind of "larger picture" Wilson yearned for seems increasingly unattainable, or is, in the face of mounting pressure, devoutly defended. Postmodern narratives of twentieth-century writing frequently posit a blurring or collapsing of the kind of boundaries between mass and high cultures that modernism once organized and held intact. It has become common to speak of a radical break with modernist strategies (Jameson 1983, 1984); of a crisis in legitimation (Lyotard 1984); of a widespread decentering of cultural production (Collins 1989; Ross 1988, 1989; Modleski 1986; Fiske 1991). Typically, mass and high culture are brought into a new relationship, either by moving to legitimate cultural productions once thought low, vulgar, or "mass" (such as Hollywood film), or, conversely, by moving to delegitimate the high cultural office of "literature." In both cases, an ideology of cultural centers and margins is replaced by a decentering of all cultural formations.

Theories of the postmodern owe much to Lyotard's influential account of the ending of *les grands recits* of Western history – marked, to quote another critic, by the "renunciation of foundational thought; of rules governing art; and of the ideological 'master discourses' liberalism and marxism" (Aronowitz 1990, 99). Such thinking is, not surprisingly, at the root of many powerful critiques of postmodern culture, whether we are speaking of the powerful conservative backlash in favor of preserving and/or restoring cultural foundations, or of a critic like Fredric Jameson, whose schizophrenic "perpetual present" of the postmodern era comprises an experience of "isolated, disconnected, discontinuous material signifiers which fail to link up into a coherent sequence" (1983, 119). Most interesting in the present context, however, are those critics who attempt to affirm and even celebrate a new cultural heterogeneity devoid of master narratives and rules governing (high) cultural production. Their work often brings Lyotard's iconoclastic work directly to mind (as in the example that ensues); more directly, their work depends on a revaluation (perhaps *invention*) of the popular. Studies of postmodernism frequently make an end of modernism by positing a momentous reconfiguring of the relationships between mass and high culture.[4] Modernist writing is held to be that which simply excludes the "other" of mass culture and which is supported by elitist critical predilections. Post-modernism then signifies the collapse or warping of such clear distinctions; texts begin to represent a multivoiced, multimedia world. Detective fiction, science fiction, rock lyrics, Hollywood script writing – none of this is any longer the automatic gainsay of "culture," though postmodern writing can be seen as the gainsay of modernist definitions of culture. Writers have crossed cultural boundaries so often, and the boundaries themselves have become so indistinct, that a narrative strategy out of James Joyce might coexist with the voice of a TV soap opera; a commercial might borrow from and improve on the work of Eisenstein.

In the fragmented marketplace, moreover, where innumerable voices struggle to be heard, no single mode of writing can lay claim to hegemony. Depending on political viewpoint, this new heteroglossia may be seen as a fatal collapse of the modernist critique of twentieth-century consumer culture (Jameson) or as the emergence of a new democratic impulse (Collins, Ross) or as a welcome end to the Western longing for controlling "master narratives" (Lyotard). In the latter cases, we should add, critics are by implication not only writing a new cultural history but practicing a new critical philosophy that refuses to be grounded in elitist ideologies of great, canonical literature(s). That democratic impulse also reinterprets the culture industry, which, no longer a monolithic manipulator of consciousness, is seen to structure yet also to be structured by the cultural practices of "the people." In this new reading of culture, popular entertainments respond to authentic desires and the mass public, far from being passive consumers of the culture industry, constitute a diverse, resistant, and remarkably discriminating audience. Hence in their Introduction to *Modernity and Mass Culture* (1991), Patrick Brantlinger and James Naremore, following the lead of theorists like Stuart Hall and Michel de Certeau, provisionally distinguish between mass and popular culture, establishing the latter as the realm of contested symbolic values whose function may lead the people (rather than the "masses") to a genuine resistance of hegemonic values. In Stuart Hall's words, popular culture is a place where a "struggle for and against a culture of the powerful is engaged" (1981, 234).

Jim Collins's recent *Uncommon Cultures* (1989) – at once a narrative of postmodernism and a postmodern narrative of twentieth-century culture – provides an uncompromising example. As I have, Collins emphasizes the compartmentalization of the marketplace for writing into a number of discrete, fragmented areas. He goes on to argue that we "need to see popular culture and Post-Modernism as a continuum because both reflect and produce the same cultural perspective – that 'culture' no longer can be conceived as a Grand Hotel, as a totalizable system that orchestrates all cultural production and reception according to one master system" (xiii). Collins dismisses the concept of a hierarchical "master system" of culture as a fiction, promulgated mostly by the interested "enlightened culture czars" (13) of academia. Contemporary North American culture, Collins writes, is characterized instead by "struggles between discourses [that] destabilize the very category of 'the dominant' by asserting multiple, competing hierarchies" (25). Each discrete cultural enterprise relates to its own center rather than to a center in some abstract master hierarchy; and without a concept of "the dominant," one cannot judge (as the "culture czars" try to do) some modes of cultural production as authentic and consign other work to the oblivion of mass, trash, or consumer-oriented writing. Each enterprise, in other words, requires one to study its laws and processes of construction in and for themselves. Moreover, Collins suggests, many modes of writing in the postmodern world function by legitimating their discourse as true and superior to all others (detective fiction is his main example), thus duplicating and subverting the truth-claims once made by "literature" alone. Most important, then, Collins questions the nature and existence of cultural authority – preferring, indeed, to postulate plural authorities, centralities, and multiple cultures. This attack on a hierarchized cultural system, which operates by distinguishing between a dominant culture (variously characterized as authentic, avant-garde, canonical, literary, and so on) and subjugated cultures (mass, mechanical, consumer-oriented, formulaic), is certainly the most unnerving of the "heretical" theories Collins promises in his Preface.

Collins's critique could be justified if literary practices in the first part of the twentieth century could be said to constitute a Grand Hotel of culture, or if, as a corollary, postmodern writing really did constitute, at some undetermined point in the middle of the century, a thoroughgoing collapse of boundaries into a continuum of popular/postmodern culture. But Collins, like many contemporary theorists who affirm a postmodern cultural heterogeneity, encounters two major problems: First, a failure to perceive, or at least to dislodge, the elitist cultural and rhetorical positions that constitute both his critique of "high culture" and his affirmation of "popular culture"; second, an understatement of the extent to which modernist work collapses categories like "high culture" and "popular culture." Actually, Collins preserves a dichotomy between literature/mass culture as an historical phenomenon that now underpins our ability to recognize postmodern work when we see it (because it transcends that dichotomy). In order to register the difference of postmodernism, newly accountable to a multivoiced, heterogeneous culture, modernism must be hypostatized as monologic. Modernism, in *Uncommon Cultures,* is totalized as a totalizing system (it is pure, complete, monologic, holding all the answers) in order to pave the way for its collapse into an anti-elitist and culturally dispersed postmodernism.[5]

In effect, I have been arguing against this modernism/postmodernism split throughout. First, I have claimed that modernist accommodations of mass cultural expressions are much more thoroughgoing and pervasive than hitherto seen, to the extent that they anticipate the radical interweaving of media, narrative modes, and voices supposedly characteristic of postmodernism, and in many cases make problematic the kind of simple high/mass culture dichotomy accepted by both adherents and detractors of the usual perspective on modernist writing. Though I claim that the process of accommodation has preserved a functioning and authoritative literary realm, the wide variety of accommodatory patterns studied in these works suggests the limitations of a margin-and-center trope. The cultural center has already been colonized, as it were, by the forces at the margins. Both proponents of modernist literature and those who accuse it of elitism thus hold an oversimplified view of the tactics whereby modernist writers engage their cultural milieu. Second, I have argued all along that what continues to grant modernist writing its authority within the academy, and what continues to grant literature an objective status within the heterogeneous culture of America, is the nature of contemporary criticism. The expertise and specialization that professionals within the academy are increasingly expected to attain requires the marking out of certain kinds of texts (though the nature of those texts might change) and the implementation of certain modes of inquiry. If, as I have argued, the institutional formations within which critics study and discuss these texts have changed little over the last hundred years, except to demand from professionals a still more rigorous training in ever more abstruse areas of discourse, postmodern critical discourse functions by reinscribing the kind of cultural segmentation and elitism it often claims is absent from the texts that are the objects of its inquiry.

Thus it comes as no surprise that Collins's postmodern critical apparatus reestablishes the rhetorical practices of the modernist literature he derides. For one thing, Collins appropriates the strategy that, he claims, characterizes elitist art. The culture czars misrepresent mass culture as mindless nonsense in order to distinguish literary work; Collins, in order to legitimate postmodern culture as truly revolutionary, registers all manner of diverse prepostmodern cultural production at the monolithic Grand Hotel. This critical posture seems quintessentially avant-garde, in the sense that an artificially narrow definition of traditional art is used to celebrate a new manifesto by virtue of its "heretical" (xiv) break with the past. As in some futurist manifesto inveighing against the moribund library, literature is hypostatized as a bundle of outdated principles while popular/postmodern culture, in its many guises, assumes the mantle of authentic work.

This latter statement is a particularly contentious one, given that Collins demolishes a variety of theories (notably the Frankfurt School's) that regard authenticity as an attribute of works opposing mass culture; even critics apparently sympathetic to popular culture are condemned for attempting to recuperate the concept of authenticity (20). But preserving a viable sense of authenticity as a function of the popular/postmodern continuum is, covertly, the crux of Collins's whole argument. To begin with, he emphasizes the seriousness of mass culture; his attack on the elitist distinction between authentic (high) and false (mass) work is clearly meant to rescue the concept of authenticity. The term swallows all others, as it were, in the sense that there are no longer grounds for viewing any fragment of the heterogeneous cultural landscape or any individual or group experience of mass culture as inauthentic. Collins covertly revalues the meaning of the word: from authenticity as a by-product of discriminatory practices to authenticity as that which cannot be discriminated. And Collins works particularly hard to counter the link between mass culture and commodification, always the particular preserve of left intellectuals. Accusations that perceived differences in mass culture are the result of "spurious product differentiation" (12), for instance, are quickly denied. Popular products establish and recognize their own discursive differences and audiences can be highly selective. Real, authentic differences thus characterize the realm of popular culture, though the nature of this authenticity is never described – let alone admitted. Instead, Collins takes a leaf out of the book of the Frankfurt School. Authenticity is defined negatively against the pronouncements of the culture czars: It is that which is not spurious. In a final tribute to the authority of making the usual kind of sense, Collins, having written off the elitist modernist texts that have for decades legitimated critical pursuits, finds that the attempt to decipher the now-secret realm of popular culture will demand still finer and more rigorous efforts on the part of the erstwhile culture czars. The postmodernist cultural context "makes ideological analysis more essential than it has ever been before in the decoding and evaluating of those diverse messages" (142).

How then can critics formulate, as West wrote of *Miss Lonelyhearts,* a "just understanding of what the book is about" in terms of its "sense of tradition, place in scheme, method"?[6] Does *Miss Lonelyhearts* answer to a postmodernist theory of adaptation whereby its own attempt to display the betrayals of mass culture is betrayed by its intimacy with that culture? Does *The Day of the Locust* conform to the expressive forms of Hollywood and thus sell out a literary heritage that is anyway uselessly elitist? Or are both texts thoroughgoing attacks from superior, "centered" perspectives on the cultural institutions that make necessary (and possible) this kind of baffled game playing? The nature of West's text and the character of our critical institutions make these questions impossible to answer, and in this sense the critical establishment stands at its own crossroads at the end of the twentieth century. On the other hand, the questions need not be answered, for both my assumption of a powerful cultural elite and Collins's assumption that it does not exist yield texts that are ambiguous, multivoiced, and authentic. What once seemed a novel problematically indifferent to cultural difference turns out to look very much like the quintessential protopostmodern text. A narrative that once seemed too beholden to the multiple (and confusing) shots and angles of Hollywood filmmaking can now be justified on the basis of its very disorganization; its sophistication arises precisely out of its foreshadowing of our loss of discernible and reliable cultural bearings. Both critical trajectories end by bestowing on these texts an extravagant potential. But though in this sense the questions I began with need not be answered, by the same token they do need to be addressed. The fierce contests now being waged in the profession are precisely what ordains the continued relevance of works like *Miss Lonelyhearts* and *The Day of the Locust*. Were those contests to cease with the collapse of our critical discourse, the promised end of the high cultural endowment might indeed become a reality.

As ever, Nathanael West anticipates and confuses these issues. A postmodernist slipping of concepts like distinction and authenticity is figured, for instance, in his tendency to describe junk heaps of cultural remains – the dream dump in *The Day of the Locust,* the "Chamber of Horrors" in *A Cool Million,* Miss Lonelyhearts at his newspaper game:

> He could not go on with it and turned again to the imagined desert where Desperate, Broken-hearted and the others were still building his name. They had run out of sea shells and were using faded photographs, soiled fans, time-tables, playing cards, broken toys, imitation jewelry – junk that memory had made precious. (26)

Mere lists, as if to emphasize the lack of hierarchies of value, compose these junk heaps of a commodified culture. Yet this detritus is still somehow redeemed as "precious." Does this signify a residual value in the encounter of humans and wasted commodities? Or does a vanishing but still-latent hierarchy of value exist in a long-term "memory" of an alternative culture? Or, as in Dos Passos's *U.S.A.,* is the required memory the act of critical remembering that allows us to read from, say, *The Waste Land* to an understanding of the irony of such junk being made precious? Again, there are no easy answers. But a persuasive answer lies in the way West's text organizes its response to the progressive disintegration of cultural orders. West's anarchic cultural vision transforms a cultural junk heap into what might be called, following Andre Malraux's terminology in *The Voices of Silence* (1953), a "museum world" of culture. According to Malraux, the museum sustains and sometimes invents the artistic character of its acquisitions. The museum may transform any cultural artifact into art; the religious icon, once intended to be the Virgin Mary, is reconstituted as a work of art bearing hitherto undiscovered stylistic resemblances to other works produced in the same period or by the same painter. And the museum homogenizes distinctively different objects from widely different cultures as "art." As Malraux writes, the "modern art-gallery not only isolates the work of art from its context but makes it forgather with rival or even hostile works. It is a confrontation of metamorphoses" (14).

It is in this sense that we may speak of *Miss Lonelyhearts* and *The Day of the Locust* as creating a museum world. In the text's "forgathering" and reconstellating of different discourses, inherited literary styles, separated from their initial context, tend toward the re-presented voices of mass culture. In the manner of

Tod Hackett's montagelike "The Burning of Los Angeles," West's novels display styles like trophies. T. S. Eliot's "voice of thunder" thus occupies its place in Shrike's quest speech beside "like a rain-washed star" and a modernist poetics of fragmentation blurs into a Hollywood idiom of repetitive disjunctions. The novel makes us aware of the modality of modes; this forced confrontation of different modes, once divorced from their institutionalized cultural significances, invites us to recognize the axiological processes that constitute literary texts as other, distinctive, and culturally authoritative.[7] By virtue of its persistent commentary on its own literariness, the text mirrors back the interpretive strategies we adduce to create it as literature, leaving us both certain that the text *is* literary and perhaps hesitant to inquire too closely into the way we register it as such.

Yet, once we do inquire, we find that the real "forgathering" occurs not inside the text but in the process whereby critics place works in particular frames of reference. We do not read *Miss Lonelyhearts* in the context of the newspaper game it describes or *The Day of the Locust* as if it were a Hollywood production; we do not take for our cultural guide the "man of letters" or Tod Hackett. Our context is the "museum world" of the academy, and our readings − like the special shows of many art museums − are capable of testing the limits of a particular discourse and still affirming that those limits are intact. A pile of bricks on the floor of the Tate Gallery in London (to cite just one notorious case) does not demolish the concept of art; it merely demonstrates how powerfully the environs of the museum, together with our expectations about its function, makes us see afresh − which is to say, makes us see a pile of bricks as art. In the same way, the profession of literary studies makes it always possible to recuperate as literature a given text; though the profession also excludes, on principles I hope the previous chapters have clarified, most published texts from consideration. Although the walls of our "museum world" (unlike an actual museum) are flexible, and never so flexible as right now, it will not accommodate an infinite number of extra wings. Professional authority depends on exclusion. Our ability to set goals, create principles and values, foreclose particular lines of argument and inquiry, and create some concept of literariness − in short, everything that preserves our right to speak as professionals − makes it mandatory to distinguish the true voices from the false. This is true even in a text as dialogically conceived as West's. Indeed, in my efforts to confront the problematic of West's attack on literature, I managed to convert *Miss Lonelyhearts* and *The Day of the Locust* into quintessential twentieth-century texts. They are literature by another name. And those critics who fail to see West's strategies as an accommodation of mass culture at all, who prefer to see these novels as plunges into the ridiculous or banal, nonetheless affirm the critical discourse that allows me to discover what is literary about Nathanael West. That professional prerogative to stake out literary territory somewhere in the shifting flux of this century's cultural significations will remain as long as our debate over culture continues.

Notes

1 I shall deal with such "common sense" critical approaches in later chapters, particularly during my reading of montage structure in Dos Passos's *U.S.A.*

2 See for instance Frederic Jameson's "Postmodernism and Consumer Society" (1983); "The Politics of Theory: Ideological Positions in the Postmodernism Debate" (1984); and "Postmodernism, or the Cultural Logic of Late Capitalism" (1984); and Jean Baudrillard's *For a Critique of the Political Economy of the Sign* (1981) and *Simulations* (1983).

3 I am thinking here of the influential work of Stuart Hall and the Birmingham School of Contemporary Cultural Studies, which draws particularly on Raymond Williams's work and on Antonio Gramsci's idea of hegemony. Work on popular culture by the likes of Tony Bennett, Tania Modleski, Dana Polan, and John Fiske begins from a similar set of assumptions.

4 Andrew Ross states his position nicely in the Introduction to *No Respect: Intellectuals and Popular Culture* (1989, 1–14). His book provides an interesting contrast to Richard Hofstadter's seminal *Anti-Intellectualism in American Life* (1962), for Ross is at once less secure about the kind of intellectual authority Hofstadter accepted unquestioningly and more confident about the present ability of the intellectual to mediate between various cultural realms.

5 See Richard Fine's *Hollywood and the Profession of Authorship, 1928–1940* (1985) for an intriguing cultural history of writers in Hollywood.

6 The "spectacular phenomenon of the period 1833–60," Frank Luther Mott argues in *American Journalism* (1947, 215), "was the advent of the penny paper"; and the same period saw the rapid expansion of the market for popular fiction.

7 See William Charvat's *The Profession of Authorship in America, 1800–1870* (1968, 84–99, 262–82); Michael Gilmore's *American Romanticism and the Marketplace* (1985); and Henry Nash Smith's *Democracy and the Novel: Popular Resistance to Classical American Authors* (1978).

8 In twenty years between 1878 and 1898 the number of high schools in the United States rose from about 800 to 5,500, increasing the number of pupils from fewer than 100,000 to half a million; in the 1890s, the Chautauqua system enrolled 100,000 Americans in courses of directed reading (Altick 1989, 217).

9 See George Juergens's *Joseph Pulitzer and The New York World* (1966, 50).

10 Contemporary reviewers of Henry James, for instance, often took issue with what they saw as the effeteness of his writing. "Who that has read the novels of Mr. James and Mr. Howells," wrote William Watson in 1889, the year following the appearance of *The Reverberator*, "can fail to observe how attenuation and depletion are becoming features of modern literature?"; and Robert Buchanan labeled James the type of the "Superfine Young Man" (Gard, 1968, 190, 187). What should give us pause in making too easy an analysis of the backlash against "superfine" writing, however, is the fact that James himself applied similar rhetoric to other writers. In a letter to T. S. Perry (February 1881), for instance, he claimed that "literature is going down in the U.S.A." and that "the stuff that is sent me seems to me written by eunuchs and sempstresses [*sic*]" (Gard 27).

11 Without possessing Wilson's theoretical underpinnings, many other writers have made similar arguments for a natural affinity at the turn of the century between journalism and literary writing. Ellen Moers, for one, has stated that

> Journalism, even more than naturalism, seems to have changed the shape of the American novel for good in the 1890s. More highly colored, more masculine, and more sketchy than before; colloquial in the American style; located on the street or the battlefield rather than in the parlor; indifferent to respectable courtship but obsessed with sex and crime; rich in sensation but poor in reflection, the novel would burst into a new growth from the seed of the newspaper sketch. (1969, 21)

A recent study by Shelley Fisher Fishkin follows naturally from such claims by stressing that, in a group of writers including Twain, Dos Passos, and Hemingway, "these apprenticeships in journalism help to explain not only the roots of the particular subjects, styles and strategies that characterize the work of these authors, but also the contours of what one might consider a distinctively American aesthetic" (1985, 5).

12 By the twenties, moreover, the insatiable demand of Hollywood script factories for new writers had occasioned a wholesale pilgrimage to Southern California. West, along with William Faulkner, Lillian Hellman, F. Scott Fitzgerald, Dorothy Parker, and many more, lived and worked in Hollywood. Theodore Dreiser, as we shall see, had extensive dealings with the Hollywood film industry; and even John Dos Passos spent a short, unhappy time there.

13 As Jacques Leenhardt has shown, any sociological analysis of reading in the twentieth century must grapple with the notion of *publics* rather than "*The* public, conceived of as an undifferentiated whole" (214).

14 T. J. Jackson Lears, as we have seen, argues for the importance of new professionals to the development of consumer capitalism, where they functioned as catalysts and facilitators, managing and providing "therapy" to the disrupted psychic economy of late-nineteenth-century America. And Magali Sarfatti Larson insists on an intimate relationship between professionalism and the organizing structures of a capitalist economy, claiming that professionalization was largely the result of economic forces working to legitimate skill and expertise as a form of capital – a "process by which producers of special services sought to constitute *and control* a market for their expertise" (1977, xvi).

15 Like most commentators on professionalism, John Higham argues that the rise of a professional outlook "was an integral part of a broad movement for the establishment of authority in American intellectual life" (1965, 8).

16 As Eliot Freidson puts it: "Originally rooted in arcane lore and in texts in ancient languages known only to a few, higher knowledge is now still expressed in terms unfamiliar to and impenetrable by the many and discussed by techniques of discourse that are opaque to outsiders" (1986, 3).

17 Thomas Haskell, for instance, defines professionalization as a "three-part process by which a community of inquirers is established, distinguishes itself from other groups and from the society at large, and enhances communication among its members, organizing and disciplining them, and heightening their credibility in the eyes of the public" (1984, 19).

18 Pierre Bourdieu's notion of "cultural capital," which he expounds in a book like *Distinction* (1984), is clearly analogous.

19 One example of how the Wilsonian model of professionalism fails to clarify the social and cultural pressures shaping the modernist text is Lisa M. Steinman's *Made in America: Science, Technology, and American Modernist Poets* (1987), which interprets the attraction to science in the work of poets like William Carlos Williams, Marianne Moore, and Wallace Stevens as an attempt to bestow on poetry the cultural prestige pertaining to scientific research. Science and technology in the "work of practical men" appeared to offer poets a way of including the "real world" in their art (5). But cultural authority accrues to the poetry of Stevens, Williams, and Moore not because of their claims for its practicality, usefulness, or scientific accuracy, but because they were able to employ scientific theories in the service of an obscure, avant-garde poetry and a specialized audience capable of reading it. Ian F. A. Bell's thorough account of Ezra Pound's recourse to scientific terminology and models as a way of emphasizing the professional qualities necessary to the *critic* negotiates similar territory more convincingly (1981, 3).

20 See Michael Schudson, *Discovering the News* (1978) and Christopher Wilson's "The Rhetoric of Consumption: Mass Market Magazines and the Demise of the Gentle Reader, 1880–1920" (1983).

21 See Sanford Levinson's "Law as Literature: Do Legal Texts Have Authoritative Interpretations?" (1984); Richard A. Posner's "Interpreting Law, Interpreting Literature" (1988); and Stanley Fish's *Doing What Comes Naturally: Change, Rhetoric, and the Practice of Theory in Literary and Legal Studies* (1989), in particular, "Working on the Chain Gang: Interpretation in Law and Literature" (87–102) and "Fish vs. Fiss" (120–40), for differing accounts of the problem of interpreting legal texts.

22 I want to emphasize that this link is far from self-conscious. The work of Michel Foucault is important to my argument at this point (as throughout), particularly because his analysis of discourse emphasizes the secret or hidden relationships among various cultural elements. As he writes, discursive practices "are not based on an agent of knowledge (historical or transcendental) who successively invents them or places them on an original footing; rather, they designate a will to knowledge that is anonymous, polymorphous, susceptible to regular transformations, and determined by the play of identifiable dependencies" (1977, 201). Foucault helps to explain, for instance, why a novel by Henry James and a critical work about Henry James may

be said to be related within the same discourse – and, moreover, may be said to arise out of the same cultural formations, and work toward the same ends of securing cultural authority.

23   Though Lawrence Levine does not specifically consider academic responses to mass culture, his recent *Highbrow/Lowbrow* (1988) details nicely the complex social transformations that led to the separation of culture into High and Low and to the progressively more powerful attempts on the parts of experts in various cultural fields (such as concert directors) to exercise authority over their audiences.

24   Those elements still empower speakers in the classroom or at a convention. That such a successful strategy should be seen as a failure is a paradox inherent in the nature of professions, where the power of specialized languages is such that, as in literary studies, the members of any "community of competence" may be very few.

25   In particular, there would not be what Alistair Fowler calls the "selective" canon of twentieth-century literature: those works within the accessible canon that are most commonly singled out as great, classic, most worthy, and most demanding of attention (1982, 213–16).

CHAPTER TWO

1   As Christopher Wilson remarks: "For Victorian Americans of the upper and middle classes, the activity of reading served as a haven of revered cultural values: tradition, restraint, cultivation. It was the archetypically private endeavor in an era when the public realm struck many as impersonal, chaotic, even debilitating. Spiral staircases, formal dining rooms, back entrances – all testified to the prescribed and intricate rituals of daily life; reading parlors and personal libraries, by contrast, were regarded as sanctuaries" (1983, 41).

2   "The Papers" (1902), James's later and more bitter analysis of newspaper culture, recalls this lament about the built-in obsolescence of print produced by the mass media. The story, concerning the bizarre self-dramatizations undertaken by Sir Beadel-Moffet in his attempt to keep his name constantly before the public, emphasizes the fact that media fame does not last in perpetuity but must be vigilantly renewed – an insight commonplace enough to our late-twentieth-century culture.

3   A suggestion of artistic sensibility obscured, interestingly, by the New York Edition's revised "I consider my guess as good as the next man's."

4   In his notebook entry, James commented that "Nothing of that sort has ever been known *dans ce monde là*" (1947, 84).

5   See Alwyn Berland's *Culture and Conduct in the Novels of Henry James* (1981, 1–29).

6   This argument is the reverse of the more common one that James's work embodies an educative principle that actually shapes a reader's responses, thus making him or her into a more sophisticated reader. William Veeder's influential *Henry James – the Lessons of the Master: Popular Fiction and Personal Style in the Nineteenth Century* (1975), which describes how James instigates a process of assimilating and transforming popular conventions in order to entice and then educate the general reader, typifies this position. The assumption that the text maneuvers any reader into more expert responses is a crucial one, for James's leanings toward an uncompromisingly high standard for literary excellence could then be democratized at a stroke, while removing the vague imputation that the Master's prestige rests upon his appeal to an

avant-garde audience. Moreover, the reader – any reader – would then be guided toward and shown how to activate literary meanings in the process of reading; the concept of literature would emerge out of the text rather than, as I have argued, being read into the text; the concept would be stable, transcendent. In the case of *The Reverberator,* however, would it not be just as likely for a reader, in the absence of authoritative statements within the narrative, to misconstrue the sign "literature" as meaning "all written documents" and thus to comprehend Flack's "Well, it's all literature" as a straightforward, accurate, and true statement? In order to avoid making that mistake, one would need a context of various definitions as well as some (preexisting) understanding of how those contexts might be activated. There is, in any case, little evidence that James ever did redeem the stupid reader in this way; indeed, since contemporaneous reviews and early criticism of James's work (as critics now are fond of pointing out) generally miss the purpose of his strategies completely, the opposite might be more accurate. Veeder's argument does work beautifully – as long as the imputed audience is a critical one and not just any audience.

7   As I argued in the first chapter, we need only situate James within the writings of those feminists who have inveighed against the patriarchal bias of the traditional canon and who claim that women writers hitherto denominated minor are as worthy to be read, or more so, than male contemporaries, to realize that the issue must at least be debated. It will not do to accept James's preeminence as absolute – as though James's magisterial presence in the canon were the only nonproblematic aspect of his work.

CHAPTER THREE

1   The narrator is also recalling the scene on page 9 of the novel ([1901] 1979).

2   As does John Carlos Rowe (235).

3   As Maxwell Geismar suggests in *Henry James and His Cults* (1964, 216).

4   Because Mrs. Brissenden may, on the contrary, have everything to tell about various relationships, it is possible that her recourse to straightforwardness is the most devious rhetorical ploy of all.

5   Three main propositions about James's relationship to his audience have been entertained in recent years. First, critics have demonstrated his desire to appeal to a popular audience, affecting his early work in particular but also arguably present in the late novels, a sign of which is his extraordinary interest in the gritty details of marketing his works (Anesko 1986; Margolis 1981; Jacobson 1983). Second, critics have suggested that dissatisfaction with the limitations and prohibitions of a popular audience led to the formulation of a dense, ironic, multivalent, and individualistic style, an act tantamount to a slap in the face of the general reading public (Baxter 1981; Nash Smith 1978). Third, James has been viewed as promoting an ethics of reading, whereby the ability to read well would resonate in every area of a person's intellectual and moral life (Veeder 1975). Susan Kappeler, as we shall see, makes similar assumptions about the educative potential of James's work in her *Writing and Reading in Henry James* (1980).

6   Quoted in Bruce McElderry, Jr.'s *Henry James* (1965, 128). Edmund Wilson likewise labeled it "mystifying" and "maddening" (1959, 25).

7   Jean Frantz Blackall in particular wants to make the novel "yield to analysis" (1965, 35). See also E. C. Curtsinger's "James's Writer at the Sacred Fount" (1982); Bruce McElderry, Jr.'s *Henry James* (1965, 128); and Elliot M. Schrero's "The Narrator's Palace of Thought in the Sacred Fount" (1971).

8   Such as Macksey and Donato's *The Structuralist Controversy* (1970), to which Rowe refers several times in his work.

CHAPTER FOUR

1   Equity refers here to a body of rules developed to "supplement and remedy the limitations and the inflexibility of the common law."

2   H. S. Kraft, for instance, believed that after the trial there was "less indifference to films and more caution on the part of novelists; the individual screen writer, often in the dual role of writer-producer, recognizes the aspiration of the novelist and approaches the screen play with greater thoughtfulness" (1946, 12–13). See also James Lund-quist's *Theodore Dreiser* (1974, 24) and W. A. Swanberg's *Dreiser* (1965, 377).

3   An argument that Dreiser in fact made at the time.

4   The attorney was certainly drawing on the depositions by well-known writers and critics whom Paramount had invited to watch the film and relate their impressions. Many were outspoken in taking Dreiser to task for his literary sins.

5   For a succinct description of the major shifts in meaning of that word, see Raymond Williams's *Keywords* (1985)

6   In a similar context, Paul A. Orlov argues that Dreiser's references to Horatio Alger novels create an ironic pattern of subversion whereby "the seeming parallels between events at a turning point in Clyde's life and those events central to the lives of Alger's heroes grotesquely emphasize the contrast between *his* quest's ending and *theirs*" (1982, 243).

7   See Philip Fisher's "Looking Around to See Who I Am: Dreiser's Territory of the Self" (1977); Paul A. Orlov's "The Subversion of the Self: Anti-Naturalist Crux in *An American Tragedy*"; and Ellen Moers's *Two Dreisers* (1969).

8   Two separate studies of Dreiser's *Sister Carrie* by Sheila Hope Jurnak (1971) and Cathy and Arnold Davidson (1977) duplicate Orlov's methodology. Jurnak, for instance, claims that "Dreiser seems to be saying that . . . true art strips away illusion and displays the actual. He uses popular art form references to dramatize both the 'fictional' and the 'actual'" (320). The Davidsons, likewise, argue that Dreiser "takes the standard, formulaic, expected episodes of so much of the popular fare of the time and then develops those situations to their realistic end rather than to their conventional conclusion" (396). Fishkin's examination of *An American Tragedy* in the light of Dreiser's newspaper days provides another example. In journalism Dreiser found a "reality that he endeavored to capture in his art" (100), even though the newspaper reports of the Gillette murder "treated the facts of the case and the trial in the conventional manner" (115) and hence had to be reworked to emphasize psychological depth and cultural context.

CHAPTER FIVE

1   Dos Passos's trilogy was published as *The 42nd Parallel* (1930); *1919* (1932); *The Big Money* (1936); and in one edition in 1938.

2   The whole scene, incidentally, is filled with echoes of the Sacco and Vanzetti case: Andrea Salsedo, whose suicide initiated the chain of events that led to the anarchists' deaths, was a printer, and Mac, as Sacco and Vanzetti had once feared themselves, is nearly arrested with radical handbills about him.

3   See also Edward Murray's *The Cinematic Imagination: Writers and the Motion Pictures* (1972, 168–178) and Gretchen Foster's "John Dos Passos's Use of Film Technique in *Manhattan Transfer* and *The 42nd Parallel*" (1986). Dos Passos had met Eisenstein and several other Soviet directors, including Dziga Vertov, during his trip to the Soviet Union in 1928.

4   We might note in passing that Carol Shloss, in positing this "larger coherence" of the novel, arrives at a diametrically opposed position from most critics, who tend to see Dos Passos as ideologically split: as, for instance, a collectivist historian and late-romantic idealist (Cowley [1932] 1974) or as a progressive and bourgeois writer (Foley 1980) or as a participant in his times and self-effacing artist (McLuhan [1951] 1974).

5   Hence for John Lydenberg (1971) the protagonist of *U.S.A.* is "the words"; for Linda Wagner, Dos Passos's success lies in stylistic innovation rather than philosophical profundity. See also John William Ward's "Dos Passos, Fitzgerald and History" ([1969] 1974) and Blanche H. Gelfaut's "The Search for Identity in the Novels of John Dos Passos" ([1945] 1972).

6   Barbara Foley, it should be added, disagrees, arguing that history profoundly informs the structure of *The Big Money,* although ultimately "history and fiction follow parallel but separate paths and reach parallel but separate conclusions" (1980, 465). See also Alfred Kazin's Introduction to *The Big Money* (1969, v–vi).

7   Dos Passos was joined in this cult of toughness, experience, and harsh reality by many writers for the *New Masses,* in which Dos Passos published frequently. His rhetoric often seems inspired by the magazine's reservations about bourgeois (effeminate) culture and its aspirations toward proletarian (masculine) culture – keeping in mind the fact that his thoughts about power, as we shall see, issue in a rather different place.

8   As if recognizing the problem of representing certain failure as work for a man, Dos Passos, in another rhetorical maneuver, ridicules the dispenser of daydreams for attempting to play the market in the first place; the "man who wants to play with the power of money," Dos Passos admonishes, "has to go out after it straight." Writing for money, in fact, is a contradiction in terms and thus "silly."

9   That probable conflict of writing experimentally for a proletarian audience was well known to the *New Masses,* whose writers argued frequently for the necessity of a plain, unembellished style.

CHAPTER SIX

1   Toward the end of his life, West felt that on completing a book he found "nowhere any just understanding of what the book is about – I mean in the sense of tradition, place in scheme, method, etc., etc" (Martin 1970, 335), as if his work eluded all possible attempts at categorization. In *Nathanael West,* Kingsley Widmer, following up West's hint, designates *Miss Lonelyhearts* a "literary flying fish," a "small odd master-piece" (1982, 49–50) – though in his Preface he also rates the book as a "highpoint of the modernist American literary imagination."

2 It is worth noting that Miss Lonelyhearts's heartfelt embrace of his would-be killer, Mr. Doyle, replays the central premise of the Krazy Kat comic strip, which is that Krazy Kat loves Ignatz Mouse, whose mission in life is to "Krease that Kat's bean with a brick."

3 Jan Gorak also emphasizes resistance in his discussion of West's art of *significant* disorder in *God the Artist: American Novelists in a Post-Realist Age* (1987, 37). Other critics show a covert pressure to account for West's technical borrowings. Randall Reid, for instance, sensitive throughout to West's relationship to popular culture, sounds oddly apologetic: "A novel in the form of a comic strip was not as strange a notion as it may seem. West was always fascinated by painting and caricature, and of course popular art was, in intellectual circles of the twenties, as fashionable as the fox trot" (1967, 85).

4 In *Discovering Modernism: T. S. Eliot and His Context,* Louis Menand has put it well: "When we examine a modernist literary work as an instance of modernist theory in practice, we can never quite be certain whether we are looking at an example of the critical prescription being applied successfully or an example of the disease the prescription is supposed to cure" (1987, 113).

CHAPTER SEVEN

1 A review by George Milburn also sees West's cinematic technique as the novel's greatest failing: The "worst part of the book is that it follows the choppy, episodical technique of a movie scenario. It has that peculiar disorganization that most movies have" (quoted in Wells 1973, 65).

2 In this case, Tod believes that Faye's South Sea story was inspired by a "large photograph that must have once been used in the lobby of a theatre to advertise a Tarzan picture" (61).

3 Donald T. Torchiana makes precisely that point in an essay on West's use of painting in *Locust:* "In evoking the painter's eye, in placing Tod Hackett's vision of traditional art in the midst of mob disorder, Nathanael West has looked both ways: at the present and at history, at a symbol and at its traditional vestiges, at an idea and at its eternal recurring images" (1973, 280–1).

4 The debate on mass culture and popular culture has moved, as Michael Denning puts it in "The End of Mass Culture," from the "fixed poles of the late 1970s" to the "contested terrain" of the present (1991, 253).

5 Astradur Eysteinsson's recent *The Concept of Modernism* (1990), which documents the labyrinth of critical positions taken up by writers on modernism, neatly suggests the difficulties posed by such totalizing accounts.

6 Letter to George Milburn, April 6, 1939; quoted in Martin 1970, 335.

7 For an opposing point of view that stresses the "absolute heterogeneity" of museum culture as it is mediated by photography, see Douglas Crimp's "On the Museum's Ruins" (1983).

Reference List

Altick, Richard D. 1989. *Writers, Readers, and Occasions: Selected Essays on Victorian Literature and Life.* Columbus: Ohio State University Press.

Anesko, Michael. 1986. *"Friction with the Market": Henry James and the Profession of Authorship.* New York: Oxford University Press.

Aronowitz, Stanley. 1990. "On Intellectuals." In *Intellectuals: Aesthetics, Politics, Academics,* edited by Bruce Robbins, 3–56. Minneapolis: Minnesota University Press.

Baker, Houston A. 1987. *Modernism and the Harlem Renaissance.* Chicago: University of Chicago Press.

Bakhtin, Mikhail. 1976. "Discourse in Life and Discourse in Art." 1926. In *Freudianism: A Marxist Critique,* translated by I. R. Titunik, 93–116. New York: Academic Press.

Baudrillard, Jean. 1981. *For a Critique of the Political Economy of the Sign.* Translated by Charles Levin. St. Louis: Telos Press.

———. 1983. *Simulations.* Translated by Philip Beitchman, Paul Foss, Paul Patton. New York: Semiotext(e).

Baxter, Charles. 1981. "'Wanting in Taste': *The Sacred Fount* and the Morality of Reading." *The Centennial Review* 25: 314–29.

Beach, Joseph Warren. 1918. *The Method of Henry James.* New Haven: Yale University Press.

Bell, Ian F. A. 1981. *Critic as Scientist: The Modernist Poetics of Ezra Pound.* London: Methuen.

Bender, Thomas. 1984. "The Erosion of Public Culture: Cities, Discourses, and Professional Disciplines." In *The Authority of Experts: Studies in History and Theory,* edited by Thomas L. Haskell, 84–106. Bloomington: Indiana University Press.

Benjamin, Walter. 1969. "The Work of Art in an Age of Mechanical Reproduction." 1936. Translated by Harry Zohn. In *Illuminations,* edited by Hannah Arendt, 217–50. New York: Schocken Books.

Berland, Alwyn. 1981. *Culture and Conduct in the Novels of Henry James.* Cambridge: Cambridge University Press.

Berry, Wendell. 1985. "The Loss of the University." In *Criticism in the University,* edited by Gerald Graff and Reginald Gibbons, 207–18. TriQuarterly Series on Criticism and Culture. Evanston, Ill.: Northwestern University Press.

Besant, Walter. 1884. *The Art of Fiction: A Lecture.* London: Chatto and Windus.

Blackall, Jean Frantz. 1965. *Jamesian Ambiguity and* The Sacred Fount. Ithaca: Cornell University Press.

Bledstein, Barton. 1976. *The Culture of Professionalism: The Middle Classes and the Development of Higher Education in America.* New York: Norton.

Bloom, Allan. 1987. *The Closing of the American Mind.* New York: Simon and Schuster.

Boorstin, Daniel. 1973. *The Image: A Guide to Pseudo-Events in America.* New York: Atheneum.

Bourdieu, Pierre. 1984. *Distinction: A Social Critique of the Judgment of Taste.* Translated by Richard Nice. Cambridge: Harvard University Press.

Boynton, Henry Walcutt. 1904. *Journalism and Literature and Other Essays.* Boston: Houghton Mifflin.

Brantlinger, Patrick, and James Naremore. 1991. *Modernity and Mass Culture.* Bloomington: Indiana University Press.

Carver, Craig. 1975. "The Newspaper and Other Sources of *Manhattan Transfer.*" *Studies in American Fiction* 3: 167–79.

Charvat, William. 1968. *The Profession of Authorship in America, 1800–1870,* edited by Matthew Bruccoli. Columbus: Ohio State University Press.

Chomsky, Noam, and Edward S. Herman. 1988. *Manufacturing Consent: The Political Economy of the Mass Media.* New York: Pantheon Books.

Collins, Jim. 1989. *Uncommon Cultures: Popular Culture and Post-Modernism.* New York: Routledge.

Cowley, Malcolm. 1974. "John Dos Passos: The Poet and the World." *The New Republic* (1932). In *Dos Passos: A Collection of Critical Essays,* edited by Andrew Hook, 76–86. Englewood Cliffs, N.J.: Prentice-Hall.

Crane, Stephen. 1968. *Great Short Works of Stephen Crane.* New York: Perennial Classic.

Crimp, Douglas. 1983. "On the Museum's Ruins." In *The Anti-Aesthetic: Essays on Postmodern Culture,* edited by Hal Foster, 43–56. Port Townsend, Wash.: Bay Press.

Crow, Thomas. 1983. "Modernism and Mass Culture in the Visual Arts." In *Modernism and Modernity: The Vancouver Conference Papers,* edited by Benjamin H. D. Buchloh, Serge Guilbaut, and David Solkin, 215–64. The Press of the Nova Scotia College of Art and Design.

Culver, Stuart. 1984. "Representing the Author: Henry James, Intellectual Property, and the Work of Writing." In *Henry James: Fiction as History,* edited by Ian F. A. Bell, 114–36. London: Barnes and Noble.

Curtsinger, E. C. 1982. "James's Writer at the Sacred Fount." *Henry James Review* 3: 117–28.

Davidson, Arnold E., and Cathy N. Davidson. 1977. "Carrie's Sisters: The Popular Prototypes for Dreiser's Heroine." *Modern Fiction Studies* 23: 395–407.

Denning, Michael. 1991. "The End of Mass Culture." In *Modernity and Mass Culture,* edited by Patrick Brantlinger and James Naremore, 253–68. Bloomington: Indiana University Press.

Dos Passos, John. 1930. "Wanted: An Ivy Lee for Liberals." *The New Republic* 63 (August): 371–2.

———. 1932. "Washington and Chicago, II: Spotlights and Microphones." *The New Republic* (June 29): 178–9.

———. 1978. *U.S.A.* New York, 1938. Reprint. New York: Penguin.

———. 1988a. "The Pit and the Pendulum." *New Masses* 1 (August 1926): 10–11, 30. In *John Dos Passos: The Major Nonfictional Prose,* edited by Donald Pizer, 85–91.Detroit: Wayne State University Press.

———. 1988b. "Toward a Revolutionary Theatre." *New Masses* 3 (December 1927): 20. In Pizer, 101–3.

———. 1988c. "Mr. Dos Passos on *Him.*" *New York Times* (22 April 1928), Sec. 9, 2. In Pizer, 110–11.

———. 1988d. "They Want Ritzy Art." *New Masses* 4 (June 1928): 8. In Pizer, 112–14.

———. 1988e. "Statement of Belief." *Bookman* 68 (September 1928): 26. In Pizer, 115.

———. 1988f. "Whom Can We Appeal To?" *New Masses* 6 (August 1930): 8. In Pizer, 131–3.

———. 1988g. Introduction to *Three Soldiers.* New York, 1932. In Pizer, 146–8.

———. 1988h. "The Writer as Technician." *American Writers' Congress,* edited by Henry Hart. New York: International Publishers, 1935. In Pizer, 169–72.

Dreiser, Theodore. 1932. "What Are America's Powerful Motion Picture Companies Doing?" (February). University of Pennsylvania, Special Collections.

———. 1948. *An American Tragedy.* New York, 1925. Cleveland, Ohio: World Publishing.

———. 1959. *Letters of Theodore Dreiser,* edited by Robert Elias. Philadelphia: University of Pennsylvania Press.

———. 1974. *Newspaper Days.* New York 1931. Reprint. New York: Beekman.

———. 1977. "I Find the Real American Tragedy." *Mystery Magazine* 11 (February 1935): 9–11, 88–90. In *Theodore Dreiser: A Selection of Uncollected Prose,* edited by Donald Pizer, 291–9. Detroit: Wayne State University Press.

Edel, Leon. 1979. Introduction to *The Sacred Fount,* v–xxxii. New York: Grove Press.

Elias, Robert. 1959. *Letters of Theodore Dreiser.* Philadelphia: University of Pennsylvania Press.

Eysteinsson, Astradur. 1990. *The Concept of Modernism.* Ithaca: Cornell University Press.

Fiedler, Leslie. 1982. *What Was Literature? Class Culture and Mass Society.* New York: Simon and Schuster.

Fine, Richard. 1985. *Hollywood and the Profession of Authorship, 1928–1940.* Ann Arbor, Mich.: UMI Research Press.

Fish, Stanley. 1980. *Is There a Text in This Class? The Authority of Interpretive Communities.* Cambridge: Harvard University Press.

———. 1989. *Doing What Comes Naturally: Change, Rhetoric, and the Practice of Theory in Literary and Legal Studies.* Durham: Duke University Press.

Fisher, Philip. 1977. "Looking Around to See Who I Am: Dreiser's Territory of the Self." *English Literary History* 44: 728–48.

Fishkin, Shelley Fisher. 1985. *From Fact to Fiction: Journalism and Imaginative Writing in America.* Baltimore: The Johns Hopkins University Press.

Fiske, John. 1991. "Popular Discrimination." In *Modernity and Mass Culture,* edited by Patrick Brantlinger and James Naremore, 103–16. Bloomington: Indiana University Press.

Foley, Barbara. 1980. "The Treatment of Time in *The Big Money:* An Examination of Ideology and Literary Form." *Modern Fiction Studies* 26: 447–67.

Foster, Gretchen. 1986. "John Dos Passos' Use of Film Technique in *Manhattan Transfer* and *The 42nd Parallel.*" *Literature/Film Quarterly* 14: 186–94.

Foucault, Michel. 1977. *Language, Counter-Memory, Practice: Selected Essays and Interviews.* Edited by Donald F. Bouchard. Translated by Donald F. Bouchard and Sherry Simon. Ithaca: Cornell University Press.

Fowler, Alistair. 1982. *Kinds of Literature: An Introduction to the Theory of Genres and Modes.* Cambridge: Harvard University Press.

Fox, Richard Wightman, and T. J. Jackson Lears. 1983. *The Culture of Consumption: Critical Essays in American History 1880–1980.* New York: Pantheon Books.

Freidson, Eliot. 1986. *Professional Powers: A Study of the Institutionalization of Formal Knowledge.* Chicago: University of Chicago Press.

Gard, Roger. 1968. *Henry James: The Critical Heritage.* London: Routledge and Kegan Paul.

Geismar, Maxwell. 1964. *Henry James and his Cult.* London: Chatto and Windus.

Gelfant, Blanche H. 1971. "The Search for Identity in the Novels of John Dos Passos." *PMLA,* 1961. In *Dos Passos, the Critics, and the Writer's Intention,* edited by Allen Belkind, 156–96. Carbondale: Southern Illinois University Press.

———. 1972. "The Fulfilment of Form in *U.S.A.*" *The American City Novel.* Oklahoma, 1954. In *Studies in U.S.A.,* edited by David Sanders, 48–54. Columbus, Ohio: Charles Merrill.

Gibbons, Tom. 1973. *Rooms in the Darwin Hotel: Studies in English Literary Criticism and Ideas 1880–1920.* Nedlands, Australia.

Gilmore, Michael. 1985. *American Romanticism and the Marketplace.* Chicago: University of Chicago Press.

Gilmore, Walker. 1970. *Horace Liveright: Publisher of the Twenties.* New York: David Lewis.

Ginsberg, Allen. 1970. "Poetry, Violence, and the Trembling Lambs." San Francisco *Chronicle,* July 26, 1959. In *A Casebook on the Beats,* edited by Thomas Parkinson, 24–7. New York: Thomas Y. Crowell.

Gorak, Jan. 1987. *God the Artist: American Novelists in a Post-Realist Age.* Urbana and Chicago: University of Illinois Press.

Graff, Gerald. 1987. *Professing Literature: An Institutional History.* Chicago: University of Chicago Press.

———, and Reginald Gibbons. 1985. *Criticism in the University.* TriQuarterly Series on Criticism and Culture. Evanston, Ill.: Northwestern University Press.

———, and Michael Warner. 1989. *The Origins of Literary Studies in America.* New York: Routledge.

Gramsci, Antonio. 1971. *Selections from the Prison Notebooks of Antonio Gramsci.* Edited and translated by Quentin Hoare and Geoffrey Nowell Smith. New York: International Publishers.

Griffin, Susan M., and William Veeder. 1986. *The Art of Criticism: Henry James on the Theory and the Practice of Fiction.* Chicago: University of Chicago Press.

Gross, John. 1969. *The Rise and Fall of the Man of Letters: A Study of the Idiosyncratic and the Humane in Modern Literature.* New York: Macmillan.

Hall, Stuart. 1981. "Notes on Deconstructing 'the Popular.'" *People's History and Socialist Theory,* edited by Raphael Samuel. London: Routledge and Kegan Paul.

Hartman, Geoffrey H. 1980. *Criticism in the Wilderness: The Study of Literature Today.* New Haven: Yale University Press.

Haskell, Thomas L. 1977. *The Emergence of a Professional Social Science: The American Social Science Association and the Nineteenth-Century Crisis of Authority.* Urbana: University of Illinois Press.

———. 1984. *The Authority of Experts: Studies in History and Theory.* Bloomington: Indiana University Press.

Henderson, W. J. 1890. "Journalism Versus Literature." *Lippincott's Monthly Magazine* 46: 712–15.

Higham, John, Leonard Krieger, and Felix Gilbert. 1965. *History: The Development of Historical Studies in the United States.* Englewood Cliffs, N.J.: Prentice-Hall.

Hirsch, E. D. 1987. *Cultural Literacy: What Every American Needs to Know.* Boston: Houghton Mifflin.

Hoffman, Frederick J., Charles Allen, and Carolyn F. Ulrich. 1947. *The Little Magazine: A History and Bibliography.* Princeton: Princeton University Press.

Hofstadter, Richard. 1962. *Anti-intellectualism in American Life.* New York: Alfred Knopf.

Howells, William Dean. 1968. "American Literary Centres." *Literature and Life.* New York: Harper, 1902. Reprint, 173–86. Port Washington, N.Y.: Kennikat Press.

Huyssen, Andreas. 1986. *After the Great Divide: Modernism, Mass Culture, Postmodernism.* Bloomington: Indiana University Press.

Jacobson, Marcia. 1983. *Henry James and the Mass Market.* Tuscaloosa: University of Alabama Press.

James, Henry. 1908. Preface. *The Novels and Tales of Henry James.* New York Edition. Vol. XIII: v–xxi. Scribner's.

———. 1947. *The Notebooks of Henry James.* Edited by F. O. Matthiessen and Kenneth B. Murdock. New York: Oxford University Press.

———. 1979a. *The Reverberator.* New York, 1888. Reprint. New York: Grove Press.

———. 1979b. *The Sacred Fount.* New York, 1901. Reprint. New York: Grove Press.

———. 1980. *Letters.* Edited by Leon Edel. Cambridge, Mass.: Belknap Press, III.

———. 1984. "The Question of the Opportunities." *Literature* (March 26, 1898). Reprint. In *Henry James: Literary Criticism,* edited by Leon Edel and Mark Wilson, 651–7. New York: Library of America.

———. 1986a. Criticism. 1893. In *The Art of Criticism: Henry James on the Theory and the Practice of Fiction,* edited by Susan M. Griffin and William Veeder, 232–6. Chicago: University of Chicago Press.

———. 1986b. "The Future of the Novel." 1899. In *The Art of Criticism: Henry James on the Theory and the Practice of Fiction,* edited by Susan M. Griffin and William Veeder, 242–51. Chicago: University of Chicago Press.

Jameson, Fredric. 1971. *Marxism and Form: Twentieth-Century Dialectical Theories of Literature.* Princeton: Princeton University Press.

———. 1981. *The Political Unconscious: Narrative as a Socially Symbolic Act.* Ithaca: Cornell University Press.

———. 1983. "Postmodernism and Consumer Society." In *The Anti-Aesthetic: Essays on Postmodern Culture,* edited by Hal Foster, 111–25. Port Townsend, Wash.: Bay Press.

———. 1984. "The Politics of Theory: Ideological Positions in the Postmodernism Debate." *New German Critique* 33: 53–65.

Juergens, George. 1966. *Joseph Pulitzer and the New York World.* Princeton: Princeton University Press.

Jurnak, Sheila Hope. 1971. "Popular Art Forms in *Sister Carrie.*" *Texas Studies in Literature and Language* 13: 313–20.

Kappeler, Susan. 1980. *Writing and Reading in Henry James.* London: Macmillan.

Kazin, Alfred. 1969. Introduction to *The Big Money.* New York: Signet.

———. 1971. "The Stature of Theodore Dreiser." 1955. In *Dreiser: A Collection of Critical Essays,* edited by John Lydenberg, 11–21. Englewood Cliffs, N.J.: Prentice-Hall.

Kenner, Hugh. 1983. "The Making of the Modernist Canon." In *Canons,* edited by Robert von Hallberg, 363–75. Chicago: University of Chicago Press.

———. 1971. *The Pound Era.* Berkeley: University of California Press.

Kernan, Alvin. 1982. *The Imaginary Library: An Essay on Literature and Society.* Princeton: Princeton University Press.

Kimball, Roger. 1990. *Tenured Radicals: How Politics Has Corrupted Our Higher Education.* New York: HarperCollins.

Klein, Marcus. 1981. *Foreigners: The Making of American Literature, 1900–1940.* Chicago: University of Chicago Press.

Kraft, H. S. 1946. "Dreiser's War in Hollywood." *The Screen Writer* 1 (March): 9–13.

Kwiat, Joseph J. 1953. "The Newspaper Experience: Crane, Norris, and Dreiser." *Nineteenth-Century Fiction* 8: 99–117.

Landsberg, Melvin. 1972. *Dos Passos' Path to* U.S.A. Boulder: The Colorado Associated University Press.

Larson, Magali Sarfatti. 1977. *The Rise of Professionalism.* Berkeley: University of California.

———. 1984. "The Production of Expertise and the Constitution of Expert Power." In *The Authority of Experts: Studies in History and Theory,* edited by Thomas Haskell, 28–80. Bloomington: Indiana University Press.

Lears, T. J. Jackson. 1981. *No Place of Grace: Antimodernism and the Transformations of American Culture 1880–1920.* New York: Pantheon Books.

———. 1983. "From Salvation to Self-Realization: Advertising and the Therapeutic Roots of the Consumer Culture." In *The Culture of Consumption: Critical Essays in American History 1880–1980,* edited by Richard Wightman Fox and T. J. Jackson Lears, 3–38. New York: Pantheon Books.

Leavis, F. R. 1974. "A Serious Artist." *Scrutiny* 1932. In *Dos Passos: A Collection of Critical Essays,* edited by Andrew Hook, 70–5. Englewood Cliffs, N.J.: Prentice-Hall.

Leenhardt, Jacques. 1980. "Toward a Sociology of Reading." In *The Reader in the Text: Essays on Audience and Interpretation,* edited by Susan R. Suleiman and Inge Crosman, 205–24. Princeton: Princeton University Press.

Lehan, Richard. 1963. Dreiser's *An American Tragedy:* A Critical Study. *College English* 25: 187–93.

———. 1971. *Theodore Dreiser: His World and his Novels.* Carbondale: Southern Illinois University Press.

Leonard, Neil. 1966. "Theodore Dreiser and the Film." *Film Heritage* 2: 7–16.

Leitch, Vincent B. 1988. *American Literary Criticism from the Thirties to the Eighties.* New York: Columbia University Press.

Levine, Lawrence. 1988. *Highbrow/Lowbrow: The Emergence of Cultural Hierarchy in America.* Cambridge: Harvard University Press.

Levinson, Sanford. 1984. "Law as Literature: Do Legal Texts have Authoritative Inter-pretations?" In *The Authority of Experts: Studies in History and Theory,* edited by Thomas Haskell. Bloomington: Indiana University Press.

Light, James. 1961. *Nathanael West: An Interpretative Study.* Evanston, Ill.: Northwestern University Press.

Ludington, Townsend. 1980. *Dos Passos: A Twentieth-Century Odyssey.* New York: E. P. Dutton.

Lundquist, James. 1974. *Theodore Dreiser.* New York: Frederick Ungar.

Lydenberg, John. 1971. "Dos Passos's *U.S.A.:* The Words of the Hollow Men." In *Dos Passos, the Critics, and the Writer's Intention,* edited by Allen Belkind, 93–105. Carbon-dale: Southern Illinois University Press.

Lyotard, Jean-Francois. 1984. *The Postmodern Condition: A Report on Knowledge.* Translated by Geoff Bennington and Brian Massumi. Minneapolis: University of Minnesota Press.

Macksey, Richard, and Eugenio Donato. 1972. *The Structuralist Controversy: The Languages of Criticism and the Sciences of Man.* Baltimore: The Johns Hopkins University Press.

Malraux, André. 1953. *The Voices of Silence.* Translated by Stuart Gilbert. Garden City, N.Y.: Doubleday.

Margolis, Anne T. 1981. *Henry James and the Problem of Audience: An International Act.* Ann Arbor, Mich.: UMI Research Press.

Martin, Jay. 1967. *Harvests of Change: American Literature 1865–1914.* Englewood Cliffs, N.J.: Prentice-Hall.

———. 1970. *Nathanael West: The Art of his Life.* New York: Farrar, Straus, Giroux.

Marz, Charles. 1979. "Dos Passos's Newsreels: The Noise of History." *Studies in the Novel* 11: 194–200.

———. 1980. "*U.S.A.:* Chronicle and Performance." *Modern Fiction Studies* 26: 398–415.

McElderry, Bruce R., Jr. 1965. *Henry James.* New York: Twayne.

McLuhan, Herbert Marshall. 1974. "John Dos Passos: Technique vs. Sensibility." 1951. In *Dos Passos: A Collection of Critical Essays,* edited by Andrew Hook, 148–61. Englewood Cliffs, N.J.: Prentice-Hall.

Menand, Louis. 1987. *Discovering Modernism: T. S. Eliot and His Context.* New York: Oxford University Press.

Mitchell, Lee Clark. 1985. "'And Then Rose for the First Time': Repetition and Doubling in *An American Tragedy.*" *Novel* 19: 39–56.

Modleski, Tania. 1986. *Studies in Entertainment: Critical Approaches to Mass Culture.* Bloom-ington: Indiana University Press.

Moers, Ellen. 1969. *Two Dreisers.* New York: Viking Press.

———, and Sandy Petrey. 1977. "Critical Exchange: Dreiser's Wisdom . . . Or Stylistic Discontinuities?" *Novel* 11: 63–69.

Mott, Frank Luther. 1947. *American Journalism.* New York: Macmillan.

Moulton, Richard G. 1989. From *Shakespeare as a Dramatic Artist: A Study of Inductive Literary Criticism,* 1888. In *The Origins of Literary Studies in America,* edited by Gerald Graff and Michael Warner, 61–74. New York: Routledge.

Mueller, Lavonne. 1973. "Malamud and West: Tyranny of the Dream Dump." In *Na-thanael West: The Cheaters and the Cheated,* edited by David Madden, 221–31. Deland, Fla.: Everett/Edwards.

Murray, Edward. 1972. *The Cinematic Imagination: Writers and the Motion Pictures*. New York: Frederick Ungar.

Nagourney, Peter. 1982. "Elite, Popular and Mass Literature: What People Really Read." *Journal of Popular Culture* 16: 99–107.

Norris, Frank. 1903. "The American Public and 'Popular Fiction.'" *The Responsibilities of the Novelist*. New York: Doubleday, Page: 103–08.

——— 1986. "The True Reward of the Novelist." 1901. In *Frank Norris: Novels and Essays,* 1147–51. New York: Library of America.

Orlov, Paul A. 1977. "The Subversion of the Self: Anti-Naturalist Crux in *An American Tragedy.*" *Modern Fiction Studies* 23: 457–72.

———. 1982. "Plot as Parody: Dreiser's Attack on the Alger Theme in *An American Tragedy.*" *American Literary Realism* 15: 239–43.

Perosa, Sergio. 1978. *Henry James and the Experimental Novel*. Charlottesville: University of Virginia Press.

Petrey, Sandy. 1977. "The Language of Realism, the Language of False Consciousness: A Reading of *Sister Carrie.*" *Novel* 10: 101–13.

Piaget, Jean. 1971. *Structuralism,* edited and translated by Chaninah Maschler. London: Routledge and Kegan Paul.

Pizer, Donald. 1976. *The Novels of Theodore Dreiser: A Critical Study*. Minneapolis: University of Minnesota Press.

———. 1988. *John Dos Passos: The Major Nonfictional Prose*. Detroit: Wayne State University Press.

Podhoretz, Norman. 1964. "Nathanael West: A Particular Kind of Joking." In *Doings and Undoings: The Fifties and Later in American Writing*. New York: Farrar, Straus, Giroux.

Poggioli, Renato. 1968. *The Theory of the Avant-Garde*. Translated by Gerald Fitzgerald. Cambridge, Mass.: Belknap Press.

Posner, Richard A. 1988. "Interpreting Law, Interpreting Literature." *The Raritan Quarterly* 7 (Spring): 1–31; 8 (Summer): 59–78.

Raban, Jonathan. 1971. "A Surfeit of Commodities: The Novels of Nathanael West." In *The American Novel and the Nineteen Twenties*. New York: Edward Arnold.

Reid, Randall. 1967. *The Fiction of Nathanael West: No Redeemer, No Promised Land*. Chicago: University of Chicago Press.

Robbins, Bruce. 1990. *Intellectuals: Aesthetics, Politics, Academics*. Minneapolis: University of Minnesota Press.

Robinson, Lillian S. 1983. "Treason Our Text: Feminist Challenges to the Literary Canon." *Tulsa Studies in Women's Literature* 2: 105–21.

Rowe, John Carlos. 1977. "The Authority of the Sign in Henry James's *The Sacred Fount.*" *Criticism* 19: 223–40.

Ross Andrew. 1988. *Universal Abandon? The Politics of Postmodernism*. Minneapolis: University of Minnesota Press.

———. 1989. *No Respect: Intellectuals and Popular Culture*. New York: Routledge.

Sanders, David. 1972. *Studies in U.S.A.* Columbus, Ohio: Charles Merrill.

Schiller, Herbert. 1989. *Culture, Inc.: The Corporate Takeover of Public Expression*. New York: Oxford University Press.

Schrero, Elliot M. 1971. "The Narrator's Palace of Thought in *The Sacred Fount.*" *Modern Philology* 68: 269–88.

Schudson, Michael. 1978. *Discovering the News: A Social History of American Newspapers.* New York: Basic Books.

Scott, Donald M. 1983. "The Profession That Vanished: Public Lecturing in Mid-Nineteenth-Century America." In *Professions and Professional Ideologies in America,* edited by Gerald L. Geison, 12–28. Chapel Hill: University of North Carolina Press.

Seed, David. 1984. "Media and Newsreels in Dos Passos's *U.S.A.*" *Journal of Narrative Technique* 14: 182–92.

Seldes, Gilbert. 1924. *The 7 Lively Arts.* New York: Harpers.

Shafer, Robert. 1971. "An American Tragedy." In *The Merrill Studies in An American Tragedy,* edited by Jack Salzman. Columbus, Ohio: Charles Merrill.

Shloss, Carol. 1987. *In Visible Light: Photography and the American Writer, 1840–1940.* New York: Oxford University Press.

Singleton, Gregory H. 1977. "Popular Culture or the Culture of the Populace?" *Journal of Popular Culture* 11: 254–64.

Smith, Barbara Herrnstein. 1989. "Breaking Up/Out/Down – The Boundaries of Literary Study." *Profession 89.* 2–3. New York: Modern Language Association.

Smith, Henry Nash. 1978. *Democracy and the Novel: Popular Resistance to Classical American Authors.* New York: Oxford University Press.

Smith, Page. 1990. *Killing the Spirit.* New York: Penguin.

Steinman, Lisa M. 1987. *Made in America: Science, Technology, and American Modernist Poets.* New Haven: Yale University Press.

Swanberg, W. A. 1965. *Dreiser.* New York: Charles Scribner's Sons.

Tebbel, John. 1974. *The Media in America.* New York: Thomas Y. Crowell.

Torchiana, Donald T. 1973. "*The Day of the Locust* and the Painter's Eye." In *Nathanael West: The Cheaters and the Cheated,* edited by David Madden, 249–82. Deland, Fla.: Everett/Edwards.

Trachtenberg, Alan. 1982. "Experiments in Another Country: Stephen Crane's City Sketches." In *American Realism,* edited by Eric J. Sundquist, 138–54. Baltimore: The Johns Hopkins University Press.

Trilling, Lionel. 1971. "Reality in America, Part II." 1968. In *Dreiser: A Collection of Critical Essays,* edited by John Lydenberg, 87–95. Englewood Cliffs, N.J.: Prentice-Hall.

Vanderwerken, David L. 1977. "*U.S.A.:* Dos Passos and the 'Old Words.'" *Twentieth Century Literature* 23: 195–228.

Veeder, William. 1975. *Henry James – The Lessons of the Master: Popular Fiction and Personal Style in the Nineteenth Century.* Chicago: University of Chicago Press.

Vertov, Dziga. 1984. *Kino-Eye: The Writings of Dziga Vertov.* Edited by Annette Michelson, translated by Kevin O'Brien. Berkeley: University of California Press.

Wagner, Linda. 1979. *Dos Passos: Artist as American.* Austin: University of Texas Press.

Ward, John William. 1974. "Dos Passos, Fitzgerald and History." 1969. In *Dos Passos: A Collection of Critical Essays,* edited by Andrew Hook, 120–7. Englewood Cliffs, N.J.: Prentice-Hall.

Webster, Grant. 1979. *The Republic of Letters: A History of Postwar American Literary Opinion.* Baltimore: The Johns Hopkins University Press.

Wells, Walter. 1973. "Shriek of the Locust." In *Tycoons and Locusts: A Regional Look at Hollywood Fiction of the 1930s.* Carbondale: Southern Illinois University Press.

West, Nathanael. 1932. "Some Notes on Violence." *Contact* 3 (October): 132.

———. 1933. "Some Notes on *Miss Lonelyhearts.*" *Contempo* 3 (15 May): 1.

———. 1957. *The Complete Works of Nathanael West.* New York: Farrar, Straus, Cudahy.

———. 1962a. *Miss Lonelyhearts,* 1933. Reprint. New York: New Directions.

———. 1962b. *The Day of the Locust,* 1939. Reprint. New York: New Directions.

Widmer, Kingsley. 1982. *Nathanael West.* Boston: Twayne Publishers.

White, Allon. 1981. *The Uses of Obscurity: The Fiction of Early Modernism.* London: Routledge and Kegan Paul.

White, Hayden. 1974. "Structuralism and Popular Culture." *Journal of Popular Culture* 7: 759–75.

Williams, Raymond. 1985. *Keywords: A Vocabulary of Culture and Society.* New York: Oxford University Press.

Wilson, Christopher. 1983. "The Rhetoric of Consumption: Mass Market Magazines and the Demise of the Gentle Reader, 1880–1920." In *The Culture of Consumption: Critical Essays in American History, 1880–1980,* edited by Richard Fox and T. J. Jackson Lears, 39–64. New York: Pantheon Books.

———. 1985. *The Labor of Words: Literary Professionalism in the Progressive Era.* Athens: University of Georgia Press.

Wilson, Edmund. 1959. "The Ambiguity of Henry James." In *A Casebook on Henry James' The Turn of the Screw,* edited by Gerald Willen. New York: Crowell.

———. 1950. "The Boys in the Back Room." In *Classics and Commercials: A Literary Chronicle of the Forties.* New York: Farrar, Straus, Giroux.

Zlotnick, Joan. 1971. "The Medium is the Message, Or Is It?: A Study of Nathanael West's Comic Strip Novel." *Journal of Popular Culture* 5: 236–40.

Index

Cambridge Studies in American Literature and Culture

Continued from the front of the book

The following books in the series are out of print